W9-APR-188

# TOEIC® EXAM

## Third Edition

From the Staff of Kaplan Test Prep & Admissions

**KAPLAN**

PUBLISHING

New York

This publication is designed to provide accurate and authoritative information in regard to the subject matter covered. It is sold with the understanding that the publisher is not engaged in rendering legal, accounting, or other professional service. If legal advice or other expert assistance is required, the services of a competent professional should be sought.

© 2009 Kaplan, Inc.

Published by Kaplan Publishing, a division of Kaplan, Inc.
1 Liberty Plaza, 24th Floor
New York, NY 10006

Printed in the United States of America

10 9 8 7 6 5 4 3 2 1

ISBN-13: 978-1-4195-5198-7

Kaplan Publishing books are available at special quantity discounts to use for sales promotions, employee premiums, or educational purposes. Please email our Special Sales Department to order or for more information at kaplanpublishing@kaplan.com, or write to Kaplan Publishing, 1 Liberty Plaza, 24th Floor, New York, NY 10006.

# Table of Contents

Kaplan English Programs
How to Use This Book

## PART 1: THE BASICS
### Chapter 1: Taking the TOEIC Exam

### Chapter 2: Preparing for Test Day

## PART 2: THE LISTENING COMPREHENSION SECTION
### Chapter 3: Photograph Questions

### Chapter 4: Question-Response

### Chapter 5: Short Conversations

**PART 6: TRANSCRIPTS**

# Kaplan English Programs

Kaplan's English Language and Test Preparation courses offer a "one-stop-shop" for international students. If you want to improve your English for academic or professional purposes, the following Kaplan courses can help you:

## GENERAL INTENSIVE ENGLISH

One of our most popular offerings, Kaplan's General Intensive English course is the fastest and most effective way for students to improve their English. This full-time program integrates the four key elements of language learning—listening, speaking, reading, and writing. Kaplan accelerates your learning by combining class time, computer lab practice, and a variety of specialized workshops that focus on specific skills. The challenging curriculum and intensive schedule are designed for both the general language learner and the academically bound student.

## GENERAL ENGLISH

Our General English course is a semi-intensive program designed for students who want to improve their listening and speaking skills without the time commitment of an intensive program. With morning class time and flexible computer lab hours throughout the week, our General English course is perfect for every schedule. You can spend your free afternoons sightseeing, visiting universities, or participating in our optional activities program.

## TOEFL AND ACADEMIC ENGLISH

Our world-famous TOEFL course prepares you for the TOEFL and also teaches you the academic language needed to succeed in a university. Designed for high-intermediate level English speakers, our course includes TOEFL-focused advanced reading, writing, listening, conversation, and grammar. You will also take simulation TOEFL tests complete with scores that monitor your progress, give feedback in areas that you should work on, and give detailed study suggestions using our computer labs and Kaplan's exclusive proprietary TOEFL software in our language lab. We'll teach you how to get a higher score!

## SAT FOR INTERNATIONAL STUDENTS

Do you want to earn a bachelor's degree from a U.S. university? Kaplan's SAT for International Students course prepares you for the SAT test with in-depth review, step-by-step guidance from Kaplan's expert teachers, intensive practice, and our structured self-study materials.

# GRE FOR INTERNATIONAL STUDENTS

Do you want to earn a master's degree in engineering, information technology, or architecture from a U.S. university? Kaplan's GRE for International Students course prepares you for the test with in-depth review, step-by-step guidance from Kaplan's expert teachers, intensive practice, and our structured self-study materials.

# GMAT FOR INTERNATIONAL STUDENTS

Do you want to get an MBA from a top business school? Kaplan's GMAT for International Students course prepares you for the test with in-depth review, step-by-step guidance from Kaplan's expert teachers, intensive practice, and our structured self-study materials.

# BUSINESS ENGLISH

This course focuses on the business-related English communication skills needed to function confidently in a business setting, while at the same time exposing participants to basic concepts of American business and corporate culture. In this course, students will actively participate in simulated business meetings and negotiations, give presentations, compose standard business correspondence and reports, and discuss business lectures in order to achieve their language-learning goals and master standard American pronunciation.

# TOEIC EXAM

Kaplan's listening and reading-based course teaches you the skills and strategies you need to raise your TOEIC exam score. This course focuses on professional English language skills and offers Kaplan's exclusive TOEIC exam test-taking strategies. You will get extensive practice with sample questions and full-length exams. Our TOEIC Exam course provides the quickest and most effective method for improving your test score.

# APPLYING TO KAPLAN ENGLISH PROGRAMS

To get more information, or to apply for admission to any of Kaplan's programs for international students or professionals, you can contact us at:

Kaplan English Programs
700 S. Flower Street, Suite 2900
Los Angeles, CA 90017
USA

Tel: (213) 452-5800 or 800-818-9128
Fax: (213) 892-1360
Email: world@kaplan.com
URL: www.kaplanenglish.com

# How to Use This Book

This book is designed to help you achieve the highest possible score on the TOEIC exam. The text includes easy-to-learn strategies, proven test-taking tips, a weekly study planner, essential vocabulary-building exercises, a CD with accompanying transcripts, and a complete practice test—all to give you the best chance on Test Day. Here's how to use the various components of this book.

## Step One: Read Chapter 1

In this section, you will get an overview of the TOEIC exam, become familiar with all the test forms to be filled out, and learn about the key Kaplan strategies for a high TOEIC exam score.

## Step Two: Fill Out Your Study Planner

Anyone who has taken the TOEIC exam will agree: You cannot squeeze all your study time into a week. Therefore, turn to chapter 2, and fill in the study planner with realistic study goals. Think about how many weeks you have until Test Day and how much time you can dedicate each day to studying. Remember that if you have worked all day, you may not have the energy to learn new vocabulary. Instead, use the time to review materials you have already mastered, and save the more difficult sections for when you are fresh and rested.

## Step Three: Sharpen Your Skills

For each section of the exam, this book provides example questions along with proven strategies for correctly answering these types of questions. It highlights the most important strategies so you can easily refer to them. After the examples, you will find practice questions.

Once you complete the questions, turn to the answer explanations; here you will find an analysis of both correct and incorrect answer choices. Be sure to read all of the explanations for each answer choice so that you understand your mistakes and learn how the test makers try to distract you. On the day of the test, you'll be able to eliminate incorrect choices more efficiently.

## Step Four: Use the Audio CD

The first four parts of the TOEIC exam test listening comprehension. The audio CD will build your listening skills while helping you become accustomed to these parts of the test. The transcripts of the CD appear in part 6 of this book.

## Step Five: Build Your Vocabulary

The wider your vocabulary, the better you will do on the TOEIC exam. Fortunately, the TOEIC exam tests the same words and phrases over and over again, which is why we have assembled word lists with the most common word families found on the TOEIC exam.

Using these lists and the practice exercises that follow will not only extend your vocabulary, but also teach you to use and understand words in their many forms—verbs, adjectives, or gerunds.

Remember: When you encounter an unfamiliar word or phrase in this book, take the time to look it up in the dictionary, study its meaning, and find a sentence—either in the dictionary or in this book—that uses the word.

## Step Six: Take Kaplan's TOEIC Exam Practice Test

After practicing the Kaplan strategies for the TOEIC exam, you should use the Practice Test as a test run for the real thing. Refer to chapter 1 to make sure you know how to fill out the answer grid. After taking the test, use the answer key to score your Practice Test.

## Step Seven: Review

Go back to parts 2 and 3 of this book, and review those sections of the test where your performance was weak. Read the Tips for the Final Week and Stress Busters chapters to make sure you are fully prepared—and relaxed—on Test Day.

Follow these seven steps, and you can be confident that you are truly ready for the TOEIC exam.

| PART ONE |

# The Basics

# Chapter 1: **Taking the TOEIC Exam**

- Understanding the TOEIC Exam
- How and Where the TOEIC Exam Is Administered
- An Overview of the TOEIC Exam
- Filling Out Forms

## UNDERSTANDING THE TOEIC EXAM

Before looking at the questions on the TOEIC exam, let's look at some background information about it.

### WHAT IS THE TOEIC EXAM?

The Test of English for International Communication (TOEIC) exam is designed to test your ability to understand English as it is used in international business and other professional situations. The TOEIC exam covers two main areas: your ability to understand real-life conversations and speeches in English (spoken English), and your ability to read and understand materials in English, such as manuals, reports, advertisements, periodicals, correspondence, and technical articles (written English). The language tested on the TOEIC exam is not specialized language. It is the everyday language that people use in the workplace to communicate about their jobs and business, and when they communicate with friends or acquaintances about common subject areas such as health, weekend activities, and travel.

## WHO PRODUCES THE TOEIC EXAM?

The TOEIC exam was developed by the Educational Testing Service (ETS), a private, not-for-profit organization located in Princeton, New Jersey, in the United States. ETS is a leading center for educational and psychometric research in the United States and is well known as an organization that prepares and administers a variety of tests for school, college, and graduate program admission as well as occupational and professional certification and licensing.

## WHO USES THE TOEIC EXAM?

Corporations and government offices worldwide use the TOEIC exam for many reasons:

* Assessing how well their current employees understand English
* Hiring new employees
* Tracking the progress of employees in English-language training programs

## WHAT KINDS OF JOBS USE THE TOEIC EXAM?

The TOEIC exam is useful for checking the English skills of desk clerks in hotels, mechanics servicing equipment sold outside the manufacturing country, foreign sales staff, customs officers, managers, bank employees, secretaries, and many other kinds of jobs in which non-native speakers interact with both native and non-native English speakers.

## WHEN WAS THE TOEIC EXAM INTRODUCED?

The TOEIC exam was first administered in Japan in 1979. In 1982, it became available in Korea. Since then, the program has expanded its services throughout Asia, Europe, and the Americas. The test makers estimate that the total number of TOEIC exams administered annually is more than 4.5 million.

## WHEN DID THE TOEIC EXAM CHANGE?

In 2005, ETS decided to make slight changes to the format of the TOEIC exam. The changes were made to align the exam with current theories about language testing. This book discusses the new TOEIC exam.

## HOW DO THE TOEIC EXAM AND THE TOEFL EXAM COMPARE?

The TOEIC exam and the TOEFL (Test of English as a Foreign Language) exam were both developed to test English listening and reading, but they differ in their purpose, content, and design.

### Purpose

The TOEFL exam is designed to determine how well a candidate can use English in colleges and universities in the United States. Its purpose is to identify candidates who can perform successfully in an academic setting. The TOEIC exam, on the other hand, tests everyday English used in business settings.

### Content

Content for TOEFL exam material is taken from lectures, texts, and other documents found in the academic environment. TOEIC exam materials reflect the needs of people accomplishing work tasks, providing services, communicating with others, traveling, and manufacturing and distributing products.

### Design

Because the primary purpose of the TOEFL exam is to identify those students who can perform successfully in an English-based academic environment, it focuses on test takers of intermediate to fluent English language ability.

The TOEIC exam, on the other hand, measures a wider range, from the lowest proficiency level to high professional-level competence. In addition, the Internet-based TOEFL (ibT) has speaking and writing sections, as well as listening and reading sections, whereas the TOEIC exam tests only listening and reading.

ETS offers separate Internet-based speaking and writing tests for TOEIC exam takers. These will not be covered in this book. For more information about TOEIC speaking and writing exams, visit www.toeic.org.

# HOW AND WHERE THE TOEIC EXAM IS ADMINISTERED

The TOEIC exam is available internationally through two separate programs. Your local representative will help you decide the best way for you to take the exam.

## CHOICE 1: TAKING THE EXAM IN AN OPEN PUBLIC SESSION

These sessions are held on selected dates at different locations across the globe. Companies might want to send their employees to an open session exam rather than administering the exam on their own premises. People who wish to take the exam but who are not affiliated with an organization that conducts on-site exam administration must take the exam at an open public session. Because public sessions are not yet available in every country, you should check with the ETS representative in your country regarding the availability of these open sessions.

## CHOICE 2: ON-SITE EXAM ADMINISTRATION

The TOEIC exam serves the needs of corporations and government organizations that have a number of people that they want tested at once. On-site exams are administered under secure conditions, supervised by both the client organization's staff and by ETS. Exams that are taken on-site or at an open session are all scored only by ETS or its representatives.

To find out more information about taking the TOEIC exam via either method, be sure to contact your TOEIC representative. Information on contacting your TOEIC representative can be found at www.toeic.org.

# AN OVERVIEW OF THE TOEIC EXAM

Total Questions  200 questions
Total Time  2.5 hours
  (includes time for
  filling out forms)
Total Score  10–990
Range

The TOEIC exam is a standardized test, meaning that it consists of certain types of multiple-choice questions, is given to a large number of people at the same time, is graded by computer, and is timed. Complex statistical procedures ensure that test scores from different forms of the test can be compared directly.

## FORMAT AND CONTENT

The TOEIC exam is approximately two hours long and consists of 200 multiple-choice questions. If you include the time it takes to fill in the answer sheet and background questions, the exam is about two and a half hours long. See the following chart for a breakdown of the exam sections.

### Section One—Listening Comprehension

| Part I | Photographs | 10 |
|---|---|---|
| Part II | Question-Response | 30 |
| Part III | Short Conversations | 30 |
| Part IV | Short Talks | 30 |
| Total Questions | | 100 |
| Total Time | | 45 minutes |
| Score Range | | 5–495 |

### Section Two—Reading Comprehension

| Part V | Incomplete Sentences | 40 |
|---|---|---|
| Part VI | Text Completion | 12 |
| Part VII | Reading Comprehension | 48 |
| Total Questions | | 100 |
| Total Time | | 75 minutes |
| Score Range | | 5–495 |

## SCORING

TOEIC scores are obtained by adding up the total number of correct responses in the Listening Comprehension Section and the Reading Comprehension Section. These two totals are converted to a scaled score ranging from 5 to 495 for each section, with a combined total from 10 to 990. These scaled scores allow scores from different TOEIC exams to be compared accurately.

Something to remember when you are looking at your TOEIC score is that there is no failing or passing score for this exam. The TOEIC exam was developed to assess the English proficiency of people who will need to use English in a professional capacity. It does not measure achievement, which is why there is no passing or failing score. Nevertheless, many companies who use the TOEIC exam to set their own standards may require employees to obtain a certain minimum score due to the corresponding level of English needed for that job. This does not mean that people pass or fail the TOEIC exam; it just means they meet or do not meet the specific standards set by a specific organization.

An important thing to note is that because the exam calculates only the number of correct responses, and because you do not lose points for incorrect responses, you should answer *every* question rather than leave any blank. This book will teach you how to narrow down the possible options for each answer so that you come closest to picking the correct one, but even if you do not know the answer, guess! After all, you may, with luck, score a point; if you leave an answer blank, however, you receive no credit.

 **ANSWER EVERY QUESTION**

On the TOEIC exam, you do not lose points for incorrect responses, so you should try to answer every question. If you do not know the answer, guess!

TOEIC exam writers recommend that a TOEIC score be considered valid for up to two years. However, if you took the TOEIC exam fewer than two years previously, and if you have greatly boosted your language skills during that period, you may find that your previous TOEIC exam score has become outdated.

Your TOEIC exam score is confidential. Information about your performance is available only to you and to the administering institution. Institutions may provide individual candidate information to staff only on a need-to-know basis and are not allowed to post scores on bulletin boards or other public places without the permission of the test takers.

## TIMING

As previously described, the TOEIC exam is timed. This means that your score greatly depends on being able to complete the questions within the time allowed.

We will indicate the amount of time you should budget for each part of the exam at the beginning of each chapter. At first, this will seem like an extremely short amount of time to answer all of the questions. However, at Kaplan, we have designed our test-taking strategies to help you eliminate incorrect answers as efficiently as possible. By practicing the strategies, you should be able to get through nearly all of the exam questions. Remember also, that even if you are not able to complete a whole section before the time limit, you should still fill in the answer grid for any unanswered questions. You may choose a correct answer by luck and get additional points; if you leave those answers choices blank, you will receive no points.

When you do the practice questions for each section, pay attention to the amount of time you spend on each question. You do not have to be strict about time at this point, but you do want to note where you are moving too slowly. Then, when you are ready to take the Practice Test, be sure to time yourself very carefully. This way, you will have as close to a real exam experience as possible, and you will see exactly where you need improvement.

## FILLING OUT FORMS

Like other standardized tests, the TOEIC exam requires you to fill out a number of forms. For all of these forms, you will need a No. 2 or HB pencil. (On Test Day, you will be given a pencil at the exam site.)

Before you even start the exam you will have to complete a background questionnaire. Practice filling it out before you take the TOEIC exam so that are fully comfortable with it on Test Day.

The next form you will use is the answer grid. On the answer grid, you will first fill in ovals to indicate your name, the center where you are taking the exam, and other identifying information. You will use the rest of the grid to indicate your answer choices.

When taking the exam, it is common to lose track of which question you are on. Check that you are on the right question after every five questions. That way, if you have accidentally skipped an oval, you have to correct only a few of them.

 **USE THE RIGHT PENCIL**

You must use a No. 2 or HB pencil. The computer that scores the exam cannot read any other type of pencil or pen.

It is important that you *fill in the ovals completely*; a check mark or an *X* will confuse the computer that scores the exam. Also, be sure that you do not go too far outside the oval and that if you erase, you do so completely. The Practice Test in the back of the book includes an answer grid. Practice filling it out so that you are prepared on Test Day.

# Chapter 2: **Preparing for Test Day**

- Study Planner
- Nine Key Strategies for the TOEIC Exam
- Tips for the Final Week
- Stress Busters

## STUDY PLANNER

You will find calendars on pages 11 and 12. Use them to fill in a specific study schedule. Be realistic about the amount of time you have to study and practice your English-language skills. Do not worry about your current level of English; just make sure that you give yourself the amount of time you need to get the most out of this book. Remember to update the schedule as necessary.

Do not forget to schedule vocabulary practice and the Practice Test along with the rest of the chapters of the book. Take the Practice Test after you have reviewed all of the other chapters of the book. Be sure to leave enough time before the exam so you will be able to review your weak areas from the Practice Test. Take the Practice Test as if it were the real thing: Find a quiet place where you will not be interrupted, and take it in one session. Time yourself accurately. In this way, you will be more prepared for your actual Test Day.

On page 10 are some broad guidelines for setting up your schedule. Remember that everyone is different and your pace may be far slower or faster than what is listed here. These are just to give you a general sense of the amount of time you will need. In addition to the hours noted here, you will want to schedule in time for a second or third review of certain chapters, depending on your strengths and weaknesses. Finally, do not schedule too much studying immediately before Test Day. As described later in this chapter, studying up to the last minute will only make you more anxious and will probably not raise your score.

## Sharpening Your Listening Comprehension and Reading Comprehension Skills

| | |
|---|---|
| Part I: Listening Comprehension: Photographs | 2 to 4 hours |
| Part II: Listening Comprehension: Question-Response | 2 to 4 hours |
| Part III: Listening Comprehension: Short Conversations | 2 to 4 hours |
| Part IV: Listening Comprehension: Short Talks | 2 to 4 hours |
| Part V: Reading Comprehension: Incomplete Sentences | 2 to 4 hours |
| Part VI: Reading Comprehension: Text Completion | 2 to 4 hours |
| Part VII: Reading Comprehension: Reading Comprehension | 2 to 4 hours |

## Vocabulary Review

| | |
|---|---|
| List 1 | 2.5 to 4 hours |
| List 2 | 2.5 to 4 hours |
| List 3 | 2.5 to 4 hours |
| List 4 | 2.5 to 4 hours |
| List 5 | 2.5 to 4 hours |

## Practice Test

| | |
|---|---|
| Practice Test | 2 hours |
| Practice Test Review | 1 to 3 hours |

# KAPLAN) **TOEIC Study Planner**

Month: _____

| Sunday | Monday | Tuesday | Wednesday | Thursday | Friday | Saturday |
|--------|--------|---------|-----------|----------|--------|----------|
|        |        |         |           |          |        |          |
|        |        |         |           |          |        |          |
|        |        |         |           |          |        |          |
|        |        |         |           |          |        |          |
|        |        |         |           |          |        |          |

To Do This Month:

# KAPLAN) **TOEIC Study Planner**

Month: _____

| Sunday | Monday | Tuesday | Wednesday | Thursday | Friday | Saturday |
|--------|--------|---------|-----------|----------|--------|----------|
|  |  |  |  |  |  |  |
|  |  |  |  |  |  |  |
|  |  |  |  |  |  |  |
|  |  |  |  |  |  |  |
|  |  |  |  |  |  |  |

To Do This Month:

# NINE KEY STRATEGIES FOR THE TOEIC EXAM

## STRATEGY 1: KNOW THE DIRECTIONS

Each part of the TOEIC exam has its own directions. Knowing what they are before you take the exam will help you manage your time—you will not have to waste valuable test time listening to or reading the directions if you already know what they are. In the Listening Comprehension Section, you will hear the directions for each part before the actual questions begin. (The directions will also be printed in your exam book.) While the directions are playing, you should look ahead at the questions that you will be asked to answer. Knowing what the questions are in advance will help you focus on what to listen for.

In the Reading Comprehension Section, the directions are printed at the beginning of each part. Again, by knowing what the directions are in advance, you will be able to begin answering the questions immediately instead of wasting time reading the directions.

## STRATEGY 2: READ EACH QUESTION CAREFULLY

Before looking at the answer choices, read the question closely to know what you are being asked. Often, incorrect answer choices are designed to trap you if you misread the question. If you do not understand a question, reread it slowly. On the exam, the language of the questions and answers is designed to be easier than the language of the material being tested. For example, if you understood the passage (conversation, short talk, reading passage) but do not understand the question, you probably need to reread the question.

## STRATEGY 3: PREDICT THE ANSWER

After you are clear on what you are required to do, try to predict the answer in your own words—before looking at the answer choices. The questions on the exam are very straightforward—there are no trick questions or any questions that require you to calculate or come to a logical conclusion. Information is provided in the listening and reading materials, and the questions try to determine whether you understood that information. If you understand the question, you should be able to answer it in your own words. Your predicted answer should be among the answer choices.

## STRATEGY 4: EVALUATE THE ANSWER CHOICES

After you have predicted the answer in your own words, check to see if your answer is among the choices. If the choices do not match your predicted answer exactly, select the choice that best matches. Reread the question to make sure it is a good match, and mark your answer choice on the answer sheet.

## STRATEGY 5: ELIMINATE WRONG ANSWER CHOICES

If the answer you have predicted is not among the answer choices, eliminate any answer choices that you know are wrong and choose the best answer from the remaining choices. If you can eliminate even one wrong choice, you will increase your chances of guessing the correct answer. When there are four answer choices, you have a one-in-four chance of guessing the correct one. By eliminating one choice, you have improved your chances to one in three. If you can eliminate two wrong choices, your chances are even better.

## STRATEGY 6: ANSWER EASY QUESTIONS FIRST

The Listening Comprehension Section of the exam is controlled by the recording. You will not be able to skip ahead, nor can you go back to review your answers. You must answer the questions in the Listening Comprehension Section in the order they are presented. In the Reading Comprehension Section, however, you may answer the questions in any order you like.

Generally, the Reading Comprehension Section is organized from easy to hard. Part V is the easiest, Part VI is more difficult, and Part VII is the most difficult. Within each part, the questions are generally ordered from easy to hard. The easiest items appear in the beginning, and the most difficult items appear at the end. For this reason, it is best to work through the Reading Comprehension Section in the order it is presented in the exam book. As you work through this section, do not spend too much time on any one question. Each question is worth the same number of points. If you spend a lot of time on one question, you will be wasting time you could spend to answer other questions. If you are having trouble answering a question, either guess at the answer choice or circle the question number on your answer sheet so that you can return to it later if there is time. When you have finished all the easy questions, go back and tackle the harder ones that you skipped earlier.

In Part VII of the Reading Comprehension Section, the reading passages have between two and five questions each. Generally, passages with fewer questions are shorter and easier than passages with more questions. Tackle the short passages first. The passages are usually grouped by the number of questions—the passages with two questions come before the passages with three questions, which come before the passages with four questions, and so on. However, this is not always the case. Try to answer all the two-question passages first, then the three-question passages, then the four-question passages, and so on. For some of the reading passages, there will be a question that asks about how a particular word is used in the passage. These are generally easy questions, and you should try to answer these first. If you are running out of time, look for these questions, find the word in the passage, and try to answer the question. Often, if you know the word being tested, you can eliminate one or two answer choices without even reading the passage.

## STRATEGY 7: ANSWER EVERY QUESTION

Do not leave any questions unanswered. There is no scoring penalty for an incorrect answer on the TOEIC exam. Your score is the total of all questions answered correctly. If you really do not know the answer to a question, guess. Choose one letter—(A, B, C, or D)—to use as a "guessing letter." Using the same letter for every guessed question ensures that, on average, 25 percent of your guesses will be correct. The TOEIC exam is designed so that in each part, the number of times each letter is correct is about equal. This means there are approximately the same numbers of As, Bs, Cs, and Ds in each part. For example, if you choose answer choice D to guess at ten questions in Part VII, you should expect at least two or three of your guesses to be correct. However, if you guess randomly—picking a different letter for every question—you might not get any correct!

## STRATEGY 8: MANAGE YOUR TIME

The TOEIC exam is a timed test; you are given 45 minutes to complete the Listening Comprehension Section and 75 minutes to complete the Reading Comprehension Section. As aforementioned, in the Listening Comprehension Section, the timing is controlled by the recording. After each question, there will be a pause of between five and eight seconds, during which you must choose and mark your answer (five seconds for Part I and eight seconds for Parts II–IV). After the pause, the next question, conversation, or passage will begin. You must work quickly so that you do not fall behind the recording. For the Reading Comprehension Section, you are given 75 minutes to finish, and you work at your own pace. Be sure to watch the clock so you know how much time you have left. Work as quickly as you can, but avoid making careless mistakes by working too fast.

## STRATEGY 9: CHECK YOUR ANSWER SHEET FOR MISTAKES OR UNANSWERED QUESTIONS

If you finish the test before time is called, check your answer sheet to make sure you have filled in each oval completely and that there are no extra marks on it. Be sure you have filled in only one answer choice for each question. Be sure that you have answered every question and that there are no unanswered questions. If time is running out and you will not be able to finish the test, pick one letter (A, B, C, or D) and fill in the remaining questions on your answer sheet. It is much better to guess at the remaining questions than to leave them unanswered. Your guesses might be correct, which would earn you score points.

## STRATEGY SUMMARY

1. Know the directions.
2. Read each question carefully before you look at the answer choices.
3. Predict the answer before looking at the choices.
4. Evaluate the answer choices and mark the answer if you know it.
5. Eliminate wrong answer choices and choose the best answer from the answer choices that remain.
6. Answer easy questions before the hard ones. Usually, Part V is easier than Part VI, which is easier than Part VII.

7. Answer every question, and choose one letter for every wild-guess answer.

8. Manage your time.

9. Check your answer sheet for mistakes or unanswered questions before you turn it in.

## TIPS FOR THE FINAL WEEK

The tendency among test takers is to study too hard during the last few days before the exam and then to forget the important practical matters until the last minute.

 **TEST KIT**

The night before the exam, collect the following items to bring with you to the exam:

- Admission ticket
- Photo ID card
- A watch (you must shut off any alarms, cell phones, or beepers while taking the exam)
- Headache medicine (Advil, Tylenol, etc.), just in case

### THE WEEK BEFORE TEST DAY

Do not try to study too hard on the days immediately before the exam. Instead, you should:

- Recheck your admission ticket for accuracy; call the TOEIC exam administrator if there are any problems.

- Visit the testing center if you can. Sometimes seeing the actual room where your exam will be administered may help to calm any anxiety. In addition, by visiting the center you can see how long it takes to arrive there, ensuring that you do not get lost on the day of the exam.

- Practice getting up early and working on exam material as if it were Test Day. Be sure to listen to the CD so that you get in the habit of listening to English early in the day.

- Evaluate thoroughly where you stand. Use the last week before Test Day to focus on your weaker points, and reread those chapters of this book. Do not neglect your strong areas, however; after all, this is where you will score most of your points.

- Practice using a timing routine that you will follow during the real exam. For instance, some students set their watch at 12:00 at the beginning of every section so they know how much time they have. Whatever your method, make sure it does not distract you from valuable exam time.

### THE DAY BEFORE TEST DAY

Try to avoid doing intensive studying the day before the exam. There is little you can do to help yourself at this late date, and you will probably exhaust yourself. Instead, review key strategies, get together everything you will need for Test Day, and then do something relaxing.

## TEST DAY

Plan to arrive early to your exam center; the administrators will not admit latecomers. Make sure you have your test kit with you (see page 16), especially your admission ticket and photo ID. Most centers have a clock, but you may still want to bring a watch, just in case.

After the exam booklets are handed out and you have filled out all the necessary forms, the TOEIC exam will begin. The administrator will either write or call out the starting time for each section and will also usually announce the time at specified intervals.

The exam begins with the Listening Comprehension Section, followed by the Reading Comprehension Section. Between the two sections, the administrator will tell you that the time has expired and it is time to go on to the next section. You must immediately go from the Listening Comprehension Section to the Reading Comprehension Section. Use this time to take a deep breath and refocus your concentration. Remember, if you finish the Reading Comprehension Section early, you will not be able to go back to the Listening Comprehension Section. Use this time to review your work on the Reading Comprehension Section.

During the exam, try not to think about how you are scoring. Instead, focus on the task of selecting the right answer. Remember, you do not have to create the correct answer—it is right there in front of you. Think about how well you have prepared, and be confident and positive about your abilities.

## AFTER THE TOEIC EXAM

After all your hard work in preparing for the TOEIC exam, be sure to celebrate once it is over. Get together with your family and friends, relax, and have fun. You have a lot to celebrate: You prepared for the exam ahead of time. You did your best. You are going to get a good score.

## STRESS BUSTERS

If you are like most people preparing for the TOEIC exam, you may be feeling anxious about it. You may be worried about your listening comprehension skills, for example, or all those new words you just learned, or what will happen if you do not get a certain score. All those stressful thoughts and fears can make you nervous, sleepless, and ultimately less able to perform well on the exam.

At Kaplan, we believe that learning to control stress and anxiety is a key part to boosting your TOEIC exam score. That is why we have included the following stress-busting techniques. By practicing them—no matter how silly they may seem—you will lessen your exam anxiety, and let all the hard studying you have done pay off.

## BEFORE THE TEST

Just as an athlete needs to train to perform well in a sports event, you can train to do your best on the TOEIC exam. Here are some tips for getting into peak condition, both mentally and physically.

### Make English a Part of Every Day

Surround yourself with the English language in the weeks and months leading up to your exam. Get in the habit of reading or listening to something in English every day, separate from your study time. Even if it is just ten or fifteen minutes a day, listening to something in English and trying to figure out who is talking, why they are talking, and what they are talking about will help you improve your listening comprehension. You can do the same thing with reading. By reading anything you see written in English, such as advertisements, signs, or directions, and by asking yourself what their meaning is, you will be working on your reading comprehension. Even more importantly, you will become more and more familiar, and therefore more comfortable, with English. The level of comfort you have with English, whether it is listening or reading, will help reduce stress and nervousness when you take the actual TOEIC exam.

### Talk

Talk to other friends or colleagues who are taking the TOEIC exam. Chances are, they are feeling the same sort of stress that you are. Sharing your fears and worries with people who can understand them is a proven way to alleviate stress.

### Think

Positive thinking is also a good way to ward off anxiety. Tell yourself things such as "I choose to take this exam," rather than "I have to"; "I will do well," rather than "I hope things go well"; "I can," rather than "I cannot." Any time a negative thought occurs, conquer it with a positive one. This builds your self-esteem and confidence.

This technique is especially useful at night when you are just about to fall asleep. Because your mind is very open to suggestion then, think about all your positive accomplishments and skills (*I performed well at work today*; *I like where I'm living*; *I relate well to my friends*; etc.). You will wake up feeling a lot more positive in the morning.

### Eat

Try to eat healthy foods before the exam: fruits and vegetables, low-fat foods, proteins, and whole grains. Do not fill up on sugary or high-fat snacks. Sugar makes stress worse and fatty foods are not healthy. Steer clear of heavily salted foods, too; they can deplete potassium, which you need for nerve function.

### Exercise

Whether it is walking, jogging, biking, swimming, skating, or aerobics, physical exercise is a proven way to stimulate your mind and body and to improve your ability to concentrate. After all, exercise pumps more oxygen into the blood, which helps you think better. Even if you do not regularly exercise, take a five- to ten-minute activity break for every hour that you study. This will help keep your body and mind in balance.

One warning about exercise: It is not a good idea to exercise vigorously immediately before bedtime.

### Take a Break

Do not study up to the moment you go to sleep. You need some time for your mind to relax; otherwise, you will lie awake worrying about your studies.

### Breathe

Breathing deeply and regularly is an excellent way to stay relaxed. Try closing your eyes and breathing in slowly and deeply through your nose. Hold the breath for a bit and then release it through your mouth. The key is to take in air slowly and to use your diaphragm. Breathing with your diaphragm encourages relaxation and helps minimize tension.

### Imagine

When you are feeling very anxious, it is helpful to take a break, find a quiet place, and sit comfortably. If you wear glasses, take them off. Then close your eyes and breathe deeply for a few minutes, as previously described. Fill your diaphragm and lungs as fully as you can and then exhale the air completely. While you're doing this, imagine yourself in a relaxing situation. It might be a special place you have visited—a garden or beach, for example—or one you have read about. Imagine the smells, the sounds, and the way things feel in that place. Stay in that place for as long as you feel comfortable. Then, take a moment to check how you are feeling. Focus on staying relaxed and then imagine you are taking the TOEIC exam with this same calm feeling.

Practice this exercise often, especially when you are starting to feel anxious. The more you practice it, the more effective the exercise will be for you.

## DURING THE TEST

The TOEIC exam requires a high level of concentration and quick responses. Your state of mind as you take the exam will affect your score. Here are some tips for performing your best as you take the TOEIC exam.

### Keep Moving

Do not get stuck on a difficult question or passage. You do not have to get everything right to achieve a good score, so do not spend an excessive amount of time on a question that is too difficult for you. Select the best possible choice, and then move on! While you cannot go back to review the listening items after the recording has played, in the Reading Comprehension Section you can always go back to the more difficult questions later.

### Concentrate

Other test takers may seem to be working more busily than you are, but do not pay attention to them! Other people's activity levels are not necessarily signs of progress or higher scores. Continue to work carefully and thoroughly, especially on the Reading Comprehension Section of the exam.

### Breathe

Weak test takers tend to share one major characteristic: They forget to breathe properly as the exam proceeds. They start holding their breath without realizing it, or they breathe without a normal rhythm. Improper breathing hurts confidence and accuracy, and it interferes with clear thinking. Breathe deeply and steadily, and remember your relaxation exercises.

### Think Positively!

If you get discouraged during the exam, remember:

- You do not have to get every single question right to achieve a high score.
- By having studied the strategies in this book, you are better prepared than the majority of other test takers are.
- You are probably doing better than you realize. Think to yourself: "I can do well on this exam!"

# PART TWO

# The Listening Comprehension Section

# Chapter 3: **Exam Part I—Photograph Questions**

- Test-Taking Strategies
- Photograph Practice Set
- Answer Key
- Answers and Explanations

🕐 **Time Budget for Part I: Approximately 10 minutes**

For this part of the TOEIC exam, you will look at ten photographs. The recording will consist of four different statements. You must decide which of the four statements best describes each photograph. There will be a five-second pause between the end of the last statement for a photograph, and the first statement of the next photograph.

## TEST-TAKING STRATEGIES

### STRATEGY 1: KNOW THE DIRECTIONS

It is important to understand what you are being asked to do before you take the test. The directions will look something like this:

#### LISTENING COMPREHENSION SECTION

In the Listening Comprehension Section, you will have the chance to demonstrate how well you understand spoken English. The Listening Comprehension Section will take approximately 45 minutes. There are four parts, and directions are given for each part. You must mark your answers on the separate answer sheet. Do not write them in the test book.

**Directions**: For each question, you will hear four statements about the photograph in your test book. When you hear the statements, choose the one statement that best describes what you see in the photograph. Then, find the number of the question on your answer sheet and mark your answer. The statements will not be written in your test book and will be spoken just once.

For the example photograph shown, you will hear:

| | |
|---|---|
| Narrator: | *A.* |
| Woman: | *They're leaving the office.* |
| Narrator: | *B.* |
| Woman: | *They're turning off the machine.* |
| Narrator: | *C.* |
| Woman: | *They're gathered around the table.* |
| Narrator: | *D.* |
| Woman: | *They're eating at a restaurant.* |

Choice (C), *They're gathered around the table,* best describes what you see in the photograph.

## STRATEGY 2: LOOK AT THE FIRST FEW PHOTOGRAPHS

Because you already know the directions, look at the first few photographs in your test book while the directions are playing. This will let you know what to expect and what you will need to listen for.

As you look at the photographs, think about what they are showing and how that might be described in English.

## STRATEGY 3: FOCUS ON THE PHOTOGRAPH

As you look at each photograph, decide what the main action or idea is. The correct statement about the photograph will almost always deal with the most important element in the photograph.

The correct answer will not usually be a minor detail; it will be the answer to this question: "What is this a photograph of?"

In the sample photograph, for example, the man who is standing is also holding a tea cup. TOEIC exam writers would not make the correct answer, *"The man is holding a tea cup."* While this statement is true, it is not the main action or element shown in the photograph. Ask yourself, "What is this a photograph of?" It is a photograph of four people around a table.

When there are people in the photographs, it can be easy to decide what the main action is. The people are usually doing something. The correct statement will probably be about whatever it is they are doing. However, some photographs on the TOEIC exam do not have any people in them; they might show a group of objects or a landscape, for example. With these photographs, it can be more difficult to determine what is being shown.

To help focus on the main action or element in a photograph without people in it, ask yourself:

- Where was the photograph taken? If the location is very obvious, such as the beach or a parking lot, then the answer may be about where the photograph was taken.
- What objects are being shown? The answer may be testing whether you know what they are called.
- How are the objects located or positioned? If the photograph shows several objects, the answer may involve the location or position of the objects; for example, whether one object is in front of, on top of, or behind another.

Look at each photograph quickly and decide in your own words what it shows. Each photograph shows one main action or idea; the answer for each photograph is the statement that best describes what is happening, which almost always refers to the most obvious action or object in the photograph.

Look again at the example photograph in the directions. What is it a photograph of? Your answer is probably something very close to this: "Four people are around a table." The correct statement is choice (C) *They're gathered around the table.*

Most of the time, your first answer to the question of what the photograph is of will be the correct answer.

## STRATEGY 4: EVALUATE THE STATEMENTS

Once you have formulated in your own words what the photograph is showing and have decided on the main action, you must listen to and evaluate the statements you hear. Because each statement will be spoken only once, you must listen carefully.

Listen for a statement that is a close match to what you decided the photograph was of. Be sure to listen to all four statements before you mark your answer sheet. If one of the statements is a close match to the answer you have been expecting, find the number for the question on your answer sheet and mark the oval for the letter that matches your answer.

## STRATEGY 5: ELIMINATE FALSE STATEMENTS

If none of the statements match your expected answer very well, then you must start eliminating any choices that are false. The best way to do that is to repeat each statement to yourself and ask whether or not it is true.

Look at directions example again.

Statement (A) *They're leaving the office.*

This is clearly false. The people are not leaving the room. You can eliminate this choice.

Statement (B) *They're turning off the machine.*

This is also false. You can eliminate this choice.

Statement (C) *They're gathered around the table.*

This is true; they are around the table. Therefore, you should keep this choice.

Statement (D) *They're eating at a restaurant.*

This is false. The people are at a table, but it is in an office, not a restaurant. You can eliminate this choice.

In this example, only choice (C), *They're gathered around the table*, is true. Choices (A), (B), and (D) can be eliminated because they are false.

In the directions example, the main action was very clear, and it was easy to identify the statements that were false. If only one or two choices seem false to you or if you cannot eliminate all the wrong answers, then you must select the best match from what is left.

You have already decided what the answer should be in your own words. Consider whether any of the answer choices contain words that are similar to what you expected the correct answer to use. In the directions example, you might expect the word *table*. The only choice that contains this word is (C), which is the correct answer. If you are unable to eliminate answer choices, select the choice that uses words or phrases that are similar to your expected answer.

## STRATEGY 6: ANSWER THE CURRENT QUESTION BEFORE THE NEXT ONE BEGINS

You should answer every question as quickly as you can. You have only about five seconds to choose your answer for each photograph. You should be finished with the current question before the next set of statements begins. If you are still answering a question when the next one begins, you might not hear the first statement.

As soon as you have finished a question, look ahead to the next photograph and ask yourself what it is a photograph of. Answer in your own words, and listen for the statement that most closely matches yours.

## STRATEGY 7: KNOW THE DISTRACTORS

There are several kinds of distractors used in Part I. Here are the most common:

- Wrong word usage
- Similar-sounding words
- Reasonable statements/assumptions
- Irrelevant statements
- Hybrids

More than one type of distractor may be used in a photograph. Not all distractors fit neatly into these categories; some may seem to belong to more than one category. Note also that each of these distractor types is similar because, in the end, they are false and do not describe what is happening in the photograph. However, it is useful to look at *why* they are false and to understand what it is you must listen for.

### Wrong Word Usage

This type of distractor essentially asks you to identify the correct vocabulary word, or the correct form of a word. Each of the choices might, for example, use the same form of a verb but change the nouns they refer to. Alternatively, they might use the correct noun throughout, but change the verbs. Prepositions can also be tested this way. This distractor type is often easy to eliminate.

**Example 1**

| Narrator: | *Look at the photograph marked number 1 in your test book.* |
| Narrator: | *A.* |
| Woman: | *They're examining the documents.* |
| Narrator: | *B.* |
| Woman: | *They're copying the documents.* |
| Narrator: | *C.* |
| Woman: | *They're writing on the documents.* |
| Narrator: | *D.* |
| Woman: | *They're emailing the documents.* |

The correct statement is choice (A), *They're examining the documents.* Choices (B), (C), and (D) all use the wrong verb to describe what is happening. This is essentially a vocabulary item.

**Similar-Sounding Words**

This type of distractor uses words that sound similar to the correct answer.

**Example 2**

| Narrator: | *Look at the photograph marked number 2 in your test book.* |
| --- | --- |
| Narrator: | *A.* |
| Woman: | *The man is changing his tie.* |
| Narrator: | *B.* |
| Woman: | *The man is putting out a fire.* |
| Narrator: | *C.* |
| Woman: | *The man is changing a tire.* |
| Narrator: | *D.* |
| Woman: | *The man is going to retire.* |

The correct statement is choice (C), *The man is changing a tire.* Choices (A), (B), and (D) all use words that sound similar to *tire* (e.g., *tie, fire, retire*). Sometimes the similar-sounding words will be nouns—as in choices (A) and (B). At other times, the similar-sounding words may be verbs—as in choice (D)—or other parts of speech.

### Reasonable Statements/Assumptions

This type of distractor may refer to objects or actions in the photograph and, therefore, may seem reasonable, but the statement does not correctly describe what you see. It may also make assumptions about what may (or may not) be happening in the photograph. When a statement makes an assumption, it is usually wrong.

### Example 3

| Narrator: | *Look at the photograph marked number 3 in your test book.* |
| Narrator: | *A.* |
| Woman: | *The man is working at his desk.* |
| Narrator: | *B.* |
| Woman: | *The man just sat down in the chair.* |
| Narrator: | *C.* |
| Woman: | *The man is installing software on his computer.* |
| Narrator: | *D.* |
| Woman: | *The man is deleting email.* |

The correct statement is choice (A), *The man is working at his desk.* Choice (B) uses the words *sat down* and *chair* because the man is, in fact, sitting in a chair; however, we do not know whether or not he *just sat down*—meaning he sat down very recently. He may have been sitting there for several hours. This is an example of a reasonable statement that also makes an assumption. Choice (C) uses the word *computer* because we can see a computer in the photograph; however, we do not know whether or not the man is *installing software*. Again, this is an example of a reasonable statement that also makes an assumption. Choice (D) uses the phrase *deleting email*, because that is an activity that can be associated with using a computer; however, we do not know whether or not he is deleting email, writing email, opening a document, or performing some other activity.

## Irrelevant Statements

This type of distractor uses statements that do not describe anything in the photograph. It often uses words or phrases that may seem like they should go with the objects or main action in the photograph.

### Example 4

| | |
|---|---|
| Narrator: | *Look at the photograph marked number 4 in your test book.* |
| Narrator: | *A.* |
| Man: | *The waiter is setting the table.* |
| Narrator: | *B.* |
| Man: | *The spoons are next to the forks.* |
| Narrator: | *C.* |
| Man: | *The food is in the refrigerator.* |
| Narrator: | *D.* |
| Man: | *The dishes are stacked on shelves.* |

The correct statement is choice (D), *The dishes are stacked on shelves.* Choice (A) refers to a *waiter* and *setting the table*, which can both be associated with *dishes*; however, this statement does not describe anything that can be seen in the photograph. Choice (B) refers to *spoons* and *forks*, which again are both associated with *dishes*; however, this statement does not describe anything that can be seen in the photograph. Choice (C) refers to *food* and a *refrigerator*, which can both be associated with *dishes*; however, this statement does not describe anything that can be seen in the photograph.

## Hybrids

This type of distractor combines similar-sounding words, references to objects that may be seen in the photograph, or words and phrases that seem like they should go with the objects or main action in the photograph. These distractors are working to distract you on several levels at once. They are very common, and they are usually the most difficult to eliminate.

### Example 5

| | |
|---|---|
| Narrator: | *Look at the photograph marked number 5 in your test book.* |
| Narrator: | *A.* |
| Woman: | *He's watering the plants.* |
| Narrator: | *B.* |
| Woman: | *He's putting on glasses.* |
| Narrator: | *C.* |
| Woman: | *He's getting some water.* |
| Narrator: | *D.* |
| Woman: | *He's spilling water from a cup.* |

The correct statement is choice (C), *He's getting some water.* Choice (A) uses the word *watering,* which is similar to the expected word, *water.* It is also an irrelevant statement because there are no *plants* in the photograph, and the statement does not describe what is happening. This hybrid distractor is a combination of similar-sounding words and an irrelevant statement. Choice (B) uses the word *glasses.* We might expect the correct answer to use the word *cup* or *glass.* The word *glasses* sounds similar to the word *glass,* but *glasses* refers in this case to *eyeglasses.* There are no *glasses* in the photograph, so the statement does not describe what is happening. This hybrid distractor is a combination of similar-sounding words and an irrelevant statement. Choice (D) uses the word *spilling,* which sounds similar to the expected word *filling.* It also uses the expected words *water* and *cup;* however, the statement does not describe what is happening. This hybrid distractor is a combination of similar-sounding words and a reasonable statement.

## STRATEGY SUMMARY

1. Know the directions.
2. Look ahead at the photographs while the directions are playing.
3. Focus on the main action and ask, "What is this a photograph of?"
4. Evaluate the answer choices.
5. Eliminate as many answer choices as you can.
6. Answer each question before the next one starts.
7. Understand the common distractor types.

# PHOTOGRAPH PRACTICE SET

Now you are ready to play your audio CD and practice some Photograph questions on your own. You may turn the CD player on and off at any point, but try playing the statements for at least two photographs at a time. You will find the script for each set of questions in part 6 of this book, but we suggest listening without the script so you will be better prepared for the real exam.

You will hear four short statements for each photograph. When you hear the four statements, look at the photograph and choose the statement that best describes what is in the photograph.

You can mark your answers in the ovals next to the photographs, and then check them against the answer key that follows the practice questions. (Remember that on Test Day you will mark your answers on the answer grid.) Once you have checked your answers, be sure to read the review that follows the answer key.

Play track 1 of Audio CD 1 to hear the statements for the Photograph practice questions.

⏱ Time Budget: 24 minutes for 24 photographs

1.

Ⓐ Ⓑ Ⓒ Ⓓ

2.

Ⓐ Ⓑ Ⓒ Ⓓ

3.

Ⓐ Ⓑ Ⓒ Ⓓ

4.

Ⓐ Ⓑ Ⓒ Ⓓ

5.

Ⓐ Ⓑ Ⓒ Ⓓ

6.

Ⓐ Ⓑ Ⓒ Ⓓ

7.

Ⓐ Ⓑ Ⓒ Ⓓ

8.

Ⓐ Ⓑ Ⓒ Ⓓ

9.

10.

11.

12.

Ⓐ Ⓑ Ⓒ Ⓓ

**KAPLAN**

13.

Ⓐ Ⓑ Ⓒ Ⓓ

14.

Ⓐ Ⓑ Ⓒ Ⓓ

15.

16.

17.

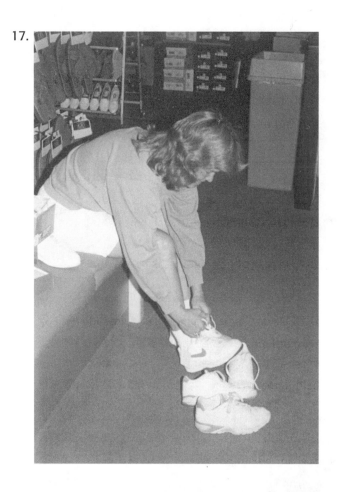

Ⓐ Ⓑ Ⓒ Ⓓ

18.

Ⓐ Ⓑ Ⓒ Ⓓ

19.

Ⓐ Ⓑ Ⓒ Ⓓ

20.

Ⓐ Ⓑ Ⓒ Ⓓ

21.

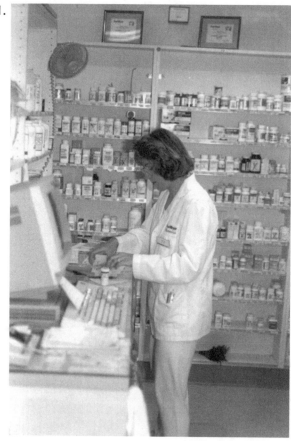

Ⓐ Ⓑ Ⓒ Ⓓ

22.

Ⓐ Ⓑ Ⓒ Ⓓ

23.

Ⓐ Ⓑ Ⓒ Ⓓ

24.

Ⓐ Ⓑ Ⓒ Ⓓ

## ANSWER KEY

| | | | |
|---|---|---|---|
| 1. | A | 13. | B |
| 2. | C | 14. | A |
| 3. | A | 15. | D |
| 4. | C | 16. | D |
| 5. | B | 17. | B |
| 6. | B) | 18. | B |
| 7. | A | 19. | D |
| 8. | D | 20. | A |
| 9. | C | 21. | D |
| 10. | D | 22. | C |
| 11. | C | 23. | C |
| 12. | D | 24. | B |

## ANSWERS AND EXPLANATIONS

All of the answer choices are included for each question, and in parentheses, there is an explanation of exactly why the wrong answer choices are incorrect. For some questions, we have left the wrong-answer explanations blank so that you can fill them in. The more you can analyze and explain the errors in the wrong answer choices, the more skillful and efficient you will become at eliminating incorrect choices and selecting the correct ones.

Sample responses for these "Identify the Error" answer explanations are included at the end of the Answers and Explanations section.

1. (A) He is sorting envelopes into the boxes. CORRECT
   (B) All of the boxes are filled to capacity. (Most of the boxes are filled, but not to capacity.)
   (C) He is writing letters to his colleagues. (He is sorting letters, not writing them.)
   (D) The squares are stacked on top of each other. (The boxes are not squares.)

2. (A) The cable is old and rusty. (The cable is not rusty in the photograph.)
   (B) The wire is in front of the school. (The photograph is of a spool, not a school.)
   (C) The cable is coiled on spools. CORRECT
   (D) The spools are being delivered by truck. (We do not know from looking at the photograph whether they are being delivered, or how they might be delivered.)

3. (A) Several parking spots are available. CORRECT

   (B) A parking attendant is counting the cars. (There is no attendant in the photograph.)

   (C) The people are getting into their cars. (There are no people in the photograph.)

   (D) The parking lot is completely filled. (You can see empty spaces in the parking lot.)

4. (A) The woman is watching television. (There is no television.)

   (B) The printer is out of paper. (The photograph is of a typewriter, not a printer.)

   (C) The typewriter is being used. CORRECT

   (D) The coffee machine is plugged in. (There is no coffee machine in the photograph.)

5. (A) He is taking inventory at the store. (There is no paperwork to suggest inventory.)

   (B) He is putting pants on the hanger. CORRECT

   (C) He is hanging the pictures on the wall. (He is hanging something, but not pictures.)

   (D) He is hemming the pants at the shop. (He is hanging pants, not hemming them.)

6. (A) He is fixing a wire in the car. (The photograph shows a tire, not a wire.)

   (B) He is putting a tire on the car. CORRECT

   (C) He is pumping air into the flat tire. (He is putting on a tire, not pumping air.)

   (D) He is tired of holding the car up. (This is the verb form of the word *tired*, not the noun form.)

7. (A) The housekeeper is making the bed. CORRECT

   (B) The woman is going to bed. _____

   (C) The sheets need changing. _____

   (D) The maid is folding towels. _____

8. (A) The equipment is full of dirt. _____

   (B) The vehicle is being driven on the highway. _____

   (C) He's working under the trees. _____

   (D) The man is operating construction equipment. CORRECT

9. (A) The man is leaving the store with the boards. (The exit is not in the photograph.)

   (B) The boards are being sawed in the back room. (Nothing is being sawed.)

   (C) The store sells lumber. CORRECT

   (D) The store is filled with many customers. (Only one customer is in the photograph.)

10. (A) The women are being shown to their table. (The women have already been seated at their table.)

    (B) The waitress has spilled soup on her sleeve. (We do not know what happened in the past.)

    (C) The women are getting ready to leave. (The women are being served dessert, not getting ready to leave.)

    (D) The waitress is serving dessert to her customers. CORRECT

11. (A) He is looking at his watch. (This is the noun form of *watch*.)

    (B) He watches his step while he walks. (He is not walking.)

    (C) He is watching something below. CORRECT

    (D) He is washing the glass under the railing. (Washing is the wrong action.)

12. (A) The nurse is entering patient information into the computer. (She is entering information into a form.)

    (B) She attends to the sick patient all by herself. (She is not helping a patient.)

    (C) She is standing patiently while she waits for the doctor. (She is writing, not standing patiently.)

    (D) The nurse is writing notes on the paper. CORRECT

13. (A) He is cooking meat at the restaurant. (He is packing meat, not cooking.)

    (B) The butcher packs meat on small trays. CORRECT

    (C) He meets his deadline for unpacking the trays. (This is using the verb *meet*, not the noun *meat*.)

    (D) The chef is chopping the meat into small pieces. (He is packing meat that is already chopped.)

14. (A) She is stacking boxes on top of each other. CORRECT

    (B) She is putting groceries on the shelf. (She is stacking boxes, not putting groceries on the shelf.)

    (C) She is getting a refund at the store. (It is not clear that she is in a store or is getting a refund.)

    (D) She is purchasing office supplies. (There are no office supplies in the photograph.)

15. (A) The man is buying a new tennis racquet. _____

    (B) The woman is writing a check for the merchandise. _____

    (C) The woman is helping a couple move furniture. _____

    (D) The woman is assisting the customers with a purchase. CORRECT

16. (A) He is driving his car to the construction site. _____

    (B) The truck is leaving the construction area. _____

    (C) He is burning garbage at the construction site. _____

    (D) The construction debris is being loaded into the trash container. CORRECT

17. (A) The shoes are stacked on the floor. (The shoes are stacked on racks and shelves.)

    (B) She is trying the shoes on for size. CORRECT

    (C) The shoes are all on sale. (We do not know whether they are on sale.)

    (D) She is walking into the shoe store. (She is already in the shoe store.)

18. (A) The material is displayed on racks. (There are no racks.)

    (B) The material is stacked on pallets. CORRECT

    (C) The stack of materials is wet. (We cannot see if it is wet in the photograph.)

    (D) The man is stacking the material. (There is no man in the photograph.)

19. (A) The package fell out of the truck. (We do not know what happened in the past.)

    (B) There is no room in the truck for the package. (There is a lot of room in the truck.)

    (C) The package has already been opened. (We cannot know whether it has been opened.)

    (D) He's loading the package into the truck. CORRECT

20. (A) He wears headphones while he is on the air. CORRECT

    (B) The air inside the studio is chilly. (We cannot know whether it is chilly. He is wearing short sleeves, so it is actually probably comfortable.)

    (C) He is using a remote to change the channel. (He is adjusting a knob, on a control panel, not changing a channel.)

    (D) He is speaking into a telephone. (He is speaking into a microphone, not a telephone.)

21. (A) The pharmacist is taking an order for a prescription. (She is not taking an order.)

    (B) The farmer is buying fertilizer for her crops. (There is no farmer, fertilizer, or crops.)

    (C) The woman is reaching for a bottle from the shelf. (She is not reaching for the shelf.)

    (D) The pharmacist is filling a customer's prescription. CORRECT

22. (A) The camera crew is carrying the equipment. (They are not carrying anything.)

    (B) The camera man is talking on the phone. (There are several people, and none is on the phone.)

    (C) The camera crew is taking a break. CORRECT

    (D) The camera man is loading film into the camera. (No one is loading film.)

23. (A) They are balancing the company's books. _____

    (B) The woman waits while the man looks. _____

    (C) The man and woman are reviewing a document. CORRECT

    (D) The woman watches the man prepare the invoice. _____

24. (A) The boys are ignoring the speaker.

    (B) The boys listen and watch while the man speaks. CORRECT

    (C) He's teaching the boys how to paint the fence. _____

    (D) The man is coaching a football team. _____

## RESPONSES FOR THE IDENTIFY THE ERROR QUESTIONS

7. (A) The housekeeper is making the bed. CORRECT

   (B) The woman is going to bed. (*She is making the bed, not getting ready to sleep.*)

   (C) The sheets need changing. (*The sheets are clean and fresh.*)

   (D) The maid is folding towels. (*She is folding the bedspread.*)

8. (A) The equipment is full of dirt. (*There is no dirt in the equipment.*)

   (B) The vehicle is being driven on the highway. (*The vehicle is not on the highway.*)

   (C) He's working under the trees. (*He is under a building structure.*)

   (D) The man is operating construction equipment. CORRECT

15. (A) The man is buying a new tennis racquet. (*There is no tennis racquet in the photograph.*)

    (B) The woman is writing a check for the merchandise. (*The woman writing is a clerk, not a buyer.*)

    (C) The woman is helping a couple move furniture. (*There is no furniture being moved.*)

    (D) The woman is assisting the customers with a purchase. CORRECT

16. (A) He is driving his car to the construction site. (*The vehicle is not a car and it is already at the site.*)

    (B) The truck is leaving the construction area. (*It is not a truck and it is not leaving.*)

    (C) He is burning the garbage at the construction site. (*There is no burning garbage seen.*)

    (D) The construction debris is being loaded into the trash container. CORRECT

23. (A) They are balancing the company's books. (*They are not doing accounting.*)

    (B) The woman waits while the man looks. (*They are interacting.*)

    (C) The man and woman are reviewing a document. CORRECT

    (D) The woman watches the man prepare the invoice. (*They are working together.*)

24. (A) The boys are ignoring the speaker. (*They are listening to him.*)

    (B) They listen and watch while the man speaks. CORRECT

    (C) He's teaching the boys how to paint the fence. (*There is a fence, but it is a minor detail in the photograph.*)

    (D) The man is coaching the football team. (*A learning activity is not necessarily a sporting activity.*)

# Chapter 4: **Exam Part II—Question-Response**

- Test-Taking Strategies
- Question-Response Practice Set
- Answer Key
- Answers and Explanations

⏱ **Time Budget for Part II: Approximately 10 minutes**

For this part of the exam, you will listen to 30 questions, and will hear three spoken responses. You must decide the best response for each question. There will be an eight-second pause between each question.

## TEST-TAKING STRATEGIES

### STRATEGY 1: KNOW THE DIRECTIONS

It is important to understand what you are being asked to do *before* you take the test. The directions will look something like this:

> **Directions:** You will hear a question or statement and three responses spoken in English. They will be spoken only once and will not be printed in your test book. Choose the best response to the question or statement and mark the letter on your answer sheet.

Listen to a sample question:

| | |
|---|---|
| Man: | *Where is the meeting room?* |
| Narrator: | *A.* |

| Woman: | To meet the new supervisor. |
| Narrator: | B. |
| Woman: | It's the second room on the left. |
| Narrator: | C. |
| Woman: | No, at three o'clock. |

Choice (B), *It's the second room on the left*, best answers the question.

## STRATEGY 2: KNOW THE QUESTION TYPES

The question types for Part II can be divided into four broad categories:

1. *Wh-* information
2. Choice
3. *Yes/No*
4. Tag

Knowing the different kinds of question types will help you to anticipate answers and to eliminate distractors.

### *Wh-* Information Questions

*Wh-* information questions are the most common type of question on the exam. They use question words (*who, what, where, why, when,* and *how*). They ask about details and require answers that provide specific information. The correct answers are usually *not* simply "yes" or "no."

| Question Word | Examples |
| --- | --- |
| *What + verb* | |
| Common verbs for *What* questions are: | |
| do | *What does Technoline Inc. charge for its services?* |
| be | *What aren't we supposed to delete?* |
| have | *What have you told Sarah regarding the mix-up?* |
| will | *What will George say about the cost overruns?* |
| can | *What can't they ship by today?* |
| could | *What could we do to improve office morale?* |
| should | *What should have been done differently?* |
| would | *What wouldn't you want to change in the contract?* |
| might | *What might be causing the delay in shipping?* |

| Question Word | Examples |
| --- | --- |
| The verbs that follow the word *what* can occur in all tenses, and they can be positive or negative. | |
| *What + verb* questions cover a large number of topics. There is no "formula" for predicting the correct answers. The answers will depend on the specific verbs used in the questions. | |

### What + noun/noun phrase

| | |
| --- | --- |
| The word *what* can be followed by singular or plural nouns or noun phrases. | *What reason did they give for not paying on time?* |
| | *What time is the meeting?* |
| *What + noun/noun phrase* questions cover a large number of topics. There is no "formula" for predicting the correct answers; the answers will depend on the specific nouns or noun phrases used in the questions. | *What day would be best for you?* |
| | *What plans do you have for expanding your market share?* |
| | *What kind of company is Troglodyne?* |
| | *What types of products does your company sell?* |
| | *What sort of person would be good at this job?* |

### What idioms

| | |
| --- | --- |
| Certain idioms or fixed expressions are formed with the word *what*. | *What about . . .* |
| | *What if . . .* |
| The words *what about* can be used to make a suggestion. The answer will usually be either an agreement or a disagreement with the suggestion, plus a reason for agreeing or disagreeing (e.g., *That's a good idea, but . . .*). The words *what about* can also be used to ask the status of something. | *What about offering a discount on volume purchases?* (Suggestion) |
| | *What about their plan to downsize the workforce?* (Asking about status) |
| The words *what if* asks about a possibility—a situation that has not happened but that is possible. | *What if we hired temporary workers over the holidays?* |
| | *What if nobody likes the new advertisement?* |

### Where + verb

Common verbs for *Where* questions are:

| | |
| --- | --- |
| do | *Where did you put the Johnson project folder?* |
| be | *Where's the best place in town to go for sushi?* |
| have | *Where have you decided to open your next store?* |
| will | *Where will the new secretary's desk go?* |
| can | *Where can I find more information on this?* |
| could | *Where could we go to get a better price?* |

| Question Word | Examples |
|---|---|
| should | *Where should I send the invoice?* |
| would | *Where would you like me to put these boxes?* |
| The verbs that follow the word *where* can occur in all tenses, and they can be positive or negative. | |
| The answer to a *Where* question will be a location, often with a preposition (e.g., *On Smith Street*; *On my desk*; *Over there*; *At the post office*; *To the warehouse*; etc.). | |

### Who + verb

Common verbs for *Who* questions are:

| | |
|---|---|
| do | *Who didn't respond to our questionnaire?* |
| be | *Who's in charge of marketing at Brayburn Inc.?* |
| have | *Who has the authority to make budget changes?* |
| will | *Who will we send to the seminar?* |
| can | *Who can we contact to get more information?* |
| could | *Who could have known about our plans?* |
| should | *Who should we call to get the copier fixed?* |
| would | *Who would be the best candidate for training?* |
| might | *Who might be interested in partnering with us on the project?* |
| The verbs that follow the word *who* can occur in all tenses, and they can be positive or negative. | |
| The answer to a *Who* question can be a person's or a company's name (e.g., *John Wilson*; *Mrs. Smith*; *Glaxon Industries*), a group (e.g., *Our customers*; *The board of directors*), or a person's title or rank (e.g., *The accountant, President Kim*). | |

### Why + verb

Common verbs for *Why* questions are:

| | |
|---|---|
| do | *Why don't all your stores carry the full product line?* |
| be | *Why were the paychecks sent out late this week?* |
| have | *Why hasn't more been done to increase production?* |
| will | *Why won't Rebecca be at the meeting?* |
| can | *Why can they make the same product for less money?* |
| could | *Why couldn't we have gotten a better discount?* |

| Question Word | Examples |
|---|---|
| should | *Why should we wait another month?* |
| would | *Why wouldn't they send the parts right away?* |
| might | *Why might Tom not like the plan?* |

The verbs that follow the word *why* can occur in all tenses, and they can be positive or negative.

The answer to a *Why* question will be a reason or explanation. Often, answers will began with *Because . . .* or *To . . .*

### When + verb

Common verbs for *When* questions are:

| | |
|---|---|
| do | *When did they sign the agreement?* |
| be | *When was Alan supposed to be here?* |
| have | *When has the meeting been scheduled for?* |
| will | *When will the next train arrive?* |
| can | *When can I expect my order to be delivered?* |
| could | *When couldn't you go?* |
| should | *When should we leave for the airport?* |
| would | *When would be a good time to call back?* |
| might | *When might the layoffs occur?* |

The verbs that follow the word *when* can occur in all tenses, and they can be positive or negative; however, negative questions are uncommon.

The answer to a *When* question will usually indicate a time (e.g., *On Friday*; *Tomorrow*; *At five o'clock*; *In six months*).

### How + verb

Common verbs for *How* questions are:

| | |
|---|---|
| do | *How did SymTech get its start?* |
| be | *How were you planning to advertise the products?* |
| have | *How have the new tax laws affected us?* |
| will | *How will we measure the plan's success?* |
| can | *How can customers contact us?* |
| could | *How could we better invest our profits?* |
| should | *How should the president have responded?* |
| would | *How would you improve our website?* |
| might | *How might we get more data about our customers?* |

| Question Word | Examples |
| --- | --- |
| The verbs that follow the word *how* can occur in all tenses, and they can be positive or negative. | |
| The answer to a *How + verb* question will indicate the way in which something is done, or it will indicate an action that can or should be taken. Often, the answer will begin with the word *by* (e.g., *By sending a fax*; *By filling out a form*; *By bus*). | |

### How + adjective

Common adjectives for *How* questions are:

| | |
| --- | --- |
| many | *How many employees does your company have?* |
| much | *How much are these?* |
| large | *How large is the freight elevator?* |
| big | *How big is your largest store?* |
| small | *How small are the rooms?* |
| fast | *How fast can you get the order out?* |
| slow | *How slow were they to pay?* |
| different | *How different are the two plans?* |
| similar | *How similar were the offers?* |
| long | *How long will it take to ship?* |
| near | *How near the airport is the hotel?* |
| far | *How far is the warehouse from here?* |
| close | *How close are they to being finished?* |

The answer to a *How + adjective* question will indicate a degree or an amount (e.g., *Very large*; *Not far*; *Ten minutes*; *Six hours*).

### How + adverb

Common adverbs for *How* questions are:

| | |
| --- | --- |
| often | *How often is website content updated?* |
| quickly | *How quickly can the project be finished?* |
| swiftly | *How swiftly can we get it done?* |
| slowly | *How slowly does the machine need to run?* |
| cheaply | *How cheaply can we make them?* |

The answer to a *How + adverb* question will indicate a degree or an amount (e.g., *Fairly often*; *In two days*; *For five dollars each*).

| Question Word | Examples |
|---|---|
| *How idioms* | |
| How come . . . | *How come nobody's ever on time to meetings?* |
| | *How come I'm always the one who has to stay late?* |
| | *How come the copier's always out of toner?* |
| How is it that . . . | *How is it that Randy did all the work, but Jared got all the credit?* |
| | *How is it that our competitors are doing so well?* |
| | *How is it that profits are down when sales are up?* |
| How about . . . | *How about offering employees more overtime opportunities?* |
| | *How about taking a break?* |
| | *How about getting John's input on this?* |

The words *how come . . .* and *how is it that . . .* can both be used to complain. Answers to these questions will usually be reasons or explanations, often using the words *because . . .* or *to . . .*

The words *how come . . .* and *how is it that . . .* are both similar to *Why* questions.

The phrase *how about* is a suggestion. The answer will usually be either an agreement or disagreement with the suggestion, plus a reason for agreeing or disagreeing (e.g., *That's a good idea, but . . .*).

## Choice Questions

Choice questions ask about choices and preferences. They require answers that provide specific information. Choice questions often use the initial question word *which*.

> *Which suit do you like better?*

The expected answer should indicate a specific choice or preference:

> *The blue one.*

Often, Choice questions present the choices using the word *or*:

> *Would you like coffee or tea?*

The expected answer should indicate a specific choice or preference:

> *Coffee, please, with a little cream.*

Common phrases used in Choice questions include:

*Which one/ones . . .*
*Which of these/those . . .*
*Which kind of/kinds of . . .*
*Which do you prefer . . .*
*Which do you like better . . .*
*Which would you choose . . .*
*Would you like A or B . . .*

Common verbs used in Choice questions include the following. These all indicate that a choice or preference is being asked about.

*like*
*prefer*
*want*
*choose*

If you hear a Choice question, listen for a response that indicates a preference or choice. The answer to a Choice question is usually not simply "yes" or "no."

### *Yes/No* Questions

*Yes/No* questions require an answer that is "yes," "no," or an expression of uncertainty, such as, "I don't know" or "I'm not sure."

*Are you going to the conference in San Francisco?*

This question requires a yes/no response—either "yes," "no," or an expression of uncertainty:

*Yes, I am.*
*No, I'm not.*
*I'm not sure.*

Of course, other information can be added to the response:

*Yes, in fact, I'll be making a presentation.*
*No, they're sending John instead.*
*I'm not sure; they might send John.*

Note that the yes/no can be implied—not stated directly:

> *I'll be making a presentation.*
> *They're sending John instead.*
> *They might send John.*

Some common ways to say or imply "yes" include:

> *Okay*
> *Sure*
> *No problem*
> *I'd be glad to*

Some common ways to say or imply "no" include:

> *Not really*
> *Unfortunately*
> *I'm afraid not*

Some common ways to say or imply uncertainty include:

> *I'm not sure*
> *I don't know*
> *I think so*
> *I don't think so*
> *Maybe*

There are many kinds of *Yes/No* questions. Following are the most common kinds that appear on the exam.

| Verb | Examples |
| --- | --- |
| ***Do + subject pronoun + infinitive*** | |
| The verb *do* can occur in the present or past tense, and it can be positive or negative. | *Do I need to work this Saturday?* |
| | *Do you go to the gym every day?* |
| | *Doesn't she work in the accounting department?* |
| | *Does it require special training to use?* |
| | *Didn't they guarantee payment within 90 days?* |
| | *Didn't we ship their order on Monday?* |

| Verb | Examples |
|---|---|
| **Do + possessive adjective + noun** | |
| The verb *do* can occur in the present or past tense, and it can be positive or negative. | *Does my staff need to attend the meeting?* |
| | *Do your records match ours?* |
| | *Does his boss know what he's been doing?* |
| | *Don't its parts need to be serviced soon?* |
| | *Didn't our order get sent out on time?* |
| | *Did their payment clear?* |
| The nouns can be singular or plural. | |
| **Do + -ing** | |
| The verb *do* can occur in the present or past tense, and it can be positive or negative. | *Does paying in cash mean we'll get a discount?* |
| | *Did hiring more workers help your production problem?* |
| | *Doesn't shipping by air cost more?* |
| | *Didn't installing the wireless network take a lot of time?* |
| **Be + subject pronouns + adjectives** | |
| The verb *be* can occur in the present or past tense, and it can be positive or negative. | *Am I late for the meeting?* |
| | *Are you happy with your new job?* |
| | *Is Mr. Murphy sick today?* |
| | *Is it faster than the old one?* |
| | *Are they expensive?* |
| | *Aren't we lucky to have Phoebe on our staff?* |
| **Be + subject pronouns + -ing** | |
| The verb *be* can occur in the present or past tense, and it can be positive or negative. | *Am I doing this correctly?* |
| | *Are you waiting to speak to Mr. Crawford?* |
| | *Isn't Julie Reiss running the department these days?* |
| | *Is it operating more efficiently since it was upgraded?* |
| | *Are they coming to the party?* |
| | *Weren't we expecting a delivery from QualComp today?* |
| **Have + subject pronoun + past participle** | |
| The verb *have* can occur in the present or past tense, and it can be positive or negative. | *Have I worked here long enough to qualify for benefits?* |
| | *Haven't you finished the Scottsdale report yet?* |
| | *Has she called you about the cost estimate?* |
| | *Hasn't it cost too much money already?* |
| | *Hadn't they asked us to bill their client directly?* |
| | *Haven't we changed vendors?* |

| Verb | Examples |
|---|---|
| *Can/Could + subject pronoun + infinitive*<br><br>The verbs *can/could* can be positive or negative. | *Can I send the documents to your home instead of your office?*<br><br>*Could you come to work a little early tomorrow?*<br><br>*Couldn't she find a cheaper apartment?*<br><br>*Can it go any faster than that?*<br><br>*Couldn't they hire you on a temporary basis?*<br><br>*Can't we return it if it's damaged?* |
| *Could + subject pronoun + have + past participle*<br><br>The verb *could* can be positive or negative. | *Couldn't I have gone with him?*<br><br>*Could you have finished quicker if you had better tools?*<br><br>*Couldn't he have gotten a better price somewhere else?*<br><br>*Could it have been due to a clerical error?*<br><br>*Couldn't they have waited a little longer?*<br><br>*Could we have raised our prices too high?* |
| *Will + subject pronoun + infinitive*<br><br>The verb *will* can be positive or negative. | *Won't I need to bring my own tools?*<br><br>*Will you take your laptop with you?*<br><br>*Will she know where to go when she gets there?*<br><br>*Will it work when the temperature is below freezing?*<br><br>*Will they have enough time to finish everything?*<br><br>*Won't we pay in cash?* |
| *Will + possessive adjective + noun*<br><br>The verb *will* can be positive or negative. | *Will my paycheck be ready by this afternoon?*<br><br>*Will your company be adding any more staff?*<br><br>*Will his plan get approval from the board?*<br><br>*Won't its sales just continue to decline?*<br><br>*Will our software work on their system?*<br><br>*Won't their website be updated daily?* |
| *Will + -ing*<br><br>The verb *will* can be positive or negative. | *Will repairing the computer be cheaper than buying a new one?*<br><br>*Won't making reservations online be faster?*<br><br>*Will taking this medicine on an empty stomach make me feel nauseated?*<br><br>*Won't traveling by yourself be lonely?* |

| Verb | Examples |
|---|---|
| **Would + subject pronoun + infinitive** | |
| The verb *would* can be positive or negative. | *Would I need to get approval first?* |
| | *Would you buy more if we lowered our price?* |
| | *Would he charge extra for overnight delivery?* |
| | *Would it look better if we painted it blue?* |
| | *Wouldn't they prefer to stay at the Wexler Hotel?* |
| | *Wouldn't we make more money by investing in high-risk bonds?* |
| **Would + possessive adjective + noun** | |
| The verb *would* can be positive or negative. | *Would my salary go up if I take the new position?* |
| | *Would your office be a more convenient place to meet?* |
| | *Would her boss really say something like that?* |
| | *Would its parts break less frequently if they were serviced more often?* |
| | *Would their services be of use to us?* |
| | *Would our staff be willing to work overtime on short notice?* |
| **Would + -ing** | |
| The verb *would* can be positive or negative. | *Would working from home be a possibility?* |
| | *Wouldn't buying in bulk quantities be less expensive?* |
| | *Would billing you monthly be more convenient?* |
| | *Wouldn't flying be quicker than driving?* |
| **Should + subject pronoun + infinitive** | |
| The verb *should* can be positive or negative. | *Should I arrange a meeting with John?* |
| | *Shouldn't you make your presentation first?* |
| | *Should Lisa call to make the reservations?* |
| | *Shouldn't it be held in the conference room, instead?* |
| | *Should they upgrade their entire manufacturing system?* |
| | *Should we go to a later show?* |
| **Should + possessive adjective + noun** | |
| The verb *should* can be positive or negative. | *Should my accountant call you back to discuss the details?* |
| | *Shouldn't your order have been delivered by now?* |
| | *Should his file be updated?* |
| | *Shouldn't its parts be oiled every day?* |
| | *Should their offer be accepted?* |
| | *Shouldn't our department handle matters like that?* |

| Verb | Examples |
|---|---|
| *Should + -ing*<br>The verb *should* can be positive or negative. | *Should smoking be banned in public places?*<br>*Shouldn't training be required for all new employees?*<br>*Should billing be quarterly?*<br>*Shouldn't buying online be cheaper?* |

## Tag Questions

Tag questions come at the end of sentences. They are used to check information, ask for agreement, or find out whether something is true. They are more common in spoken English than they are in written English.

> *Chris works in the accounting department, doesn't he?*

In this case, the question is checking whether or not Chris works in the accounting department. The speaker thinks this might be true but is not sure. Notice that the expected answer is "yes," "no," or an expression of uncertainty:

> *No, he works in the marketing department.*

Tag questions repeat the auxiliary verb used in the sentence:

> *David can come on Friday, can't he?*
> *The capital of France is Paris, isn't it?*
> *You don't take the subway to work, do you?*
> *You haven't seen my glasses anywhere, have you?*

Notice that the tag is negative when the sentence verb is positive, and it is positive when the sentence verb is negative:

> *John Mayer is the CEO of Exitron, isn't he?*
>     [+]            [−]

> *John Mayer isn't the CEO of Exitron, is he?*
>     [−]            [+]

If the sentence does not have an auxiliary verb, the question tag always uses a form of *do*:

> *You remembered to send the invoices, didn't you?*
> *Sarah made the reservations, didn't she?*
> *Mr. Lee likes to play golf, doesn't he?*
> *Mark goes on vacation next week, doesn't he?*

## STRATEGY 3: KNOW THE DISTRACTORS

There are four basic types of distractors for Part II questions:

1. **Similar-sounding words**—This type of distractor uses words and phrases that sound similar to the expected correct response.
2. **Repetition of question words**—This type of distractor repeats words and phrases used in the question or statement.
3. **Irrelevant responses**—This type of distractor responds to a common misunderstanding of the question or statement. Also included in this category are yes/no answers to *Wh-* information questions and *Wh-* information answers to *Yes/No* questions.
4. **Hybrid distractors**—This type of distractor uses combinations of the first three distractor types.

Look at the Part II directions example again. You will hear:

| | |
|---|---|
| Man: | *Where is the meeting room?* |
| Narrator: | *A.* |
| Woman: | *To meet the new supervisor.* |
| Narrator: | *B.* |
| Woman: | *It's the second room on the left.* |
| Narrator: | *C.* |
| Woman: | *No, at three o'clock.* |

Choice (A) uses the word *meet*, which is a repetition of the word *meeting* in the question. This is an example of a repetition distractor. Choice (C) does not answer the question; however, if you misunderstood the question as "When is the meeting?" this would be an appropriate response. This is an example of an irrelevant response distractor.

Here is another example.

| | |
|---|---|
| Woman: | *How many cups of coffee do you usually drink each day?* |
| Narrator: | *A.* |
| Man: | *No more than two.* |
| Narrator: | *B.* |
| Man: | *I have two copies.* |
| Narrator: | *C.* |
| Man: | *I think that's too many.* |

The correct response is (A), *No more than two.* Choice (B) uses the word *copies*, which sounds similar to *coffee* or *coffees*. This is an example of a similar-sounding distractor. Choice (C) repeats the question word *many*, and it uses the word *too*, which sounds like the expected word *two*. This is an example of a hybrid distractor using repetition of a question word and a similar-sounding word.

A set of responses may use more than one type of distractor at a time. Not all distractors fit neatly into the categories we have outlined; some may seem to belong to more than one category. Note also that each of these distractor types is similar because, in the end, they are inappropriate responses to the question or statement. However, it is useful to look at *why* they are inappropriate and to understand what it is you must listen for.

## Similar-Sounding Words

This type of distractor uses words and phrases that sound similar to the expected correct response. For example, you will hear:

| | |
|---|---|
| Man: | *How many pairs of tickets do we need?* |
| Narrator: | *A.* |
| Woman: | *I eat chicken two or three times a week.* |
| Narrator: | *B.* |
| Woman: | *Four should be enough.* |
| Narrator: | *C.* |
| Woman: | *Get some pears, some apples, and some cherries, too.* |

The correct response is (B), *Four should be enough.* Choice (A) uses the word *eat*, which sounds a little like *need*, and *chicken*, which sounds a little like *ticket*. This is an example of a similar-sounding distractor. Choice (C) uses the word *pears*, which sounds like the word *pairs*. This is another example of a similar-sounding distractor.

## Repetition of Question Words

This type of distractor repeats words and phrases used in the question or statement.

| | |
|---|---|
| Man: | *Are there any more copies of the annual report left?* |
| Narrator: | *A.* |
| Woman: | *Yes, there should be a few left on the shelf in the library.* |
| Narrator: | *B.* |
| Woman: | *No, I'm afraid he left early this afternoon.* |
| Narrator: | *C.* |
| Woman: | *Yes, turn left at the next traffic light.* |

The correct response is (A), *Yes, there should be a few left on the shelf in the library.* Choice (B) repeats the question word *left,* but here it has a different meaning. This is an example of a repetition distractor. Choice (C) repeats the question word *left,* but again, it has a different meaning. This is another example of a repetition distractor.

### Irrelevant Responses

This type of distractor responds to a common misunderstanding of the question or statement.

You will hear:

| | |
|---|---|
| Woman: | *Where will you stay when you go to London?* |
| Narrator: | *A.* |
| Man: | *I'm leaving on the tenth.* |
| Narrator: | *B.* |
| Man: | *At my cousin's house.* |
| Narrator: | *C.* |
| Man: | *Yes, I'm going there for a conference.* |

The correct response is choice (B) *At my cousin's house.* Choice (A) answers the question, *When will you go to London?* Choice (C) answers the *Yes /No* question, *Will you go to London?* Both choices (A) and (C) are irrelevant response distractors.

### Hybrid Distractor

This type of distractor uses combinations of the first three distractor types.

You will hear:

| | |
|---|---|
| Man: | *When's the deadline for submitting contract bids?* |
| Narrator: | *A.* |
| Woman: | *They need to be in by five P.M. on Friday.* |
| Narrator: | *B.* |
| Woman: | *No, not until all the contract bids are in.* |
| Narrator: | *C.* |
| Woman: | *You can submit your contact information by email.* |

The correct response is (A), *They need to be in by five P.M. on Friday.* Choice (B) repeats the question words *contract bids,* and it uses the word *until,* which might be expected in a response to a *When* question. The response is also a Yes/No answer to an *Wh*-information question. This distractor is a hybrid distractor combining repetition and an irrelevant response. Choice (C) repeats the question word *submit*, and it uses the word *contact*, which sounds similar to *contract*. It also uses the phrase *by email*, because an expected response to a *When* question often takes the form of *by + time* word. This is an example of a hybrid distractor using repetition and similar-sounding words.

## STRATEGY 4: FOCUS ON THE PURPOSE

Listen carefully to the question or statement that the first speaker makes. Ask yourself what the intent of the first speaker is. Examine what kind of response the speaker expects. Determine whether the response should be "yes" or "no," provide new information, or indicate an opinion or offer advice.

Listen especially to the first word for clues as to whether the question is *Yes/No* or *Wh-* information. Knowing the intent of the first speaker is a key step in the process of choosing the correct response.

## STRATEGY 5: EVALUATE THE STATEMENTS

Listen closely to the first word to determine what kind of question it is and to decide what the speaker's intent is. Once you know the intent of the question or statement, you must listen to and evaluate the responses you hear. Because each response will be spoken only once, you must listen carefully.

Listen for a response that closely matches the intent of the question. After you hear a statement that is a close match to the answer you have been expecting, find the number for the question on your answer sheet and mark the oval for the letter that matches your answer. Be sure to listen to all three responses before you mark you answer sheet.

## STRATEGY 6: ELIMINATE STATEMENTS THAT DO NOT FIT

If none of the responses match your expected answer very well, then you must eliminate any choices that do not fit the situation. Listen carefully to the first word to determine what kind of question it is. Eliminate any answers that are inappropriate. For example, eliminate a yes/no answer to a *Wh-* information question.

Listen carefully to the tense used in the question and in the responses. Eliminate any answer choices that use the wrong tense; for example, a past tense response to a question about a future action.

If you must guess, eliminate the answer choices that repeat words from the question. Very often, these are distractors. Not always, but often.

## STRATEGY 7: ANSWER THE CURRENT QUESTION BEFORE THE NEXT ONE BEGINS

Make sure you answer every question as quickly as you can. You have only about eight seconds to choose your answer for each question or statement. You should be finished with the current question before the next one begins. If you are still answering a question when the next one begins, you might not hear the beginning of the question.

As soon as you have finished with a question, get ready to listen for the next one.

## STRATEGY SUMMARY

1. Know the directions.
2. Know the different kinds of question types.
3. Understand the basic types of distractors.
4. Focus on the purpose of the question or statement.
5. Evaluate the statements you hear and mark the answer if you know it.
6. Eliminate statements that do not fit the situation and select the best match from what is left.
7. Be sure to answer the current question before the next question begins.

# QUESTION-RESPONSE PRACTICE SET

 Play track 2 on Audio CD 1 to hear the questions.

🕑 **Time Budget: 8 minutes for 24 questions**

1. Mark your answer on your sheet.  Ⓐ Ⓑ Ⓒ
2. Mark your answer on your sheet.  Ⓐ Ⓑ Ⓒ
3. Mark your answer on your sheet.  Ⓐ Ⓑ Ⓒ
4. Mark your answer on your sheet.  Ⓐ Ⓑ Ⓒ
5. Mark your answer on your sheet.  Ⓐ Ⓑ Ⓒ
6. Mark your answer on your sheet.  Ⓐ Ⓑ Ⓒ
7. Mark your answer on your sheet.  Ⓐ Ⓑ Ⓒ
8. Mark your answer on your sheet.  Ⓐ Ⓑ Ⓒ
9. Mark your answer on your sheet.  Ⓐ Ⓑ Ⓒ
10. Mark your answer on your sheet.  Ⓐ Ⓑ Ⓒ
11. Mark your answer on your sheet.  Ⓐ Ⓑ Ⓒ
12. Mark your answer on your sheet.  Ⓐ Ⓑ Ⓒ
13. Mark your answer on your sheet.  Ⓐ Ⓑ Ⓒ
14. Mark your answer on your sheet.  Ⓐ Ⓑ Ⓒ
15. Mark your answer on your sheet.  Ⓐ Ⓑ Ⓒ
16. Mark your answer on your sheet.  Ⓐ Ⓑ Ⓒ
17. Mark your answer on your sheet.  Ⓐ Ⓑ Ⓒ
18. Mark your answer on your sheet.  Ⓐ Ⓑ Ⓒ
19. Mark your answer on your sheet.  Ⓐ Ⓑ Ⓒ
20. Mark your answer on your sheet.  Ⓐ Ⓑ Ⓒ
21. Mark your answer on your sheet.  Ⓐ Ⓑ Ⓒ
22. Mark your answer on your sheet.  Ⓐ Ⓑ Ⓒ
23. Mark your answer on your sheet.  Ⓐ Ⓑ Ⓒ
24. Mark your answer on your sheet.  Ⓐ Ⓑ Ⓒ

## ANSWER KEY

| | | | |
|---|---|---|---|
| 1. A | | 13. C | |
| 2. C | | 14. A | |
| 3. C | | 15. C | |
| 4. B | | 16. B | |
| 5. C | | 17. A | |
| 6. C | | 18. C | |
| 7. C | | 19. C | |
| 8. C | | 20. B | |
| 9. B | | 21. B | |
| 10. A | | 22. C | |
| 11. A | | 23. A | |
| 12. C | | 24. A | |

## ANSWERS AND EXPLANATIONS

For each question, we have identified the question type (*Wh-*, Choice, *Yes/No*, or Tag). All of the answer choices are included for each question, and in parentheses, there is an explanation of exactly why the wrong answer choices are incorrect. For some questions, we have left the wrong-answer explanations blank so that you can fill them in. The more you can analyze and explain the errors in the wrong answer choices, the more skillful and efficient you will become at eliminating incorrect choices and selecting the correct ones.

Sample responses for these Identify the Error answer explanations are included at the end of the Answers and Explanations section.

1. Is there anything good on TV tonight? (*Yes/No*)
   (A) The news comes on in about an hour. CORRECT
   (B) Yes, the plant is on top of the television. (Double repetition of the words *on* and *TV/television*)
   (C) Please find a different station. (Does not relate to the question)

2. Why did they cancel the reception for Mr. Chang? (*Why*)
   (A) Her secretary did. (Answers a *Who* question)
   (B) He received the invitation. (Does not answer the question)
   (C) He got sick. CORRECT

3. Where can I buy a magazine? (*Where*)

    (A) A cab just went by. (Plays on the words *by* and *buy*)

    (B) The store takes credit cards, I think. (Irrelevant)

    (C) The newsstand on the corner. CORRECT

4. What type of business are you in? (*What*)

    (A) Because I sold the house. (Irrelevant)

    (B) I'm a banker. CORRECT

    (C) I'll type it tomorrow. (Uses the verb form of the word *type*)

5. Would you like to work overtime tonight? (*Yes/No*)

    (A) No thanks, I have one. (Answers a question offering something)

    (B) I'd rather begin at 8. (Plays on the word *work*: *begin work/work overtime*)

    (C) Sure, I need the hours. CORRECT

6. Where is your final destination today? (*Where*)

    (A) I'll be flying there. (Does not include a location; answers a *How* question)

    (B) I'm leaving this afternoon. (Does not include a location; answers a *When* question)

    (C) I'm going to Rome. CORRECT

7. It'll be a long trip, won't it? _____

    (A) She tripped on the stairs, yes. _____

    (B) No, I leave next week. _____

    (C) Yes, about four weeks. CORRECT

8. Why don't we take a short break? _____

    (A) My car got new brakes last summer. _____

    (B) Yes, Lisa broke the plate by accident. _____

    (C) Good idea, I'm getting tired. CORRECT

9. When will the earnings report be issued? (*When*)

    (A) It will be published in the newspaper. (Does not include a time reference; answers a *Where* question)

    (B) At the end of the first quarter. CORRECT

    (C) Because the stock went up last week. (Wrong subject; wrong tense)

10. You subscribe to *Business Monthly* Magazine, don't you? (Tag)
    (A) No, but my office does. CORRECT
    (B) Yes, I heard the news on the radio. (Irrelevant)
    (C) The mail is late today. (Wrong subject)

11. How are the contract negotiations coming along? (*How*)
    (A) Our attorneys are reviewing the proposed changes. CORRECT
    (B) We're almost finished with the progress report. (Irrelevant)
    (C) They returned the rental car last night. (Answers a *When* question; irrelevant)

12. Who should we send to Buenos Aires? (*Who*)
    (A) I'd recommend next week. (Answers a *When* question)
    (B) Let's send out for lunch. (Answer repeats the word *send*)
    (C) Jaime should go. CORRECT

13. Does Ali rent that house, or does he own it? (Choice)
    (A) He used to rent a house in Alexandria. (Plays on the words *Alexandria* and *Ali*; wrong tense)
    (B) His cousin just bought a home downtown. (Irrelevant)
    (C) He has a one-year lease. CORRECT

14. Has Ms. Matala finished with the samples? (*Yes/No*)
    (A) Yes, she was right on schedule. CORRECT
    (B) No, she was born in Finland. (Plays on the words *finished* and *Finland*)
    (C) She felt his action was justified. (Irrelevant)

15. What's the training workshop about? _____
    (A) Sometime tomorrow afternoon. _____
    (B) Somewhere in the new building. _____
    (C) Something to do with team building. CORRECT

16. Why don't you apply for that new job posting? _____
    (A) I worked on the second shift. _____
    (B) I don't think I'm qualified. CORRECT
    (C) I'm walking to the post office. _____

17. Is that pollution or just morning haze? (*Choice*)

    (A) The latter; it should be gone by noon. CORRECT

    (B) The industrial zone is located in the valley. (Answers a *Where* question)

    (C) The afternoon rain keeps the air clean. (Wrong subject)

18. Why don't we take a cruise for vacation? (*Why*)

    (A) Because the food is so good. (Does not make sense because the question is formed negatively)

    (B) So that we can get a free ticket. (Does not answer a negative question)

    (C) That might be a nice change. CORRECT

19. Will Mr. Yoon write the report, or does he want me to do it? (*Choice*)

    (A) He was right last time. (Plays on the words *right* and *write*)

    (B) I think he reports directly to Mr. Yoon. (Verb form of the word *report*, not the noun form)

    (C) He'll do it himself. CORRECT

20. How many workers will we need for the Johnston building? (*How*)

    (A) Construction has been ongoing for two years. (Refers to time, not to an amount)

    (B) I estimate around a hundred. CORRECT

    (C) We'll need to work overtime to finish. (Repeats the words *need* and *work*)

21. Why don't you think about taking early retirement? (*Why*)

    (A) I thought you retired. (Repeats part of *retirement*)

    (B) Actually, I've been considering it. CORRECT

    (C) I've worked for over thirty years. (Irrelevant)

22. Who's your favorite author? (*Who*)

    (A) I prefer short stories over novels. (Answers a *What* question)

    (B) Her favorite books are usually fiction. (Repeats the word *favorite*; wrong subject)

    (C) It's hard for me to pick just one. CORRECT

23. Don't you think interest rates will continue to go up? _____

    (A) In the short term, I suppose so. CORRECT

    (B) No, I am very interested. _____

    (C) I had to drive up the hill. _____

24. What should we do with these files for the Wallrock lease? _____

    (A) Leave them until Tuesday. CORRECT

    (B) Your secretary has them. _____

    (C) No, I sent them to Mr. Wallrock. _____

## RESPONSES FOR IDENTIFY THE ERROR QUESTIONS

7. It'll be a long trip, won't it? (*Yes/No*)

    (A) She tripped on the stairs, yes. (*Play on the word trip; confusing verb/noun forms*)

    (B) No, I leave next week. (*Confusion between the time the trip starts and how long it lasts*)

    (C) Yes, about four weeks. CORRECT

8. Why don't we take a short break? (*Yes/No*)

    (A) My car got new brakes last summer. (*Play on the words break and brakes*)

    (B) Yes, Lisa broke the plate by accident. (*Play on the words break and broke*)

    (C) Good idea, I'm getting tired. CORRECT

15. What's the training workshop about? (*What*)

    (A) Sometime tomorrow afternoon. (*Answers When question*)

    (B) Somewhere in the new building. (*Answers Where question*)

    (C) Something to do with team building. CORRECT

16. Why don't you apply for that new job posting? (*Why*)

    (A) I worked on the second shift. (*Irrelevant; wrong verb and tense*)

    (B) I don't think I'm qualified. CORRECT

    (C) I'm walking to the post office. (*Play on the words posting and post office*)

23. Don't you think interest rates will continue to go up? (*Yes/No*)

    (A) In the short term, I suppose so. CORRECT

    (B) No, I am very interested. (*Play on the words interest and interested*)

    (C) I had to drive up the hill. (*Play on the words go up and drive up*)

24. What should we do with these files for the Wallrock lease? (*What*)

    (A) Leave them until Tuesday. CORRECT

    (B) Your secretary has them. (*Answers a Who question*)

    (C) No, I sent them to Mr. Wallrock. (*Repeats the word Wallrock; answers a Where question*)

# Chapter 5: **Exam Part III—Short Conversations**

- Test-Taking Strategies
- Short Conversations Practice Set
- Answer Key
- Answers and Explanations

**Time Budget for Part III: Approximately 12 minutes**

For this part of the exam, you will listen to ten short conversations. There will be two speakers in each conversation. In your exam booklet, you will see three questions, each with four responses; you will also hear the *question*, but *not* the answer choices. For each question, you must pick the response that best answers the question. There will be an eight-second pause between questions, and an eight-second pause between the end of the last question and the start of the next conversation.

## TEST-TAKING STRATEGIES

### STRATEGY 1: KNOW THE DIRECTIONS

It is important to understand what you are being asked to do, and to be sure you know the directions before you take the test. The directions will look something like this:

**Directions:** You will now hear a number of conversations between two people. You will be asked to answer three questions about what the speakers say. Select the best response to each question and mark the letter on your answer sheet. The conversations will be spoken only once and will not be printed in your test book.

Please note that for this part of the TOEIC exam, the test maker will not provide sample questions, as it does in Parts I and II.

However, here is an example illustrating the format of a typical Short Conversation, so you can start becoming familiar with it.

Narrator:  *Questions 41 through 43 refer to the following conversation.*

Woman:  *Something smells delicious in here . . . what is it?*

Man:  *It's vegetable lasagna. I made it for dinner last night. I made too much, and there's a lot left over, so I brought some for today's lunch.*

Woman:  *Well, it really does smell wonderful. How did you learn to make this?*

Man:  *It's my mother's family recipe—she got it from her grandmother. I'd be happy to bring the recipe to work tomorrow, if you'd like.*

Narrator:  *Number 41: What are the speakers mainly discussing?*

You will be able to read the first question and the four answer choices in your test book:

41.  What are the speakers mainly discussing?

(A) The man's family

(B) A problem the woman has

(C) The food the man has made

(D) The restaurants in the area

There will be an eight-second pause after the first question. Then you will hear:

Narrator:  *Number 42: What does the man offer to do for the woman?*

You will be able to read the second question and the four answer choices in your test book:

42.  What does the man offer to do for the woman?

(A) Take her to lunch.

(B) Bring her his recipe.

(C) Introduce her to his family.

(D) Drive her to work the next day.

There will be an eight-second pause after the second question. Then you will hear:

Narrator:  *Number 43: What is probably true about the speakers?*

You will be able to read the third question and the four answer choices in your test book:

43. What is probably true about the speakers?

    (A) They are neighbors.

    (B) They are coworkers.

    (C) They are in a restaurant.

    (D) They are talking on the telephone.

Each question is spoken once, followed by an eight-second pause. This means for each question you have only eight seconds to read the question and answer choices and mark your answer sheet.

Usually, there are two speakers, and each speaker has two turns at speaking. This is the four-line format. Occasionally, however, you will hear the second speaker only once; this is the three-line format.

**Part III: Short Conversations**
**Two Formats**

| 4-line format | 3-line format |
| --- | --- |
| *Speaker A* | *Speaker A* |
| *Speaker B* | *Speaker B* |
| *Speaker A* | *Speaker A* |
| *Speaker B* | |

Almost all the short conversations are in the four-line format. Both formats (four-line and three-line) are followed by three questions.

## STRATEGY 2: READ THE FIRST FEW QUESTIONS

Because you already know what the directions are, look at the first few questions in your test book while the directions are playing. This will let you know what to expect and what you will need to listen for.

Because the directions for Part III are short, there is not much time to read ahead. However, try to read as many questions as you can.

## STRATEGY 3: KNOW THE QUESTION TYPES AND ORDER

In Part III, the questions usually ask for information in the order in which it was presented in the conversation. This means that the first question will usually ask about something mentioned near the beginning, the second question will ask about something that was mentioned in the middle, and the third question will ask about something mentioned near the end.

There are three basic categories of questions for Part III:

1. **Gist**—Gist questions will ask what the main topic is, where the conversation takes place, or who the speakers are. They ask about the overall situation, rather than about specific details. Common Gist questions include:

   > *What are the speakers mainly discussing?*
   > *Where does this conversation probably take place?*
   > *Where do the speakers probably work?*
   > *Who are the speakers?*

2. **Detail**—Detail questions ask about details mentioned in the conversation, such as what someone did or has been asked to do; how a problem is being handled; or the order in which things are to be done. They can ask about general information or very specific details. Common Detail questions include:

   > *What did the man do?*
   > *What did the woman ask the man to do?*
   > *How did the speakers solve their problem?*
   > *Which will the man do first?*
   > *When is the report due?*

3. **Implication/Inference**—Implication/Inference questions ask about things that are not stated directly by either of the speakers. They can ask about the speaker's intentions, emotions, expectations, or probable future actions. Common Implication/Inference questions include:

   > *What does the woman intend to do next week?*
   > *Why is the man disappointed?*
   > *What does the woman expect the man to do?*
   > *What will the man probably do next?*

Some Implication/Inference and Gist questions may seem to be similar. For example, a Gist question that asks about where the conversation takes place requires an inference, in that the conversation will provide enough information to make the location or setting of the conversation obvious, but this information will not be stated directly. However, while some Gist questions require you to understand an implication or make an inference, Gist questions focus on the larger picture or the overall situation. Implication/Inference questions deal with details about the speakers or the situation.

### Common Part III Question Patterns

The most common patterns for Part III questions are:

| A | B | C |
|---|---|---|
| Gist | Gist | Detail |
| Detail | Detail | Detail |
| Implication/Inference | Detail | Detail |

Other patterns are possible, but these are the three most common.

## STRATEGY 4: KNOW THE DISTRACTORS

To understand the kinds of Part III distractors, and how they work, you first need to understand how TOEIC exam writers write TOEIC items.

All Part III distractors must answer the question *plausibly*, that is, they must be possible answers to the question. When you look at a Part III question and the answer choices by themselves—without hearing the conversation—each choice must answer the question in a logical and realistic way. For example:

What did the man do on Monday?

(A) He left work early.

(B) He finished a report.

(C) He ate lunch at his desk.

(D) He replied to John's email.

Without hearing the conversation, none of the answer choices can be eliminated. Each choice is a plausible answer to the question, and there are no "impossible" answer choices. All Part III items are written in this way.

Another feature of Part III items is that none of the questions is linked in any way. That is, the information contained in a set of question and answer choices will not help you to answer any other questions.

There are four basic types of distractors for Part III questions:

1. **Not mentioned**—This type of distractor uses words, phrases, and ideas that are not mentioned in the conversation. There is no connection to the language used in the conversation. The distractor answers the question plausibly but does not relate to the conversation.

2. **Repeated words**—This type of distractor uses words, phrases, and ideas that are mentioned in the conversation but changes them so that they are not true. The distractor answers the question plausibly but is incorrect.

3. **New words**—This type of distractor introduces new words, phrases, or ideas that may be associated with or implied by language and ideas expressed in the conversation but that are untrue. The distractor answers the question plausibly but is incorrect.

4. **Rephrase/paraphrase**—This type of distractor takes the original language used in the conversation and rephrases or paraphrases it in a way that makes it untrue. The distractor answers the questions plausibly, but incorrectly.

Note that a set of answer choices may use more than one type of distractor at a time. Not all distractors fit neatly into the categories outlined here; some may seem to belong to more than one category. Note also that each of these distractor types is similar because, in the end, they are incorrect answers to the question. However, it is useful to look at *why* they are incorrect and to understand what you must listen for.

Look at the Part III directions example again. (Material in *italics* indicates what you will hear; material in **bold** indicates what is printed in your test book.)

| | |
|---|---|
| Narrator: | *Questions 41 through 43 refer to the following conversation.* |
| Woman: | *Something smells delicious in here . . . what is it?* |
| Man: | *It's vegetable lasagna. I made it for dinner last night. I made too much, and there's a lot left over, so I brought some for today's lunch.* |
| Woman: | *Well, it really does smell wonderful. How did you learn to make this?* |
| Man: | *It's my mother's family recipe—she got it from her grandmother. I'd be happy to bring the recipe to work tomorrow, if you'd like.* |
| Narrator: | *Number 41: What are the speakers mainly discussing?* |

41. **What are the speakers mainly discussing?**

(A) **The man's family**

(B) **A problem the woman has**

(C) **The food the man has made**

(D) **The restaurants in the area**

This is a Gist question. The correct answer is choice (C). Choice (A) uses words, phrases, and ideas mentioned in the conversation (*mother, family, grandmother*), but the main topic of discussion is not the man's family. This is an example of a repeated words distractor. Choice (B)

is not mentioned or implied. This is an example of a not mentioned distractor. Choice (D) is not mentioned, but it uses the word *restaurant*, which is associated with food and cooking. This is an example of a new words distractor.

> Narrator: *Number 42: What does the man offer to do for the woman?*

42. What does the man offer to do for the woman?

   (A) Take her to lunch.
   (B) Bring her his recipe.
   (C) Introduce her to his family.
   (D) Drive her to work the next day.

This is a Detail question. The correct answer is (B). Choice (A) repeats the conversation word *lunch,* but the man has not offered to take the woman to lunch. This is an example of a repeated words distractor. Choice (C) repeats the conversation word *family*, which is also associated with the conversation words *mother* and *grandmother.* This is an example of a repeated words distractor but could also be seen as a rephrase/paraphrase distractor. Choice (D) plays on a rephrasing or paraphrasing of the words *I'd be happy to bring the recipe to work tomorrow . . .* The man offers to bring his recipe to work the next day, not drive the woman to work. This is an example of a rephrase/paraphrase distractor.

> Narrator: *Number 43: What is probably true about the speakers?*

43. What is probably true about the speakers?

   (A) They are neighbors.
   (B) They are coworkers.
   (C) They are in a restaurant.
   (D) They are talking on the telephone.

This is an Inference/Implication question. The correct answer is choice (B). Choice (A) is not mentioned or implied and is an example of a not mentioned distractor. Choice (C) is not mentioned, but it uses the word *restaurant*, which is associated with the topics of food and cooking. This is an example of a new words distractor. Choice (D) is not mentioned or implied. Because the woman can smell the food, they must be in the same room at the same time. This is an example of a not mentioned distractor.

Notice that for each question, all the distractors are plausible answers, and that none of the questions or answer choices are of any help in answering other questions.

## STRATEGY 5: LISTEN FOR THE INFORMATION

By reading the questions in your test book, you will know what information to listen for in the conversation. For example, if the first question is a Detail question asking about what one of the speakers has done, you should listen carefully for words and phrases that indicate what that speaker has done.

The conversations will often contain a lot of information that is *not* tested. However, because you have the questions in front of you in your test book, you will know what information to be listening for.

Note that the questions for Part III are all *Wh-* questions. There are no *Yes/No* questions. Review the *Wh-* question material in chapter 4 to help you focus on the kinds of information the questions ask for and on the format of the expected answers. You should know, for example, that a *When* question deals with time and that you will need to listen for time words (e.g., *today, yesterday, this afternoon, at 10 o'clock*).

You will have to listen carefully to the conversation to get information you need. You will not be able to read the questions and apply logic to answer the questions. Remember, the question and answer choices used in one question will *not* help you to answer another question. The TOEIC exam writers are very careful to avoid letting the information in one question and answer choice set help to answer another question and answer choice set.

Pay attention to who each speaker is. Often, the relationship between the speakers is made very clear, and there may be a question to test whether you understood this information. Sometimes the distractors will use information that is true for one of the speakers but not the other. For example, a man and woman might be discussing the man's vacation plans. For the question "What are the speakers mainly discussing?" one of the distractors may refer to the woman's vacation plans.

## STRATEGY 6: ANSWER EACH QUESTION IN YOUR OWN WORDS

Read each question and predict the answer in your own words *before* reading the answer choices. If you understand the conversation, you should be able to answer all the questions in your own words. For each question, your predicted answer—or one very closely matching it—should be among the answer choices. Remember, there are no trick questions on the TOEIC exam. All the information needed to answer the questions is presented in the conversation.

If you read the answer choices first without answering the question in your own words, you will be tempted to choose one of the distractors. It is much better to have your own idea about the correct answer first, *before* looking at the answer choices.

## STRATEGY 7: EVALUATE THE ANSWER CHOICES

If one of the answer choices is a close match to the answer you expect, mark the oval for that letter. If none of the responses matches your expected answer very well, you must eliminate as many choices as you can. Remember, one question and answer choice set will not help you answer another, so do not look at answer choices from one question for clues to answer another question.

Often, each answer choice uses words and phrases as they were spoken in the conversation. However, if only one of the answer choices uses words and phrases from the conversation, this is likely to be the correct one.

## STRATEGY 8: ELIMINATE ANSWER CHOICES

If none of the answer choices matches your expected answer very well, then you must eliminate as many wrong choices as you can. If you must guess, eliminate any choices that do not use words and phrases from the conversation—the not mentioned distractor type. (Unless there is only *one* choice that uses words and phrases from the conversation, in which case you should choose this as the correct answer.) The not mentioned distractors are often the easiest to eliminate.

## STRATEGY 9: MANAGE YOUR TIME

Remember that there are only eight seconds between questions. There is also an eight-second pause between the end of the last question and the introduction for the next conversation. If you spend too much time on one set of questions, you may miss the beginning of the next conversation. You will need to select your answer choice and mark it on your answer sheet as quickly as you can to keep up with the test. Because you will hear the conversations only once, you must not allow yourself to fall behind.

If you find yourself running out of time, mark your answer sheet with your wild-guess letter (see strategy 7 from chapter 2). Do not leave any questions unanswered.

## STRATEGY 10: READ THE QUESTIONS FOR THE NEXT CONVERSATION

For each conversation, there is a brief introduction. For example, you will hear: *"Questions 44 through 46 refer to the following conversation."* Ideally, you should have answered all three questions for the current conversation before you hear the introduction for the next conversation. You should then immediately begin to read as many of the next set of questions as you can before the conversation begins. This will help you focus on the information you need to listen for.

## STRATEGY SUMMARY

1. Know the directions.
2. Read the first few questions while the directions are playing.
3. Understand the question types and how questions are ordered.
4. Understand the basic types of distractors.
5. Listen for the information in the questions.
6. Answer each question in your own words before reading the choices.
7. Evaluate the answer choices and mark the answer if you know it.
8. Eliminate answer choices that are wrong and select the best match from what is left.
9. Manage your time and be sure to answer all three questions before the next conversation begins.
10. Read the questions for the next conversation before it starts.

# SHORT CONVERSATIONS PRACTICE SET

 Play track 3 of Audio CD 1 to hear the Short Conversations.

🕑 **Time Budget: Approximately 12 minutes for 24 questions**

**Practice 1**

1. What are the speakers mainly discussing?

   (A) Where they go on vacation
   (B) When they take time off work
   (C) What they do every weekend
   (D) How many hours they work each week

2. What about the woman surprised the man?

   (A) She seems to have a lot of vacation.
   (B) She never works on Mondays.
   (C) She never takes days off work.
   (D) She works a lot of hours.

3. How is the man's job different from the woman's?

   (A) He has less vacation.
   (B) He has more vacation.
   (C) He can work on weekends.
   (D) He cannot work on weekends.

## Practice 2

4. Who is the man?

   (A) An employer
   (B) A job applicant
   (C) A recruitment officer
   (D) A personnel manager

5. What kind of experience are the speakers talking about?

   (A) Public speaking
   (B) Project management
   (C) Organizing events
   (D) Computer repairs

6. What kind of job is being offered?

   (A) Computer repair technician
   (B) IT project manager
   (C) Computer programmer
   (D) University lecturer

## Practice 3

7. Why is the man annoyed?

   (A) A filing cabinet has been moved.
   (B) He cannot find a document.
   (C) He cannot understand a document.
   (D) There is a mistake in the contract.

8. What has the woman changed?

(A) The text of a contract

(B) The furniture

(C) The finance files

(D) The filing system

9. Where is the JDK contract file?

(A) In the top drawer of a cabinet

(B) In the third drawer from the top

(C) In the filing cabinet near the window

(D) In the filing cabinet near Mike's desk

**Practice 4**

10. What is the woman learning about?

(A) A camera

(B) A projector

(C) A printer

(D) A photocopier

11. What does the green button do?

(A) It switches off the equipment.

(B) It puts the machine on standby.

(C) It switches on the equipment.

(D) It changes the brightness.

12. How can users change the size of the image?

(A) By pressing the "resize" button

(B) By pressing the blue arrows

(C) By pressing the red button

(D) By turning the wheel

**Practice 5**

13. What do the speakers want to reserve?

    (A) A room for an office party

    (B) A conference room

    (C) A car

    (D) A table at a restaurant

14. When was the reservation made?

    (A) Monday

    (B) Tuesday

    (C) Thursday

    (D) Friday

15. How long do the speakers need to wait?

    (A) Half an hour

    (B) Forty-five minutes

    (C) An hour

    (D) More than an hour

**Practice 6**

16. Whom is the woman speaking to?

    (A) A policeman

    (B) A bus driver

    (C) A passenger

    (D) A travel agent

17. Where does the woman want to go?

    (A) A train station

    (B) The airport

    (C) The bus station

    (D) A subway station

18. How many minutes will the woman need to wait for the next bus?

   (A) 3
   (B) 5
   (C) 8
   (D) 15

## Practice 7

19. What are the speakers mainly discussing?

   (A) New safety rules
   (B) Rescheduling a meeting
   (C) Preparing for an inspection
   (D) Ordering plastic

20. Who will Rory call?

   (A) The client
   (B) The rest of their team
   (C) The safety inspector
   (D) The consultant

21. How will Rory contact their team?

   (A) By memo
   (B) By phone
   (C) By email
   (D) By text message

## Practice 8

22. Where does Tony work?

   (A) In the maintenance department
   (B) On the shop floor
   (C) In the product training department
   (D) In the service supplies department

23. What is Tony's problem?

   (A) He does not know what to order.

   (B) He does not know how to order.

   (C) He is not sure if he should order.

   (D) He does not know where Mr. Logan's order is.


24. Why are Mr. Logan and Tony not together?

   (A) Mr. Logan is ill.

   (B) Mr. Logan is in another city.

   (C) Tony is on the shop floor.

   (D) Tony is in a meeting.

## ANSWER KEY

1. B
2. A
3. D
4. B
5. B
6. C
7. B
8. D
9. C
10. B
11. B
12. D

13. D
14. D
15. A
16. A
17. A
18. A
19. B
20. A
21. C
22. D
23. C
24. B

## ANSWERS AND EXPLANATIONS

All of the answer choices are included for each question, and in parentheses, there is an explanation of exactly why the wrong answer choices are incorrect. For some questions, we have left the wrong-answer explanations blank so that you can fill them in. The more you can analyze and explain the errors in the wrong answer choices, the more skillful and efficient you will become at eliminating incorrect choices and selecting the correct ones.

Sample responses for these Identify the Error answer explanations are included at the end of the Answers and Explanations section.

### Practice 1

1. What are the speakers mainly discussing?

    (A) Where they go on vacation. (This repeats the word *vacation*.)

    (B) When they take time off work. CORRECT

    (C) What they do every weekend. (The woman says she works some weekends, but we do not hear what the speakers do every weekend.)

    (D) How many hours they work each week. (They talk about work, but do not mention this detail.)

2.  What about the woman surprised the man?

    (A) She seems to have a lot of vacation. CORRECT

    (B) She never works on Mondays. (She does not take only Mondays off.)

    (C) She never takes days off work. (In fact, she seems to take more time off than he does.)

    (D) She works a lot of hours. (They talk about work, but do not mention this detail.)

3.  How is the man's job different from the woman's?

    (A) He has less vacation. (This is what he thinks at first, but then we learn that she has the same number of vacation days as he does.)

    (B) He has more vacation. (The topic of the conversation is vacation time, but this is not a true statement.)

    (C) He can work on weekends. (Working on weekends is mentioned, but this is not a true statement.)

    (D) He cannot work on weekends. CORRECT

## Practice 2

4.  Who is the man?

    (A) An employer (The woman is a potential employer, but the man is not.)

    (B) A job applicant CORRECT

    (C) A recruitment officer (This is not mentioned.)

    (D) A personnel manager (This repeats the words *project management*.)

5.  What kind of experience are the speakers talking about?

    (A) Public speaking (This repeats the word *speaking*.)

    (B) Project management CORRECT

    (C) Organizing events (This repeats the word *organizational*.)

    (D) Computer repairs (They are talking about programming, not making repairs.)

6.  What kind of job is being offered?

    (A) Computer repair technician (They are talking about programming, not repairs.)

    (B) IT project manager (The woman would prefer someone with management potential, but the current job is for a programmer.)

    (C) Computer programmer CORRECT

    (D) University lecturer (This repeats the word *university*.)

### Practice 3

7. Why is the man annoyed?

    (A) A filing cabinet has been moved. (The files have been moved, but not the cabinet.)

    (B) He cannot find a document. CORRECT

    (C) He cannot understand a document. (He says "I can't understand it," but he is not referring to the document.)

    (D) There is a mistake in the contract. (This repeats the word *contract.*)

8. What has the woman changed?

    (A) The text of a contract (This repeats the word *contract.*)

    (B) The furniture (The files have been moved but not the cabinet.)

    (C) The finance files (This repeats the word *files.*)

    (D) The filing system CORRECT

9. Where is the JDK contract file?

    (A) In the top drawer of a cabinet (The top drawer is mentioned, but the file is not there.)

    (B) In the third drawer from the top (This repeats the phrase *drawer from the top.*)

    (C) In the filing cabinet near the window CORRECT

    (D) In the filing cabinet near Mike's desk (This is mentioned, but the file is not there.)

### Practice 4

10. What is the woman learning about?

    (A) A camera (This repeats the word *camera.*)

    (B) A projector CORRECT

    (C) A printer (This is clearly a related technology, but it is not mentioned.)

    (D) A photocopier (This plays on the words *photo* and *copy.*)

11. What does the green button do?

    (A) It switches off the equipment. (The red button does this.)

    (B) It puts the equipment on standby. CORRECT

    (C) It switches on the equipment. (The red button does this.)

    (D) It changes the brightness. (The blue button does this.)

12. How can users change the size of the image?

    (A) By pressing the "resize" button (This is not mentioned.)

    (B) By pressing the blue arrows (These control brightness and color.)

    (C) By pressing the red button (The red button switches the machine on and off.)

    (D) By turning the wheel CORRECT

## Practice 5

13. What do the speakers want to reserve?

    (A) A room for an office party (This repeats the word *party*.)

    (B) A conference room (This is not mentioned.)

    (C) A car (This repeats the word *car*.)

    (D) A table at a restaurant CORRECT

14. When was the reservation made?

    (A) Monday (This repeats the word *Monday*.)

    (B) Tuesday (This repeats the word *Tuesday*.)

    (C) Thursday (This is not mentioned.)

    (D) Friday CORRECT

15. How long do the speakers need to wait?

    (A) Half an hour CORRECT

    (B) Forty-five minutes (This is not mentioned.)

    (C) An hour (This is not mentioned.)

    (D) More than an hour (This is not mentioned.)

## Practice 6

16. Whom is the woman speaking to?

    (A) A policeman CORRECT

    (B) A bus driver (Buses are mentioned, but we do not address a driver as "officer.")

    (C) A passenger (She is traveling, but we would not address another passenger as "officer.")

    (D) A travel agent (The topic is travel, but she is clearly in the middle of her journey, not arranging it.)

17. Where does the woman want to go?

   (A) A train station CORRECT
   (B) The airport (She has just come from the airport.)
   (C) The bus station (This repeats the word *bus*.)
   (D) A subway station (This repeats the words *subway station*.)

18. How many minutes will the woman need to wait for the next bus?

   (A) 3 CORRECT
   (B) 5 (This repeats the word *five*.)
   (C) 8 (This repeats the word *eight*.)
   (D) 15 (This repeats the word *fifteen*.)

**Practice 7**

19. What are the speakers mainly discussing?

   (A) New safety rules _____
   (B) Rescheduling a meeting CORRECT
   (C) Preparing for an inspection _____
   (D) Ordering plastic _____

20. Who will Rory call?

   (A) The client CORRECT
   (B) The rest of their team _____
   (C) The safety inspector _____
   (D) The consultant _____

21. How will Rory contact their team?

   (A) By memo _____
   (B) By phone _____
   (C) By email CORRECT
   (D) By text message _____

## Practice 8

22. Where does Tony work?

    (A) In the maintenance department _____

    (B) On the shop floor _____

    (C) In the product training department _____

    (D) In the service supplies department CORRECT

23. What is Tony's problem?

    (A) He does not know what to order. _____

    (B) He does not know how to order. _____

    (C) He is not sure if he should order. CORRECT

    (D) He does not know where Mr. Logan's order is. _____

24. Why are Mr. Logan and Tony not together?

    (A) Mr. Logan is ill. _____

    (B) Mr. Logan is in another city. CORRECT

    (C) Tony is on the shop floor. _____

    (D) Tony is in a meeting. _____

## RESPONSES FOR IDENTIFY THE ERROR QUESTIONS

### Practice 7

19. What are the speakers mainly discussing?

    (A) New safety rules (*This repeats the word safety.*)

    (B) Rescheduling a meeting CORRECT

    (C) Preparing for an inspection (*This repeats the word inspection.*)

    (D) Ordering plastic (*This repeats the word plastic.*)

20. Who will Rory call?

    (A) The client CORRECT

    (B) The rest of their team (*He will contact them, but not by phone.*)

    (C) The safety inspector (*This repeats the words safety inspection.*)

    (D) The consultant (*She is mentioned, but the man is not asked to contact her.*)

21. How will Rory contact their team?

  (A) By memo (*This is a common method to contact people, but this is not mentioned.*)

  (B) By phone (*He will contact the client by phone, not the team.*)

  (C) By email CORRECT

  (D) By text message (*This repeats the word message.*)

**Practice 8**

22. Where does Tony work?

  (A) In the maintenance department (*This repeats the words maintenance department.*)

  (B) On the shop floor (*This repeats the words shop floor.*)

  (C) In the product training department (*This repeats the words product training department.*)

  (D) In the service supplies department CORRECT

23. What is Tony's problem?

  (A) He does not know what to order. (*He says what he needs, but does not know if he should order.*)

  (B) He does not know how to order. (*This is not the problem.*)

  (C) He is not sure if he should order. CORRECT

  (D) He does not know where Mr. Logan's order is. (*This is not mentioned.*)

24. Why are Mr. Logan and Tony not together?

  (A) Mr. Logan is ill. (*This is not mentioned.*)

  (B) Mr. Logan is in another city. CORRECT

  (C) Tony is on the shop floor. (*This is true, but that is not the reason why they are not together.*)

  (D) Tony is in a meeting. (*This is not mentioned.*)

# Chapter 6: **Exam Part IV—Short Talks**

- Test-Taking Strategies
- Short Talks Practice Set
- Answer Key
- Answers and Explanations

🕐 **Time Budget for Part IV: Approximately 13 minutes**

For this part of the TOEIC exam, you will hear ten short talks. There is only one speaker in each talk. In your exam booklet, you will see three written questions, each with four written responses; you will also hear the question (but not the answer choices). For each question, you must pick the response that best answers the question. There will be an eight-second pause between questions, and an eight-second pause between the end of the last question and the start of the next talk.

## TEST-TAKING STRATEGIES

### STRATEGY 1: KNOW THE DIRECTIONS

It is important to understand what you are being asked to do and to be sure you know the directions before you take the test. The directions will look something like this:

**Directions:** You will now hear short talks given by a single speaker. You will be asked to answer three questions about what the speaker says. Select the best response to each question and mark the letter on your answer sheet. The talks will be spoken only once and will not be printed in your test book.

Please note that for this part of the TOEIC exam, sample questions are not provided, as they were in Parts I and II. However, here is an example illustrating the format of a typical Short Talk, so you can start becoming familiar with it.

You will hear:

| | |
|---|---|
| Narrator: | *Questions 71 through 73 refer to the following talk.* |
| Man: | *Good morning everyone. Today I'd like to discuss our strategy for the New York City area. As I'm sure you're all aware, real estate prices there are among the highest in the nation and are continuing to rise. On the one hand, this is good news in the short term because it means that the company's rental properties there will continue to be profitable. On the other hand, if the trend continues, it means that acquiring and developing new residential and business properties will become more costly; and because rents are so high already, we won't be able to charge what we need to maintain our current return on investment—over time, returns will fall. There are also some signs that the New York market may be turning around—houses and apartments are staying on the market an average of two days longer now than they did six months ago. While sellers are still getting contracts at the prices they want, it's taking longer to get them. This could mean that housing prices and rents are poised to come down soon. The situation is rather mixed and difficult to read. What I'd like us to do is formulate a revised strategy that balances the rewards we now enjoy in the current boom market against the future risks of a soft housing market.* |
| Narrator: | *Number 71: What does the speaker say could happen if the current trend in real estate prices continues?* |

You will be able to read the first question and the four answer choices in your test book:

71. What does the speaker say could happen if the current trend in real estate prices continues?

    (A) Return on investment could fall.
    (B) Development opportunities could increase.
    (C) Fewer residential properties could be available.
    (D) Selling commercial properties could become more difficult.

There will be an eight-second pause after the first question. Then you will hear:

> Narrator: *Number 72: What does the speaker claim regarding New York City real estate?*

You will be able to read the second question and the four answer choices in your test book:

72. What does the speaker claim regarding New York City real estate?

    (A) Prices have fallen in the past six months.

    (B) Houses and apartments are taking longer to sell.

    (C) Apartment sales have doubled in the past six months.

    (D) Commercial properties are a good long-term investment.

There will be an eight-second pause after the second question. Then you will hear:

> Narrator: *Number 73: What does the speaker want to change?*

You will be able to read the third question and the four answer choices in your test book:

73. What does the speaker want to change?

    (A) A project schedule

    (B) A meeting agenda

    (C) A company strategy

    (D) A real estate contract

Each question is spoken once, followed by an eight-second pause. This means for each question you have only eight seconds to read the question and answer choices, and mark your answer sheet.

## STRATEGY 2: READ THE FIRST FEW QUESTIONS

Because you already know what the directions are, look at the first few questions in your test book while the directions are playing—just as you did for Part III. This will let you know what to expect and what you will need to listen for.

Because the directions for Part IV are short, there is not much time to read ahead. However, try to read as many questions as you can.

## STRATEGY 3: KNOW THE QUESTION TYPES

The organization of Part IV questions is similar to that for Part III. The questions generally ask for information in the order in which it is presented in the talk: The first question will usually ask about something mentioned near the beginning, the second question will ask about something mentioned in the middle, and the third question will ask about something mentioned near the end.

There are three basic categories of questions for Part IV. (These are essentially the same categories found in Part III).

1. **Gist**—Gist questions will ask what the main topic is, where the talk takes place, or who the intended audience is. Gist questions ask about the overall situation rather than about specific details. For example:

   *Who is the speaker?*

   *Who is the intended audience?*

   *What is the speaker mainly discussing?*

   *What is the purpose of the announcement?*

   *Where does this talk probably take place?*

2. **Detail**—Detail questions ask about information mentioned in the short talk. They can ask about general information or very specific details. Examples include what a speaker has said about something or someone; when an action or event will take place; what role, function, or responsibility people will have; how a problem or situation is being handled; the order in which things are to be done; or what products or services a company provides. For example:

   *What does the speaker say about Starboard Enterprises?*

   *What will happen the next day?*

   *What will David Johnson's role be?*

   *Where will the old files be kept?*

   *When should the first locking nut be removed?*

   *What service does Travis Consulting provide?*

3. **Implication/Inference**—Implication/Inference questions ask about things that are not stated directly by the speaker, such as the speaker's intentions, emotions, expectations, or probable future actions. Common Implication/Inference questions include:

   *What does the speaker intend to do next week?*

   *Why is the speaker surprised?*

   *What does the speaker expect managers to do?*

   *What will the speaker probably do next?*

   *What does the speaker imply about the new rules?*

Some Implication/Inference and Gist questions might seem to be similar. For example, a Gist question that asks about who the talk is intended for requires an inference, in that the talk will provide enough information about the location, setting, or situation to make the intended audience obvious, but the identity of the audience will not likely be stated directly. However, while some Gist questions require you to understand an implication or make an inference, they generally focus on the larger picture or the overall situation. Implication/Inference questions tend to deal with implied details about something the speaker is discussing, expecting, planning, or intending to do, or about details that concern the situation or context itself.

## COMMON PART IV QUESTION PATTERNS

Part IV questions patterns are essentially the same as those for Part III. The most common patterns for Part IV questions are:

| A | B | C |
|---|---|---|
| Gist | Gist | Detail |
| Detail | Detail | Detail |
| Implication/Inference | Detail | Detail |

Other patterns are possible, but these are the three most common.

## STRATEGY 4: KNOW THE DISTRACTORS

The distractors for Part IV are essentially the same as those used in Part III. As was the case for Part III, all Part IV distractors will answer the question plausibly, that is, they will be possible answers to the question. When you look at a Part IV question and the answer choices by themselves—without hearing the talk—each choice will answer the question in a logical and realistic way, and no choice can be eliminated using logic or common sense. Each option will be a plausible answer to the question, and there are no impossible answer choices. All TOEIC exam Part IV items are written in this way.

As was described for Part III, none of the Part IV questions are linked in any way, that is, the information contained in a set of question and answer choices will not help you to answer any other questions.

There are four basic types of distractors for Part IV questions:

1. **Not mentioned**—This type of distractor uses words, phrases, and ideas that are not mentioned in the talk, but there is no connection to the language used in the talk. The distractor answers the question plausibly but does not relate to the talk.
2. **Repeated words**—This type of distractor uses words, phrases, and ideas that are mentioned in the talk, but it changes them so that they are not true. The distractor answers the question plausibly but is incorrect.

3. **New words**—This type of distractor introduces new words, phrases, or ideas that may be associated with or implied by language and ideas expressed in the talk, but that are untrue. The distractor answers the question plausibly but is incorrect.

4. **Rephrase/Paraphrase**—This type of distractor takes the original language used in the talk and rephrases or paraphrases it in a way that makes it untrue. The distractor answers the question plausibly but is incorrect.

Note that a set of answer choices may use more than one type of distractor at a time. Not all distractors fit neatly into the categories outlined here; some may seem to belong to more than one category. Note also that each of these distractor types is similar because, in the end, they are incorrect answers to the question. However, it is useful to look at *why* they are incorrect and to understand what you must listen for.

Look at the Part IV directions example again. (Material in *italics* indicates what you will hear; material in **bold** indicates what is printed in your test book.)

| | |
|---|---|
| Narrator: | *Questions 71 through 73 refer to the following talk.* |
| Man: | *Good morning everyone. Today I'd like to discuss our strategy for the New York City area. As I'm sure you're all aware, real estate prices there are among the highest in the nation and are continuing to rise. On the one hand, this is good news in the short term because it means that the company's rental properties there will continue to be profitable. On the other hand, if the trend continues, it means that acquiring and developing new residential and business properties will become more costly; and because rents are so high already, we won't be able to charge what we need to maintain our current return on investment—over time, returns will fall. There are also some signs that the New York market may be turning around—houses and apartments are staying on the market an average of two days longer now than they did six months ago. While sellers are still getting contracts at the prices they want, it's taking longer to get them. This could mean that housing prices and rents are poised to come down soon. The situation is rather mixed and difficult to read. What I'd like us to do is formulate a revised strategy that balances the rewards we now enjoy in the current boom market against the future risks of a soft housing market.* |
| Narrator: | *Number 71: What does the speaker say could happen if the current trend in real estate prices continues?* |

71. **What does the speaker say could happen if the current trend in real estate prices continues?**

(A) **Return on investment could fall.**

(B) **Development opportunities could increase.**

(C) **Fewer residential properties could be available.**

(D) **Selling commercial properties could become more difficult.**

The correct answer is choice (A). This is a Detail question. Choice (B) uses the word *development* from the talk, but it also introduces the idea of an increase in development opportunities, which is not mentioned, and is therefore a false statement. Choice (C) uses the words *residential properties* from the talk, but the idea that fewer of them will be available is not mentioned and is therefore incorrect. Choice (D) uses words, phrases, and ideas mentioned or implied in the talk (*commercial properties, difficult*), but it rephrases them in a way that is not true.

Narrator:          *Number 72: What does the speaker claim regarding New York City real estate?*

72. What does the speaker claim regarding New York City real estate?

(A) Prices have fallen in the past six months.

(B) Houses and apartments are taking longer to sell.

(C) Apartment sales have doubled in the past six months.

(D) Commercial properties are a good long-term investment.

The correct answer is (B). This is a Detail question. Choice (A) takes words, phrases, and ideas that are mentioned in the talk (*prices, fall, six months*) and rephrases them to make a false statement. Choice (C) uses words from the talk (*apartment, six months*) but combines them in a way that is incorrect. Choice (D) takes words, phrases, and ideas that are mentioned or implied in the conversation (*commercial properties, long-term investments*) and rephrases them to make a false statement.

Narrator:          *Number 73: What does the speaker want to change?*

73. What does the speaker want to change?

(A) A project schedule

(B) A meeting agenda

(C) A company strategy

(D) A real estate contract

The correct choice is (C). This is a Detail question. Choice (A) is not mentioned or implied, and is an example of a not mentioned distractor. Choice (B) is not mentioned or implied, and is an example of a not mentioned distractor. Choice (D) repeats words and phrases from the talk (*real estate, contract*), but this is not what the speaker wants to change.

Notice that for each question, all the distractors are plausible answers, and none of the questions or answer choices are of any help in answering other questions.

## STRATEGY 5: LISTEN FOR THE INFORMATION IN THE QUESTIONS

As was described in relation to Part III of the TOEIC exam, by reading the questions in your test book, you will know what information you need to be listening for. For example, if the first question is a Gist question asking about whom the audience is, you should listen carefully for words and phrases that indicate where the talk takes place and who the audience is most likely to be.

The talks will often contain a lot of information that is *not* tested. However, because you are able to read the questions in your test book, you will know what information to be listening for, and you should focus on finding what you need to answer each question.

Note that the questions for Part IV are all *Wh-* information questions—as was the case for Part III. There are no *Yes/No* questions. Go back and review the Question-Response *Wh-* information question material on pages 50–61. Be sure you understand the kinds of information the question types ask for and the format of the expected answers. You should know, for example, that a *When* question deals with time and that you will need to listen for time words (e.g., *today, yesterday, this afternoon, at 10 o'clock*).

You will have to listen carefully to the talk to get information you need. Remember, the question and answer choices used in one question set will *not* help you to answer another question.

Pay attention to the context of the talk. Know who the speaker is and what his or her relationship to the audience is. Listen for clues that tell you where the talk is likely to take place. If a speaker is addressing an audience, the setting and relationship between the speaker and the audience is usually made very clear, and there is often a question that tests whether you have understood this.

Be sure you also understand the purpose of the talk. If, for example, a speaker is addressing an audience, understand why the speaker is addressing this particular audience. If an announcement is being made, listen for clues to its purpose to understand *why* the announcement is being made.

## STRATEGY 6: ANSWER EACH QUESTION IN YOUR OWN WORDS

Read each question and predict the answer in your own words *before* reading the answer choices. If you understand the talk, you should be able to answer each question in your own words. Your predicted answer—or one very closely matching—should be among the answer choices. Remember, there are no trick questions on the TOEIC exam. All the information needed to answer the questions is presented in the talk.

It is much better to have your own idea about the correct answer first, *before* looking at the answer choices. If you look at the answer choices first, you might be attracted to an incorrect choice and wind up listening to the talk for that information, which might not even be mentioned.

## STRATEGY 7: EVALUATE THE ANSWER CHOICES

As you did with Part III, find the answer choice that is a close match to the one you expect and mark your answer sheet. Be sure to fill in the oval completely, as shown in the test directions.

If no answer choice matches your expected answer very well, eliminate as many choices as you can. Remember, because one question and answer choice set will not help you answer another, do not look at answer choices from one question for clues to answer another question.

Often, each answer choice uses words and phrases used in the talk. However, if there is only *one* answer choice that uses words and phrases from the talk, this is very likely the correct one.

## STRATEGY 8: ELIMINATE ANSWER CHOICES

If none of the answer choices matches your expected answer very well, then you must eliminate as many wrong choices as you can. If you find you have to guess, the same guessing strategy used for Part III works for Part IV, too. Eliminate any choices that do not use words and phrases from the talk—the not mentioned distractor type. (Unless there is only *one* choice that uses words and phrases from the talk, in which case you should choose this as the correct answer.) The not mentioned distractors are often the easiest to eliminate.

## STRATEGY 9: MANAGE YOUR TIME

Remember that there are only eight seconds between questions. There is also an eight-second pause between the end of the last question and the introduction for the next talk. You will need to work quickly to keep up with the test, and you will hear the short talks only once. Do not waste time answering any individual question—you risk missing the beginning of the next talk, which could contain information you need to answer the questions that follow. Select your answer choice and mark it on your answer sheet as quickly as you can.

If you find yourself running out of time, mark your answer sheet with your wild-guess letter. Do not leave any questions unanswered.

## STRATEGY 10: READ THE QUESTIONS FOR THE NEXT TALK BEFORE IT STARTS

Just as each Part III Short Conversations had a brief introduction, each Short Talk in Part IV does, too. For example, you will hear:

Narrator:         *Questions 71 through 73 refer to the following voicemail message.*

You should try to answer all three questions for the current talk before you hear the introduction for the next talk. Then, while the introduction is playing, immediately begin reading as many of the next set of questions as you can before the actual talk begins. This will help you focus on what information you need to listen for.

## STRATEGY SUMMARY

1. Know the directions.
2. Read the first few questions while the directions are playing.
3. Understand question types and how questions are ordered.
4. Understand the basic types of distractors.
5. Listen for the information in the questions.
6. Answer each question in your own words before reading the answer choices.
7. Evaluate the answer choices and mark the answer if you know it.
8. Eliminate answer choices that are wrong and select the best match from what is left.
9. Manage your time and be sure to answer all three questions before the next talk begins.
10. Read the questions for the next talk before it starts.

## SHORT TALKS PRACTICE SET

Now you are ready to do the Short Talks practice, for which you will need the CD. Choose the best answer from the choices listed and mark it in your book (on Test Day, you will mark your answers on the answer grid). You will find the transcript for the Short Talks in part 6 of this book, but try these first without the transcript so you will be better prepared for the exam.

When you have listened to all of the talks and answered all of the questions, check your answers against the answer key. Then, be sure to read the explanations that follow the answer key.

 Play track 4 on Audio CD 1 to hear the Short Talks.

### Practice 1

1. What is the speaker promoting?

   (A) International capital
   (B) Increased imports
   (C) Foreign investment
   (D) Increased export

2.  Where does this talk take place?

    (A) At a trade conference
    (B) At a business school
    (C) At a corporate board meeting
    (D) At a local government meeting

    Ⓐ Ⓑ Ⓒ Ⓓ

3.  According to the speaker, why are foreign buyers interested in Irish products?

    (A) They are reasonably priced.
    (B) They are high quality.
    (C) They are organic.
    (D) They are easily available.

    Ⓐ Ⓑ Ⓒ Ⓓ

**Practice 2**

4.  Why is the SmartShares company in the news?

    (A) It has laid off a large part of its workforce.
    (B) It has been involved in a criminal court case.
    (C) It has expanded into the East Asian market.
    (D) It has won an important industry award.

    Ⓐ Ⓑ Ⓒ Ⓓ

5.  According to the report, what is improving for workers in Thailand?

    (A) Salaries
    (B) Benefits packages
    (C) Working conditions
    (D) Productivity

    Ⓐ Ⓑ Ⓒ Ⓓ

6.  What will Mark Francis discuss?

    (A) Stock news
    (B) Developments in technology
    (C) Local news
    (D) Travel and tourism tips

    Ⓐ Ⓑ Ⓒ Ⓓ

**KAPLAN**

### Practice 3

7.  What kind of store is Dunthorps?

    (A) Clothing
    (B) Kitchenware
    (C) Department
    (D) Furniture

    Ⓐ Ⓑ Ⓒ Ⓓ

8.  What is learned about the sale at Dunthorps?

    (A) It includes items sold online.
    (B) It is held every year.
    (C) It celebrates the opening of a new store.
    (D) It limits the number of items that can be bought.

    Ⓐ Ⓑ Ⓒ Ⓓ

9.  When does the sale end?

    (A) End of June
    (B) July 1st
    (C) End of July
    (D) Mid-August

    Ⓐ Ⓑ Ⓒ Ⓓ

### Practice 4

10. Where did the artist get the idea for his piece?

    (A) France
    (B) The Caribbean
    (C) Austria
    (D) New Zealand

    Ⓐ Ⓑ Ⓒ Ⓓ

11. What kind of artwork is being discussed?

    (A) Sculpture
    (B) Pencil drawing
    (C) Painting
    (D) Photograph

    Ⓐ Ⓑ Ⓒ Ⓓ

12. Who is the speaker addressing?

   (A) Buyers at an art sale
   (B) An audience at a lecture
   (C) Artists at a workshop
   (D) Visitors to a museum

   Ⓐ Ⓑ Ⓒ Ⓓ

## Practice 5

13. Who is Ira Levinson?

   (A) The speaker
   (B) The building's architect
   (C) A new employee
   (D) The company founder

   Ⓐ Ⓑ Ⓒ Ⓓ

14. How many people will work in the building?

   (A) 250
   (B) 500
   (C) 750
   (D) 1,000

   Ⓐ Ⓑ Ⓒ Ⓓ

15. What is the purpose of the talk?

   (A) To dedicate a building
   (B) To introduce a new employee
   (C) To announce plans for a new building
   (D) To discuss a change in company policy

   Ⓐ Ⓑ Ⓒ Ⓓ

## Practice 6

16. For how many years have traffic violations been decreasing nationally?

   (A) 1
   (B) 3
   (C) 5
   (D) 8

   Ⓐ Ⓑ Ⓒ Ⓓ

17. Why is the number of traffic violations dropping?

   (A) There are fewer offenders.
   (B) There are fewer police officers.
   (C) Policing is more efficient.
   (D) Fines are stricter.

   Ⓐ Ⓑ Ⓒ Ⓓ

18. What did the police spokesperson say about the figures?

   (A) They indicate that drivers are becoming more careful.
   (B) They show that policing methods are improving.
   (C) They might not say anything about drivers' behavior.
   (D) They are probably not very accurate.

   Ⓐ Ⓑ Ⓒ Ⓓ

**Practice 7**

19. Which number should a customer press for checking account access?

   (A) 1
   (B) 2
   (C) 3
   (D) 4

   Ⓐ Ⓑ Ⓒ Ⓓ

20. What does pressing 5 allow customers to do?

   (A) Access their credit card accounts.
   (B) Speak to a customer service representative.
   (C) Repeat the menu options.
   (D) Transfer funds between accounts.

   Ⓐ Ⓑ Ⓒ Ⓓ

21. What do customers find out?

   (A) The menu options will change.
   (B) Their calls may be recorded.
   (C) They can access their accounts online.
   (D) New services have been added.

   Ⓐ Ⓑ Ⓒ Ⓓ

## Practice 8

22. Who is the intended audience for the advertisement?

    (A) First-time flyers
    (B) Commuters
    (C) Business travelers
    (D) Students and young people

    Ⓐ Ⓑ Ⓒ Ⓓ

23. What do Jet Lines executive lounges have?

    (A) Large-screen TVs
    (B) Internet access
    (C) Luggage storage areas
    (D) Exercise facilities

    Ⓐ Ⓑ Ⓒ Ⓓ

24. What did Jet Lines win an award for?

    (A) Cabin crew
    (B) Executive lounges
    (C) Meals
    (D) Customer service

    Ⓐ Ⓑ Ⓒ Ⓓ

## Practice 9

25. What relationship does Mr. Rushman have with Seiler Logistics?

    (A) He is an employee.
    (B) He is a customer.
    (C) He is a security guard.
    (D) He is a driver.

    Ⓐ Ⓑ Ⓒ Ⓓ

26. Why has Amy Richardson called Mr. Rushman?

    (A) To update him about a delivery problem
    (B) To apologize for not returning his call earlier
    (C) To make a change to her order
    (D) To request his help with a problem

    Ⓐ Ⓑ Ⓒ Ⓓ

**KAPLAN**

27.  When has Amy Richardson probably called Mr. Rushman?

(A) In the middle of the afternoon

(B) During his lunch time

(C) Early in the morning

(D) At the end of the day

Ⓐ Ⓑ Ⓒ Ⓓ

**Practice 10**

28.  How long does it take to get to the airport?

(A) 20 minutes

(B) 25 minutes

(C) 30 minutes

(D) 35 minutes

Ⓐ Ⓑ Ⓒ Ⓓ

29.  What is true about the single-fare tickets?

(A) They cannot be purchased aboard the train.

(B) They can be paid for with a credit card.

(C) They cost more during rush hour.

(D) They are cheaper if they are bought at the station.

Ⓐ Ⓑ Ⓒ Ⓓ

30.  What is learned about the advance-purchase discount tickets?

(A) They are available only online.

(B) They are good for three months from the date of purchase.

(C) They discount fares by ten percent.

(D) They cost $25 each.

Ⓐ Ⓑ Ⓒ Ⓓ

## ANSWER KEY

| | | | |
|---|---|---|---|
| 1. D | | 16. C | |
| 2. A | | 17. B | |
| 3. A | | 18. C | |
| 4. B | | 19. B | |
| 5. D | | 20. D | |
| 6. A | | 21. C | |
| 7. C | | 22. C | |
| 8. B | | 23. B | |
| 9. C | | 24. C | |
| 10. B | | 25. B | |
| 11. C | | 26. A | |
| 12. D | | 27. D | |
| 13. D | | 28. D | |
| 14. A | | 29. B | |
| 15. A | | 30. C | |

## ANSWERS AND EXPLANATIONS

All of the answer choices are included for each question, and in parentheses, there is an explanation of exactly why the wrong answer choices are incorrect. For some questions, we have left the wrong-answer explanations blank so that you can fill them in. The more you can analyze and explain the errors in the wrong answer choices, the more skillful and efficient you will become at eliminating incorrect choices and selecting the correct ones.

Sample responses for these Identify the Error questions are included at the end of the Answers and Explanations section.

### Practice 1

1. What is the speaker promoting? (Main idea/*What*)

   (A) International capital (This is not mentioned.)

   (B) Increased imports (This is not mentioned.)

   (C) Foreign investment (This is not mentioned.)

   (D) Increased export CORRECT

2. Where does this talk take place? (Main idea/*Where*)

   (A) At a trade conference CORRECT

   (B) At a business school (The speaker welcomes the audience to a trade conference.)

   (C) At a corporate board meeting (The speaker welcomes the audience to a trade conference.)

   (D) At a local government meeting (The speaker welcomes the audience to a trade conference.)

3. According to the speaker, why are foreign buyers interested in Irish products? (Detail/*What*)

   (A) They are reasonably priced. CORRECT

   (B) They are high quality. (This is not mentioned.)

   (C) They are organic. (This is not mentioned.)

   (D) They are easily available. (This is not mentioned.)

## Practice 2

4. Why is the SmartShares company in the news? (Detail/*Why*)

   (A) It has laid off a large part of its workforce. (This is not mentioned.)

   (B) It is has been involved in a criminal court case. CORRECT

   (C) It has expanded into the East Asian market. (This repeats the words *East Asia.*)

   (D) It has won an important industry award. (This is not mentioned.)

5. According to the report, what is improving for workers in Thailand? (Detail/*What*)

   (A) Salaries (This is not mentioned.)

   (B) Benefits packages (This is not mentioned.)

   (C) Working conditions (This is not mentioned.)

   (D) Productivity CORRECT

6. What will Mark Francis discuss? (Detail/*What*)

   (A) Stock news CORRECT

   (B) Developments in technology (Gadgets are mentioned.)

   (C) Local news (The program focuses on business news.)

   (D) Travel and tourism tips (The program implies reporters are traveling.)

**Practice 3**

7. What kind of store is Dunthorps? (Main idea/*What kind*)

    (A) Clothing (Clothing is mentioned, but the store sells more than clothes.)

    (B) Kitchenware (This repeats the word *kitchen*.)

    (C) Department CORRECT

    (D) Furniture (This is a play on the word *furnishings*.)

8. What is learned about the sale at Dunthorps? (Detail/*What*)

    (A) It includes items sold online. (This is not mentioned.)

    (B) It is held every year. CORRECT

    (C) It celebrates the opening of a new store. (This is not mentioned.)

    (D) It limits the number of items that can be bought. (This is not mentioned.)

9. When does the sale end? (Detail/*When*)

    (A) End of June (This is not mentioned.)

    (B) July 1st (This is when the sale begins.)

    (C) End of July CORRECT

    (D) Mid-August (This is not mentioned.)

**Practice 4**

10. Where did the artist get the idea for his piece? (Detail /*Where*)

    (A) France (Paris is mentioned, but this is not the answer.)

    (B) The Caribbean CORRECT

    (C) Austria (Austria is mentioned, but this is not the answer.)

    (D) New Zealand (This is not mentioned.)

11. What kind of artwork is being discussed? (Main idea/*What kind*)

    (A) Sculpture (This is not mentioned.)

    (B) Pencil drawing (This is not mentioned.)

    (C) Painting CORRECT

    (D) Photograph (This is not mentioned.)

12. Who is the speaker addressing? (Main idea/*Who*)

   (A) Buyers at an art sale (The talk is about art, but the setting is not a sale.)
   (B) An audience at a lecture (The speaker says the words *in the next gallery*, suggesting that the group is moving.)
   (C) Artists at a workshop (The speaker refers to *the museum*.)
   (D) Visitors to a museum CORRECT

### Practice 5

13. Who is Ira Levinson? (Detail/*Who*)

   (A) The speaker (The speaker refers to Ira Levinson, and is not talking about himself.)
   (B) The building's architect (This is not mentioned.)
   (C) A new employee (This is not mentioned.)
   (D) The company founder CORRECT

14. How many people will work in the building? (Detail/*How many*)

   (A) 250 CORRECT
   (B) 500 (This is not mentioned.)
   (C) 750 (This is not mentioned.)
   (D) 1,000 (This repeats *a thousand*.)

15. What is the purpose of the talk? (Main idea/*What*)

   (A) To dedicate a building CORRECT
   (B) To introduce a new employee (This is not mentioned.)
   (C) To announce plans for a new building (This repeats the words *new building*.)
   (D) To discuss a change in company policy (This is not mentioned.)

### Practice 6

16. For how many years have traffic violations been decreasing nationally? (Detail/*How many*)

   (A) 1 (This is not mentioned.)
   (B) 3 (This is not mentioned.)
   (C) 5 CORRECT
   (D) 8 (This is not mentioned.)

17. Why is the number of traffic violations dropping? (Main idea/*Why*)

    (A) There are fewer offenders. (The figures seem to show this, but the transportation department doesn't think this is the reason.)

    (B) There are fewer police officers. CORRECT

    (C) Policing is more efficient. (This is not mentioned.)

    (D) Fines are stricter. (This is not mentioned.)

18. What did the police spokesperson say about the figures? (Detail/*What*)

    (A) They indicate that drivers are becoming more careful. (The speaker asks if this is the case, but this is not what the police say.)

    (B) They show that policing methods are improving. (This is not mentioned.)

    (C) They might not say anything about drivers' behavior. CORRECT

    (D) They are probably not very accurate. (This is not mentioned.)

**Practice 7**

19. Which number should a customer press for checking account access? (Detail/*Which*)

    (A) 1 (This is to access savings.)

    (B) 2 CORRECT

    (C) 3 (This is to access credit cards.)

    (D) 4 (This is to access retirement and investment accounts.)

20. What does pressing 5 allow customers to do? (Detail/*What*)

    (A) Access their credit card accounts. (Customers must press 3 for this.)

    (B) Speak to a customer service representative. (Customers must press 0 for this.)

    (C) Repeat the menu options. (Customers must press 9 for this.)

    (D) Transfer funds between accounts. CORRECT

21. What do customers find out? (Detail/*What*)

    (A) The menu options will change. (This is not mentioned.)

    (B) Their calls may be recorded. (This is not mentioned.)

    (C) They can access their accounts online. CORRECT

    (D) New services have been added. (This is not mentioned.)

## Practice 8

22. Who is the intended audience for the advertisement?(Main idea/*Who*)

    (A) First-time flyers (This is not mentioned.)

    (B) Commuters (This is not mentioned.)

    (C) Business travelers CORRECT

    (D) Students and young people (This is not mentioned.)

23. What do Jet Lines executive lounges have? (Detail/*What*)

    (A) Large-screen TVs (This is not mentioned.)

    (B) Internet access CORRECT

    (C) Luggage storage areas (This is not mentioned.)

    (D) Exercise facilities (This is not mentioned.)

24. What did Jet Lines win an award for? (Detail/*What*)

    (A) Cabin crew (This repeats the word *crew*.)

    (B) Executive lounges (This repeats the word *lounge*.)

    (C) Meals CORRECT

    (D) Customer service (This is not mentioned.)

## Practice 9

25. What relationship does Mr. Rushman have with Seiler Logistics? (Detail/*What*)

    (A) He is an employee. (This not logical.)

    (B) He is a customer. CORRECT

    (C) He is a security guard. (This repeats the words *security guard*.)

    (D) He is a driver. (This repeats the word *driver*.)

26. Why has Amy Richardson called Mr. Rushman? (Main idea/*Why*)

    (A) To update him about a delivery problem CORRECT

    (B) To apologize for not returning his call earlier (She apologizes for missing his call, but that's not why she has called.)

    (C) To make a change to her order (This is not logical.)

    (D) To request his help with a problem (This is not mentioned.)

27. When has Amy Richardson probably called Mr. Rushman? (Detail/*When*)

    (A) In the middle of the afternoon (This repeats the word *afternoon*.)
    (B) During his lunch time (This is not mentioned.)
    (C) Early in the morning (The package was delivered at 7:30 A.M.)
    (D) At the end of the day CORRECT

## Practice 10

28. How long does it take to get to the airport? _____

    (A) 20 minutes _____
    (B) 25 minutes _____
    (C) 30 minutes _____
    (D) 35 minutes CORRECT

29. What is true about the single-fare tickets? _____

    (A) They cannot be purchased aboard the train. _____
    (B) They can be paid for with a credit card. CORRECT
    (C) They cost more during rush hour. _____
    (D) They are cheaper if they are bought at the station. _____

30. What is learned about the advance-purchase discount tickets? _____

    (A) They are available only online. _____
    (B) They are good for three months from the date of purchase. _____
    (C) They discount fares by ten percent. CORRECT
    (D) They cost $25 each. _____

## ANSWERS FOR IDENTIFY THE ERROR QUESTIONS

### Practice 10

28. How long does it take to get to the airport? (*Detail/How long*)

  (A) 20 minutes (*This is not mentioned.*)

  (B) 25 minutes (*This is not mentioned.*)

  (C) 30 minutes (*This is not mentioned.*)

  (D) 35 minutes CORRECT

29. What is true about the single-fare tickets? (*Detail/What*)

  (A) They cannot be purchased aboard the train. (*They can be purchased onboard.*)

  (B) They can be paid for with a credit card. CORRECT

  (C) They cost more during rush hour. (*This is not mentioned.*)

  (D) They are cheaper if they are bought at the station. (*This is not mentioned.*)

30. What is learned about the advance-purchase discount tickets? (*Detail/What*)

  (A) They are available only online. (*This is not mentioned.*)

  (B) They are good for three months from the date of purchase. (*This is not mentioned.*)

  (C) They discount fares by ten percent. CORRECT

  (D) They cost $25 each. (*This is not mentioned.*)

# PART THREE

# The Reading Comprehension Section

# Chapter 7: **Exam Part V–Incomplete Sentences**

- Test-Taking Strategies

- Incomplete Sentences Practice Set

- Answer Key

- Answers and Explanations

⏱ **Time budget for Part V: Approximately 17 minutes**

Time management is very important on the Reading Comprehension Section of the TOEIC exam. You are given a total of 75 minutes to work through the 100 questions on these three parts. There will be no indicator on the day you take the exam for when you should move from Part V to Part VI, and from Part VI to Part VII. You do not want to spend too much time on any one part. That is why this practice is very important.

For Part V, you will read 40 incomplete sentences. Beneath each sentence, you will see four words or phrases; you must pick the word or phrase that best completes the sentence.

## TEST-TAKING STRATEGIES

### STRATEGY 1: KNOW THE DIRECTIONS

It is important to understand what you are being asked to do, and to be sure you know the directions before you take the test.

Unlike the Listening Comprehension Section—where you must keep pace with the recording to avoid falling behind—you must pace yourself in the Reading Comprehension Section. You have 75 minutes to complete Parts V, VI, and VII. When you finish Part V, you can immediately begin Part VI; when you have finished Part VI, you can immediately begin Part VII.

By knowing the Reading Comprehension Section directions and the directions for Part V in advance, you do not need to waste valuable time reading what you already know. As soon as you are told to begin the Reading Comprehension Section, skip the directions and begin working on the Incomplete Sentence questions. The directions will look something like this:

### READING COMPREHENSION SECTION

In the Reading Comprehension Section, you will read a variety of texts and answer different types of reading comprehension questions. The Reading Comprehension Section will last 75 minutes. There are three parts, and directions are given for each part. You are encouraged to answer as many questions as possible within the allotted time. Mark your answers on the separate answer sheet. Do not write them in the test book.

**Directions:** A word or phrase is missing in the following sentences. Four answer choices are given below each of the sentences. Choose the best answer to complete the sentence. Then mark the letter on your answer sheet.

Here is an example illustrating the format of a typical Incomplete Sentence question, so that you can start becoming familiar with it.

101. In the fourth quarter of 2007, Taylor Airlines reported net _____ of $82.5 million.

(A) flights

(B) revenues

(C) services

(D) quantities

The sentence should read: *In the fourth quarter of 2007, Taylor Airlines reported net revenues of $82.5 million.* Therefore, you would mark (B) on your answer sheet.

## STRATEGY 2: DECIDE WHETHER THE SENTENCE TESTS *VOCABULARY* OR *GRAMMAR*

The sentences can be divided into two types of questions, based on what the answer choices are.

### Vocabulary Questions

All the choices are from different word families but have similar meanings. In the following example sentence, the answer choices are all nouns and are not part of the same word family. They do not share a common root, prefix, or suffix. Each word is different from the others in terms of its form. However, all of the words share a common theme: They are all related to money and payments. This is a classic example of a vocabulary question. To answer a vocabulary question, you must choose the word that completes the sentence *based on its meaning.* These questions test the depth of your vocabulary.

102. A late payment _____ of $25 will be applied to all accounts more than 30 days overdue.

    (A) fee
    (B) fare
    (C) cost
    (D) price

## Grammar Questions

All the word choices are from the same word family. In the following example sentence, the answer choices all contain the same word *open*. This is a classic example of a grammar question. To answer a grammar question, you must choose the word that completes the sentence *based on its form*. These questions test your command of grammar and structure.

103. Trillium Incorporated plans _____ branch offices in both Seoul and Pusan before the end of the year.

    (A) open
    (B) to open
    (C) opened
    (D) to be opened

Note that vocabulary and grammar are not always so easily separated; some questions may test vocabulary and grammar at the same time. Pronouns, comparatives, and other kinds of words can have different forms but still be related to each other. However, it is easiest to think in terms of two basic categories.

The ways vocabulary and grammar questions are approached are slightly different.

- **For vocabulary questions**—Look for words and phrases that provide clues to the answer. Often, words or phrases in the sentence will help you eliminate distractors and point you toward the correct choice. In the first example, the words *late* and *overdue* make choices (B) *fare*, (C) *cost*, and (D) *price* less attractive. The words *fares*, *costs*, and *prices* are not usually "late" or "overdue."

- **For grammar questions**—Focus on the words before and after the blank to determine which part of speech is required. Most often, the words immediately before and after the blank determine which part of speech the correct choice must be. Knowing this helps you to eliminate distractors. In the second example, the word *plans* appears immediately before the blank must be followed by an infinitive, *to*. This eliminates choices (A) *open* and (C) *opened*.

## Strategy 3: Predict the Answer

Read each sentence and try to fill the blank with your own word or phrase *before* reading the answer choices. If you understand the sentence, you should be able to correctly predict the word or phrase required to fill the blank. If your predicted answer is among the answer choices, this is likely to be the correct answer.

It is much better to have your own idea about the correct answer *before* looking at the answer choices. If you look at the answer choices first, you might be attracted to an incorrect choice.

## Strategy 4: Evaluate the Answer Choices

Find the answer choice that matches the answer you predicted. Before you mark your answer sheet, reread the sentence to make sure the option you are choosing fills the blank the correctly.

If no answer choice matches your expected answer, eliminate as many choices as you can by doing the following:

- For vocabulary questions, read the sentence for context clues that may point to the correct answer or help to eliminate distractors.
- For grammar questions, focus on the words and phrases around the blank to determine the part of speech required, and eliminate distractors that do not fit.

After eliminating as many distractors as possible, select the best choice from what is left.

If you cannot eliminate any distractors, choose one letter (A), (B), (C), or (D) and use this for every guessed answer. Using one letter consistently is better than guessing at random.

When you have decided on an answer choice, mark your answer sheet. Be sure to fill in the oval completely, as shown in the test directions.

## Strategy 5: Manage Your Time; Answer Every Question

Time management is very important in the Reading Comprehension Section. In the Listening Comprehension Section, the timing is controlled by the audio recording. In the Reading Comprehension Section, you have 75 minutes to complete Parts V, VI, and VII. How quickly you move through each part is up to you. However, because Part VII—the last part of the test—is usually the most difficult and time-consuming, you will want to go through Parts V and VI as quickly as you can so that you will have enough time left to finish Part VII.

Do not waste time working on any individual sentence. Although each sentence is worth the same amount, you should treat them all equally. Select your answer choice and mark it on your answer sheet as quickly as you can so that you can keep up with the timing of this section of the TOEIC exam.

If you find yourself running out of time, mark your answer sheet with your wild-guess letter. Do not leave any questions unanswered.

## STRATEGY SUMMARY

1. Know the directions.
2. Decide whether the sentence tests *vocabulary* or *grammar.*
   a. For vocabulary questions—Look for words and phrases that provide clues to the answer.
   b. For grammar questions—Focus on the words before and after the blank to determine which part of speech is required.
3. Predict the answer for each sentence in your own words before reading the choices.
4. Evaluate the answer choices and mark the answer.
5. Manage your time and be sure to answer every question.

## INCOMPLETE SENTENCES PRACTICE SET

🕐 **Time budget for Incomplete Sentence Practice: 24 minutes for 54 questions**

When you have answered all of the questions, check your answers against the answer key. Then read the explanations that follow the answer key.

1. The long-time employee was faithful and _____.

   (A) honestly
   (B) honest
   (C) honor
   (D) honesty

2. Next week, a computer trainer will be here to _____ to any questions you may have.

   (A) provide
   (B) request
   (C) respond
   (D) answer

3. He was going to meet us _____ at the restaurant or here.

   (A) but
   (B) yet
   (C) neither
   (D) either

4. The board of directors tried to think _____ all possible options before reaching a decision.

   (A) of
   (B) at
   (C) by
   (D) as

5. If the information is public, _____ is neither unreasonable nor unethical to share it.

   (A) his
   (B) him
   (C) its
   (D) it

6. Timing is _____ important when soliciting contributions for political campaigns.

   (A) accurately
   (B) extremely
   (C) quickly
   (D) hotly

7. Andrew lives quite a _____ from where he works.

   (A) closeness
   (B) space
   (C) distance
   (D) length

8. We are able to _____ your conditions of delivery per your proposal.

   (A) accepts
   (B) accept
   (C) accepting
   (D) accepted

9. Next week's seminar ought to provide _____ with a lot of new information.

   (A) we
   (B) our
   (C) ourselves
   (D) us

10. The paper division is showing an increased _____.

    (A) profit
    (B) profiting
    (C) profitable
    (D) profits

11. Dr. Woo left very early this morning, but _____ because he forgot his briefcase.

    (A) revolved
    (B) returned
    (C) recalled
    (D) remembered

12. Payment is due in full within 30 days upon _____ of this invoice.

    (A) receipt
    (B) receive
    (C) reception
    (D) receiving

13. Doctors have _____ that stress from work can cause other medical problems.

    (A) find

    (B) finding

    (C) found

    (D) finds

14. The warehouse employees have worked overtime every day _____ the last week.

    (A) until

    (B) along

    (C) before

    (D) for

15. We do not provide third _____ with biographical information about our clients.

    (A) parties

    (B) people

    (C) impressions

    (D) dealings

16. He _____ forgot my name at the company dinner last year.

    (A) complete

    (B) completed

    (C) completely

    (D) completeness

17. Attitude is an essential ingredient in finding the _____ possible job.

    (A) good

    (B) best

    (C) higher

    (D) easier

18. Ms. Napier chose to travel by bus _____ of taking a taxi.

    (A) except

    (B) but

    (C) besides

    (D) instead

19. Mr. Fisher wants us to exchange ideas _____ the proposed reorganization of the Adele Company.

    (A) around

    (B) between

    (C) into

    (D) about

20. Realco made _____ offer for the purchase of the Wincorp property.

    (A) a grateful

    (B) a generous

    (C) a wealthy

    (D) an attentive

21. The firm was to receive full payment upon _____ of the project.

    (A) completion

    (B) complexion

    (C) complication

    (D) commitment

22. After the governor raised taxes, his _____ declined rapidly.

    (A) populated

    (B) popular

    (C) popularity

    (D) populate

23. After finishing the week-long seminar, Ms. Beyer packed her suitcase and checked _____ of the hotel.

    (A) over

    (B) out

    (C) in

    (D) or

24. Employee handbooks that are _____ written can improve morale and prevent disagreements.

    (A) careful

    (B) caring

    (C) carefulness

    (D) carefully

25. When the chairman announced _____ retirement, the board of trustees launched a nationwide search for a replacement.

    (A) his

    (B) our

    (C) its

    (D) him

26. Even a company with an excellent image and _____ can fail if it does not meet market standards.

    (A) reputedly

    (B) reputable

    (C) repute

    (D) reputation

27. Mr. and Mrs. Kuo are confident that _____ will locate the site themselves.

    (A) them

    (B) they

    (C) themselves

    (D) their

28. There are several factors to think about _____ deciding which method of distribution to pursue.

    (A) when
    (B) what
    (C) why
    (D) where

29. In an exclusive interview, Mr. Stanowitz _____ that his company would post a loss this quarter.

    (A) confided
    (B) confidence
    (C) confide
    (D) confidential

30. The requirements for new food service products were _____ debated at the franchise meeting.

    (A) manually
    (B) patently
    (C) exhaustively
    (D) firstly

31. The engineers will all need to stay there _____ the Spanning project is finished.

    (A) for
    (B) about
    (C) until
    (D) toward

32. New approaches to mass communication _____ the limits of traditional media channels.

    (A) transcend
    (B) transcends
    (C) transcending
    (D) to transcend

33. Airline reservation _____ are being revised to include extensive traveler demographics.

   (A) telephones
   (B) employees
   (C) counters
   (D) systems

34. The date for the new product launch has been _____ because of problems in production.

   (A) advertised
   (B) delayed
   (C) produced
   (D) mobilized

35. He was asked to testify before the committee _____ his expertise.

   (A) since
   (B) further
   (C) inasmuch as
   (D) because of

36. I know we have _____ types of payment plans available for our customers.

   (A) much
   (B) many
   (C) mostly
   (D) much more

37. The new shopping center offers free parking and easy access _____ the highway.

   (A) to
   (B) with
   (C) of
   (D) for

38. This brochure provides a brief description of some of the _____ features of the insurance policy.

    (A) stately
    (B) sporadic
    (C) slantwise
    (D) salient

39. It is the ability to perform _____ over time that distinguishes great companies.

    (A) consistent
    (B) consistently
    (C) consistency
    (D) consisting

40. The growth of the waste disposal industry is being driven by demographics _____ by economic forces.

    (A) in order to
    (B) as well as
    (C) additionally
    (D) furthermore

41. The ideal _____ will have a strong sales background and in-country contacts.

    (A) position
    (B) procedure
    (C) expectation
    (D) candidate

42. Our consultants can help you _____ employee attitudes and assess training needs.

    (A) network
    (B) request
    (C) survey
    (D) volunteer

43. The reports on construction materials, including _____ on cement and ready-mixed concrete, are available in PDF format.

    (A) them

    (B) that

    (C) those

    (D) this

44. Sky Travel Air is known for being on time and having few customer _____.

    (A) complaints

    (B) complain

    (C) complaining

    (D) complainer

45. Innovative technology _____ by General Car Company debuted in new models last year.

    (A) contained

    (B) involved

    (C) pioneered

    (D) performed

46. Good graphic designers can save their clients _____ amounts of money on printing and artwork.

    (A) signify

    (B) significant

    (C) significance

    (D) signification

47. The small film company _____ had annual revenues of over four million euros.

    (A) previously

    (B) someday

    (C) along

    (D) yet

48. Mergers, takeovers, deregulation, and downsizing have created much _____ in the business world.

    (A) uncertain

    (B) uncertainly

    (C) uncertainties

    (D) uncertainty

49. The network will permit communication _____ devices such as a desktop computer and a document retrieval system.

    (A) around

    (B) between

    (C) over

    (D) above

50. All directors _____ attend this important board meeting.

    (A) must

    (B) ought

    (C) have been

    (D) should be

51. The presentation focuses on the fund's benefit to shareholders _____ than on the company's history.

    (A) rather

    (B) instead

    (C) whereas

    (D) although

52. Vendors of security services have reported a sharp increase in demand for video _____ equipment.

    (A) negligence

    (B) pilot

    (C) leakage

    (D) surveillance

53. Managers need reference materials that are easy for _____ to understand.

    (A) them
    (B) they
    (C) themselves
    (D) theirs

54. Each month, the meat packing plant rewards one employee for _____ the idea that saves the most money.

    (A) receiving
    (B) submitting
    (C) transferring
    (D) installing

# ANSWER KEY

| | |
|---|---|
| 1. B | 28. A |
| 2. C | 29. A |
| 3. D | 30. C |
| 4. A | 31. C |
| 5. D | 32. A |
| 6. B | 33. D |
| 7. C | 34. B |
| 8. B | 35. D |
| 9. D | 36. B |
| 10. A | 37. A |
| 11. B | 38. D |
| 12. A | 39. B |
| 13. C | 40. B |
| 14. D | 41. D |
| 15. A | 42. C |
| 16. C | 43. C |
| 17. B | 44. A |
| 18. D | 45. C |
| 19. D | 46. B |
| 20. B | 47. A |
| 21. A | 48. D |
| 22. C | 49. B |
| 23. B | 50. A |
| 24. D | 51. A |
| 25. A | 52. D |
| 26. D | 53. A |
| 27. B | 54. B |

# ANSWERS AND EXPLANATIONS

In the parentheses next to each question, we have identified them as being focused either on vocabulary or grammar with a *V* or a *G*. We have also included the part of speech required by the sentence.

For some of the questions, we have left this blank so that you can fill them in. The better you are at identifying the focus of each question stem, the more skillful and efficient you will become at eliminating incorrect choices and selecting the correct ones.

Sample responses for these Identify the Question Type questions are included at the end of the Answers and Explanations section.

1. The long-time employee was faithful and _____. (*G*—adjective)

    (A) honestly

    (B) honest CORRECT

    (C) honor

    (D) honesty

2. Next week, a computer trainer will be here to _____ to any questions you may have. (*V*—verb)

    (A) provide

    (B) request

    (C) respond CORRECT

    (D) answer

3. He was going to meet us _____ at the restaurant or here. (*V*—conjunction)

    (A) but

    (B) yet

    (C) neither

    (D) either CORRECT

4. The board of directors tried to think _____ all possible options before reaching a decision. (*V*—preposition)

    (A) of CORRECT

    (B) at

    (C) by

    (D) as

5. If the information is public, _____ is neither unreasonable nor unethical to share it. (*G*—pronoun)

    (A) his

    (B) him

    (C) its

    (D) it CORRECT

6. Timing is _____ important when soliciting contributions for political campaigns. (*V*—adverb)

    (A) accurately

    (B) extremely CORRECT

    (C) quickly

    (D) hotly

7. Andrew lives quite a _____ from where he works. (*V*—noun)

    (A) closeness

    (B) space

    (C) distance CORRECT

    (D) length

8. We are able to _____ your conditions of delivery per your proposal. (*G*—verb)

    (A) accepts

    (B) accept CORRECT

    (C) accepting

    (D) accepted

9. Next week's seminar ought to provide _____ with a lot of new information. (*G*—pronoun)

    (A) we

    (B) our

    (C) ourselves

    (D) us CORRECT

10. The paper division is showing an increased _____. (*G*—noun)

    (A) profit CORRECT

    (B) profiting

    (C) profitable

    (D) profits

11. Dr. Woo left very early this morning, but _____ because he forgot his briefcase. (*V*—verb)

    (A) revolved

    (B) returned CORRECT

    (C) recalled

    (D) remembered

12. Payment is due in full within 30 days upon _____ of this invoice. (*G*—noun)

    (A) receipt CORRECT

    (B) receive

    (C) reception

    (D) receiving

13. Doctors have _____ that stress from work can cause other medical problems. (*G*—verb)

    (A) find

    (B) finding

    (C) found CORRECT

    (D) finds

14. The warehouse employees have worked overtime every day _____ the last week. (*V*—preposition)

    (A) until

    (B) along

    (C) before

    (D) for CORRECT

15. We do not provide third _____ with biographical information about our clients. _____

    (A) parties CORRECT

    (B) people

    (C) impressions

    (D) dealings

16. He _____ forgot my name at the company dinner last year. _____
_____

    (A) complete
    (B) completed
    (C) completely CORRECT
    (D) completeness

17. Attitude is an essential ingredient in finding the _____ possible job.
_____

    (A) good
    (B) best CORRECT
    (C) higher
    (D) easier

18. Ms. Napier chose to travel by bus _____ of taking a taxi. _____
_____

    (A) except
    (B) but
    (C) besides
    (D) instead CORRECT

19. Mr. Fisher wants us to exchange ideas _____ the proposed
    reorganization of the Adele Company. (*V*—preposition)

    (A) around
    (B) between
    (C) into
    (D) about CORRECT

20. Realco made _____ offer for the purchase of the Wincorp property.
    (*V*—adjective)

    (A) a grateful
    (B) a generous CORRECT
    (C) a wealthy
    (D) an attentive

21. The firm was to receive full payment upon _____ of the project.
    (V—noun)

    (A) completion CORRECT

    (B) complexion

    (C) complication

    (D) commitment

22. After the governor raised taxes, his _____ declined rapidly. (G—noun)

    (A) populated

    (B) popular

    (C) popularity CORRECT

    (D) populate

23. After finishing the week-long seminar, Ms. Beyer packed her suitcase and checked
    _____ of the hotel. (V—preposition)

    (A) over

    (B) out CORRECT

    (C) in

    (D) for

24. Employee handbooks that are _____ written can improve morale and
    prevent disagreements. (G—adverb)

    (A) careful

    (B) caring

    (C) carefulness

    (D) carefully CORRECT

25. When the chairman announced _____ retirement, the board of
    trustees launched a nationwide search for a replacement. (G—pronoun)

    (A) his CORRECT

    (B) our

    (C) its

    (D) him

26. Even a company with an excellent image and _____ can fail if it does not meet market standards. (*G*—noun)

   (A) reputedly

   (B) reputable

   (C) repute

   (D) reputation CORRECT

27. Mr. and Mrs. Kuo are confident that _____ will locate the site themselves. (*G*—pronoun)

   (A) them

   (B) they CORRECT

   (C) themselves

   (D) their

28. There are several factors to think about _____ deciding which method of distribution to pursue. (*V*—conjunction)

   (A) when CORRECT

   (B) what

   (C) why

   (D) where

29. In an exclusive interview, Mr. Stanowitz _____ that his company would post a loss this quarter. (*G*—verb)

   (A) confided CORRECT

   (B) confidence

   (C) confide

   (D) confidential

30. The requirements for new food service products were _____ debated at the franchise meeting. (*V*—adverb)

   (A) manually

   (B) patently

   (C) exhaustively CORRECT

   (D) firstly

31. The engineers will all need to stay there _____ the Spanning project is finished. (*V*—preposition)

    (A) for

    (B) about

    (C) until CORRECT

    (D) toward

32. New approaches to mass communication _____ the limits of traditional media channels. (*G*—verb)

    (A) transcend CORRECT

    (B) transcends

    (C) transcending

    (D) to transcend

33. Airline reservation _____ are being revised to include extensive traveler demographics. _____

    (A) telephones

    (B) employees

    (C) counters

    (D) systems CORRECT

34. The date for the new product launch has been _____ because of problems in production. _____

    (A) advertised

    (B) delayed CORRECT

    (C) produced

    (D) mobilized

35. He was asked to testify before the committee _____ his expertise. _____

    (A) since

    (B) further

    (C) inasmuch as

    (D) because of CORRECT

36. I know we have _____ types of payment plans available for our customers. _____

    (A) much

    (B) many CORRECT

    (C) mostly

    (D) much more

37. The new shopping center offers free parking and easy access _____ the highway. (*V*—preposition)

    (A) to CORRECT

    (B) with

    (C) of

    (D) for

38. This brochure provides a brief description of some of the _____ features of the insurance policy. (*V*—adjective)

    (A) stately

    (B) sporadic

    (C) slantwise

    (D) salient CORRECT

39. It is the ability to perform _____ over time that distinguishes great companies. (*G*—adverb)

    (A) consistent

    (B) consistently CORRECT

    (C) consistency

    (D) consisting

40. The growth of the waste disposal industry is being driven by demographic _____ _____ by economic forces. (*V*—conjunction)

    (A) in order to

    (B) as well as CORRECT

    (C) additionally

    (D) furthermore

41. The ideal _____ will have a strong sales background and in-country contacts. (*V*—noun)

    (A) position

    (B) procedure

    (C) expectation

    (D) candidate CORRECT

42. Our consultants can help you _____ employee attitudes and assess training needs. (*V*—verb)

    (A) network

    (B) request

    (C) survey CORRECT

    (D) volunteer

43. The reports on construction materials, including _____ on cement and ready-mixed concrete, are available in PDF format. (*G*—pronoun)

    (A) them

    (B) that

    (C) those CORRECT

    (D) this

44. Sky Travel Air is known for being on time and having few customer _____.
    (*G*—noun)

    (A) complaints CORRECT

    (B) complain

    (C) complaining

    (D) complainer

45. Innovative technology _____ by General Car Company debuted in new models last year. (*V*—verb)

    (A) contained

    (B) involved

    (C) pioneered CORRECT

    (D) performed

46. Good graphic designers can save their clients _____ amounts of money on printing and artwork. (*G*—adjective)

    (A) signify

    (B) significant CORRECT

    (C) significance

    (D) signification

47. The small film company _____ had annual revenues of over four million euros. (*V*—adverb)

    (A) previously CORRECT

    (B) someday

    (C) along

    (D) yet

48. Mergers, takeovers, deregulation, and downsizing have created much _____ in the business world. (*G*—noun)

    (A) uncertain

    (B) uncertainly

    (C) uncertainties

    (D) uncertainty CORRECT

49. The network will permit communication _____ devices such as a desktop computer and a document retrieval system. (*V*—preposition)

    (A) around

    (B) between CORRECT

    (C) over

    (D) above

50. All directors _____ attend this important board meeting. (*G*—verb)

    (A) must CORRECT

    (B) ought

    (C) have been

    (D) should be

**KAPLAN**

51. The presentation focuses on the fund's benefit to shareholders _____
than on the company's history. _____

(A) rather CORRECT

(B) instead

(C) whereas

(D) although

52. Vendors of security services have reported a sharp increase in demand for video _____
_____ equipment. _____

(A) negligence

(B) pilot

(C) leakage

(D) surveillance CORRECT

53. Managers need reference materials that are easy for _____ to
understand. _____

(A) them CORRECT

(B) they

(C) themselves

(D) theirs

54. Each month, the meat packing plant rewards one employee for _____
the idea that saves the most money. _____

(A) receiving

(B) submitting CORRECT

(C) transferring

(D) installing

## ANSWERS FOR THE IDENTIFY THE QUESTION TYPE QUESTIONS

15. We do not provide third _____ with biographical information about
our clients. (*V—noun*)

(A) parties CORRECT

(B) people

(C) impressions

(D) dealings

16. He _____ forgot my name at the company dinner last year. (*G—modifier*)

    (A) complete
    (B) completed
    (C) completely CORRECT
    (D) completeness

17. Attitude is an essential ingredient in finding the _____ possible job. (*V—modifier*)

    (A) good
    (B) best CORRECT
    (C) profitable
    (D) easier

18. Ms. Napier chose to travel by bus _____ of taking a taxi. (*V—preposition*)

    (A) except
    (B) but
    (C) besides
    (D) instead CORRECT

33. Airline reservation _____ are being revised to include extensive traveler demographics. (*V—noun*)

    (A) telephones
    (B) employees
    (C) counters
    (D) systems CORRECT

34. The date for the new product launch has been _____ because of problems in production. (*V—verb*)

    (A) advertised
    (B) delayed CORRECT
    (C) produced
    (D) mobilized

35. He was asked to testify before the committee _____ his expertise. (*G—conjunction*)

    (A) since
    (B) further
    (C) inasmuch as
    (D) because of CORRECT

36. I know we have _____ types of payment plans available for our customers. (*G—modifier/adjective*)

    (A) much
    (B) many CORRECT
    (C) mostly
    (D) much more

51. The presentation focuses on the fund's benefit to shareholders _____ than on the company's history. (*V—conjunction*)

    (A) rather CORRECT
    (B) instead
    (C) whereas
    (D) although

52. Vendors of security services have reported a sharp increase in demand for video _____ _____ equipment. (*V—noun*)

    (A) negligence
    (B) pilot
    (C) leakage
    (D) surveillance CORRECT

53. Managers need reference materials that are easy for _____ to understand. (*G—pronoun*)

    (A) them CORRECT
    (B) they
    (C) themselves
    (D) theirs

54. Each month, the meat packing plant rewards one employee for _____ the idea that saves the most money. (*V—verb*)

   (A) receiving

   (B) submitting CORRECT

   (C) transferring

   (D) installing

# Chapter 8: **Exam Part VI—Text Completion**

- Test-Taking Strategies
- Text Completion Practice Set
- Answer Key
- Answers and Explanations

⏱ **Time Budget for Part VI: Approximately 17 minutes**

For this part of the TOEIC exam, you will read four short texts. Each text has three incomplete sentences marked with a dashed line ( ----------- ), indicating where a word or phrase from the sentence is missing. For each incomplete sentence, you must choose the correct word or phrase. For each question, you are given four answer choices.

## TEST-TAKING STRATEGIES

### STRATEGY 1: KNOW THE DIRECTIONS

It is important to understand what you are being asked to do and to be sure you know the directions before you take the test. The directions will look something like this:

**Directions:** Read the texts found in the following pages. A word or phrase is missing in the sentences that follow the texts. Four answer choices are given below each of the sentences. Choose the best answer to complete the sentence. Then mark the letter on your answer sheet.

Here is an example illustrating the format of a typical Part VI passage.

Questions 141–143 refer to the following course description.

---

Course Description:

Photography 120: Basic Photography for Everyone

Come to class prepared to have fun while learning to use your 35mm SLR film camera.

(Digital photography will NOT be covered in this class. See Course 121: *Basic Digital Imaging for Everyone*, or Course 122: *Turning Your Computer into a Digital Darkroom*.)

The course covers f-stops, shutter speeds, exposure, metering, film types, lenses, filters, flash photography, simple lighting techniques, composition and ways of "seeing," and handheld and tripod shooting techniques.

There will be a different assignment each week. You will shoot both print and slide film, and work in color and black-and-white. You will be encouraged to share your photographs in class to receive feedback from your _____.

141. (A) films
     (B) cameras
     (C) classmates
     (D) photographs

To complete all the assignments, you will _____ a minimum of six rolls of film. (The approximate cost for film and processing is $85.)

142. (A) shot
     (B) shoot
     (C) shoots
     (D) shooting

Bring your 35 mm SLR camera to the first class, as well as your enthusiasm for learning a new skill. No experience necessary!

Required textbook: *Introduction to Photography, 2nd edition* by Don Hasbrook (Note: A 35mm camera is the only equipment required for this class. If you do not own a _____,

143. (A) car
     (B) camera
     (C) scanner
     (D) laptop

or have access to one, you may rent one from the school for an additional fee. Subject to availability. Call the main office for details.)

---

# STRATEGY 2: DECIDE WHETHER THE SENTENCE TESTS *VOCABULARY* OR *GRAMMAR*

As stated earlier, the main difference between Part V and Part VI of the TOEIC exam is that some of the questions in Part VI need information that is found in other sentences in the passage. This means that, in addition to deciding whether a question tests vocabulary or grammar, you will need to determine *whether the question requires information from other parts of the passage.*

You may be tempted to read each Part VI passage from beginning to end. However, because most of the questions can be answered using only the information in the gapped sentences, you can use your time more effectively by focusing on reading only what you need to read to answer the questions.

You should look at the question sentences first, to determine whether you can answer them without reading the rest of the passage. This will allow you to focus on reading only what you need to read to answer the questions.

Look at the questions in the example passage again.

## Question 141

The answer choices are all nouns and are not part of the same word family. They do not share a common root, prefix, or suffix. Each word is different from the others in terms of its form. This is a vocabulary question.

While the answer choices are all words associated with the theme of the passage, this question can be answered using only the information contained in the gapped sentence. It does not require reading any of the surrounding contexts. In this sense, it is really like a Part V vocabulary question.

## Question 142

The answer choices are all forms of the word *shoot*. This is a grammar question. Again, this question can be answered using only the information in the gapped sentence. None of the surrounding context is required. It is similar to a Part V grammar question.

## Question 143

The answer choices are all nouns and are not part of the same word family. This is a vocabulary question. However, each of the answer choices completes the sentence in a grammatical and logical way. None of the answer choices can be eliminated based only on the question sentence itself. This kind of question is unlike the questions found in Part V. You will need to look at the surrounding context to determine which of the answer choices is consistent with the passage text.

Once you have determined whether a question tests vocabulary or grammar, you can follow the same steps that you did for Part V:

- **Vocabulary questions**—Look for words and phrases that provide clues to the answer. Often, words or phrases in the sentence will help you eliminate distractors and will point you toward the correct choice. In question 141 from the previous example, the phrase *to receive feedback from* makes choices (A) *films*, (B) *cameras*, and (D) *photographs* less attractive. *Films, cameras,* and *photographs* cannot provide feedback.

- **Grammar questions**—Focus on the words before and after the blank to determine which part of speech is required. Most often, the words immediately before and after the blank determine which part of speech the correct choice must be. Knowing this helps you to eliminate distractors. In question 142 from the previous example, the words *you will* immediately before the blank must be followed by an infinitive, *to*. This eliminates choices (A) *shot*, (C) *shoots*, and (D) *shooting*.

- **Questions that require information from other parts of the passage**—First look at the sentences that precede it. The information you need will most often be found near the gapped sentence, usually one or two sentences before it. If you do not find the information you need there, look one or two sentences past the gapped sentence. If you still cannot find the information, try reading the passage from the beginning. Usually, you will not need to do this.

## STRATEGY 3: PREDICT THE ANSWER

Just as you did for Part V, read each question and try to fill the blank with your own word or phrase *before* reading the answer choices. Because many of the questions do not actually require the surrounding passage text, you will often be able to read the question sentence by itself and correctly predict the word or phrase required to fill the blank. If your predicted answer is among the answer choices, this is likely to be the correct answer.

It is much better to have your own idea about the correct answer *before* looking at the answer choices. If you look at the answer choices first, you might be attracted to an incorrect choice.

## STRATEGY 4: EVALUATE THE CHOICES

Find the answer choice that matches the answer you predicted. Before you mark your answer sheet, reread the sentence to make sure the option you are choosing fills the blank the correctly.

If no answer choice matches your expected answer, eliminate as many choices as you can by doing the following:

- For vocabulary questions, read the sentence for context clues that may point to the correct answer or help to eliminate distractors.

- For grammar questions, focus on the words and phrases around the blank to determine the part of speech required and eliminate distractors that do not fit.

- Look at the sentences around the gapped sentence to see if there is any additional information you can use.

After eliminating as many distractors as possible, select the best choice from what is left.

If you cannot eliminate any distractors, choose one letter—(A), (B), (C), or (D)—and use this for every wild-guess answer. Using one letter consistently is better than guessing at random.

When you have decided on an answer choice, mark your answer sheet. Be sure to fill in the oval completely, as shown in the test directions.

## STRATEGY 5: MANAGE YOUR TIME; ANSWER EVERY QUESTION

Time management is very important in the Reading Comprehension Section. In the Listening Comprehension Section, the timing is controlled by the audio recording. In the Reading Comprehension Section, you have 75 minutes to complete Parts V, VI, and VII. How quickly you move through each part is up to you. Part VII, the last part of the test, is usually the most difficult and time-consuming, so you will want to leave enough time to finish it.

If you use apply strategy 2 and determine whether you can answer a question using only the information in the sentence, you should be able to avoid reading too much. This will save you time.

Do not spend too much time working on any individual question. Each question is worth the same amount, so you should treat them all equally. You must not allow yourself to fall behind by laboring too long with any one question. Select your answer choice and mark it on your answer sheet as quickly as you can so that you can keep up with the timing on the TOEIC exam.

If you find yourself running out of time, mark your answer sheet with your wild-guess letter. Do not leave any questions unanswered.

## STRATEGY SUMMARY

1. Know the directions.
2. Look at the sentences for the individual questions first: Decide whether they test *vocabulary* or *grammar,* and whether they require information found in other parts of the passage.
   - **Vocabulary questions**—Look for words and phrases that provide clues to the answer.
   - **Grammar questions**—Focus on the words before and after the blank to determine which part of speech is required.
   - **Questions that require information from other parts of the passage**—Look for the information in the sentences that comes immediately *before* the gapped sentence first:
     • Predict the answer for each sentence in your own words before reading the choices.
     • Evaluate the answer choices and mark the answer.
     • Manage your time and be sure to answer every question.
3. Predict the answer for each question in your own words before reading the choices.
4. Evaluate the answer choices and mark the answer.
5. Manage your time and be sure to answer every question.

# TEXT COMPLETION PRACTICE SET

Time Budget: 16 minutes for 21 questions

### Practice 1

Questions 1–3 refer to the following email message.

To: Mike Jasper <m_jasper@reprographica.com>
From: Jane Willis <j_willis@colorperfect.com>
Date: January 10, 2009 09:28:17 A.M.
Subject: Our meeting
Attachments: meeting summary.doc

Dear Mike,

It was so nice to be able to meet you last week. It's been almost a year now that we have _____ by

1. (A) writing
   (B) mailed
   (C) messaged
   (D) corresponded

email, but meeting face to face always makes a difference. I hope that you found last Friday's meeting as useful as we did. I think it was good for you to be able to see our production processes firsthand. If you need any further _____ regarding our color calibration system, or any other aspect of the process, please

2. (A) processes
   (B) documentation
   (C) aspects
   (D) indication

don't hesitate to drop me a line. The _____ I've included with this message summarizes the key points we agreed on during Friday's

3. (A) attachment
   (B) enclosure
   (C) meeting
   (D) amendment

discussion. Please take a look and see if you think there need to be any additions or amendments. I look forward to hearing from you soon with details of your proposal.

Kind regards,

Jane

**Practice 2**

Questions 4–6 refer to the following form.

---

### HOW TO COMPLETE YOUR FORMS

All passengers are required to complete the customs declaration form before entering the United States. You should find a copy of this form inside the seat pocket in front of you; _____, if there is no form,

    4. (A) despite the fact

        (B) additionally

        (C) however

        (D) even though

please ask a member of the cabin crew for one before arrival at your final destination. Passengers who are not U.S. citizens or who are not permanent residents of the United States are required to fill out either a white I-94 form _____ a green I-94W form. Passengers traveling on a visa must complete the white form.

    5. (A) either

        (B) and

        (C) or

        (D) also

If you do not require a visa, you must still have a valid machine-readable passport and complete the green I-94 form. All forms must be _____ in block capitals using a black or blue pen.

    6. (A) completed

        (B) completing

        (C) complete

        (D) being completed

---

## Practice 3

Questions 7–9 refer to the following passage.

---

**MADRID—THE PLACE TO BE**

Madrid is fast becoming one of Europe's most important business centers. Many of the continent's most innovative companies and dynamic businesses are already located here. Many more are joining _____,

             7. (A) it
                (B) them
                (C) those
                (D) that

from cutting-edge IT start-ups to well-established corporate finance institutions. In its new role as innovation hub of Europe, Madrid today boasts several world-class conference _____.
Add to this

                                    8. (A) calls
                                      (B) tools
                                      (C) facilities
                                      (D) localities

excellent infrastructure and first-class hospitality and it's easy to see why the city is now host to some of the world's most important trade fairs. In addition to all of this, _____, Madrid remains one of the

                                9. (A) simply
                                  (B) needless
                                  (C) of course
                                  (D) in spite of

world's great cultural cities, offering any and every form of culture and entertainment imaginable. Just one more reason to reconsider Madrid.

---

**Practice 4**

Questions 10–12 refer to the following brochure.

---

**BUSINESS OPPORTUNITIES WORLDWIDE**

LightWorld was established in the U.K. in 1997 and has _____ grown into an international franchising

  10. (A) while
      (B) for
      (C) then
      (D) since

network of over 50 stores in eight countries. LightWorld is a market leader in providing lighting solutions for the home and office _____ are practical, stylishly designed, and economical. We are currently

  11. (A) that
      (B) who
      (C) these
      (D) whose

inviting expressions of interest from potential franchisees. LightWorld is interested to hear from you if you would like to open your own _____ or if you would like to run a LightWorld network within your own

  12. (A) opening
      (B) light
      (C) outlet
      (D) setting

country or territory. For more details about this offer or more about our company, please email info@lightworld.com.eu.

---

**Practice 5**

Questions 13–15 refer to the following brochure.

---

**MORE AMERICAN HOUSEHOLDS BANKING ONLINE**

The number of American households doing their banking online grew by 39.2 percent last year. Experts predict that number to increase by a _____ 22.5 percent this year, and

      13.  (A)  more
            (B)  larger
            (C)  further
            (D)  superior

another 17.6 percent the year after. A total of 33.2 million American households are currently banking online. Young adults ages 24 to 35 with household incomes of $75,000 or higher are most likely to do their banking online. Today, nearly _____ that group (48 percent) views

      14.  (A)  half
            (B)  twice
            (C)  double
            (D)  two times

bills online, and 46 percent pays bills online. Older adults, those over 65, at all income levels, are the least likely to bank online.

A representative for the American Association of Online Bankers says banks _____ their customers to bank online,

      15.  (A)  to encourage
            (B)  encouragement
            (C)  are encouraging
            (D)  have been encouraged

"because online banking is much cheaper for banks to provide than traditional in-perso teller services."

---

## Practice 6

Questions 16–18 refer to the following memo.

---

**MEMORANDUM**

To: All TigerNet employees

From: John Sullivan, CEO

Date: April 4, 2010

Subject: Our Future

The recent collapse of our biggest competitor has many of you wondering whether the same thing could happen here. I would like to set the record straight.

Today, TigerNet is positioned for _____.

16. (A) success
    (B) pleasure
    (C) collapse
    (D) disappointment

We are the market leader with the highest quality, most functionally complete products and proven technology, the strongest balance sheet and financial viability, the most experienced and dedicated workforce, and the most tried, tested, and proven management team in the industry.

While the severe current conditions have weakened many of our competitors—dozens of Internet service providers both small and large have _____

17. (A) isolated
    (B) decreased
    (C) withdrawn
    (D) consolidated

from the marketplace—we are increasing our market share. As the market continues to consolidate, TigerNet will actually grow. We see enormous business opportunities ahead, and expect _____

18. (A) the company
    (B) a balance sheet
    (C) our competitors
    (D) their market share

to thrive for at least the next several years.

Our future is bright.

-JS-

---

### Practice 7

Questions 19–21 refer to the following brochure.

---

**TROUBLESHOOTING YOUR DSL MODEM**

Most connection problems _____

        19.  (A) does solve

             (B) are solving

             (C) could solve

             (D) can be solved

by trying one of the following.

19. Power cycle: Shut off both the modem and the computer and wait for 30 seconds. Turn the modem back on first, and then turn on the computer. After the PPPoE light stops blinking and stays on, you can reconnect to the Internet. NOTE: If your modem does not have an on/off switch, _____

      20.  (A) insert

            (B) depart

            (C) unplug

            (D) enclose

the modem from the electrical wall outlet to turn it off.

20. Check for line interference: Make sure your modem is not on or _____

                        21.  (A) in

                            (B) off

                            (C) near

                            (D) throughout

other electrical devices that may interfere with the signal. This includes your computer monitor, stereo speakers, cordless phone (or its base), or a halogen light.

21. Call the Peacelink Telephone Support Center: You can talk to a technical support representative. Hours of operation are Monday through Friday, 7:00 a.m to midnight, Eastern time, and Saturday and Sunday 9:00 a.m to 10:00 p.m Eastern. 800-555-HELP.

---

# ANSWER KEY

## Practice 1

1. D
2. B
3. A

## Practice 2

4. C
5. C
6. A

## Practice 3

7. B
8. C
9. C

## Practice 4

10. D
11. A
12. C

## Practice 5

13. C
14. A
15. C

## Practice 6

16. A
17. C
18. A

## Practice 7

19. D
20. C
21. C

## ANSWERS AND EXPLANATIONS

In the parentheses next to each answer, we have identified them as being focused either on vocabulary (*V*) or grammar (*G*). For some answers, we have left this blank, so that you can fill them in. The more you know about what is going on in the answer choices, the more skillful and efficient you will become at eliminating incorrect choices and selecting the correct ones.

Sample responses for these Identify the Question Type answer explanations are included in the Answers and Explanations section.

### Practice 1

1. D _____
2. B _____
3. A _____

### Practice 2

4. C (*G*)
5. C (*G*)
6. A (*G*)

### Practice 3

7. B (*G*)
8. C (*V*)
9. C (*V*)

### Practice 4

10. D (*G*)
11. A (*G*)
12. C (*V*)

### Practice 5

13. C (*V*)
14. A (*V*)
15. C (*G*)

### Practice 6

16. A (*V*)
17. C (*V*)
18. A (*V*)

### Practice 7

19. D (*G*)
20. C (*V*)
21. C (*V*)

## ANSWERS FOR THE IDENTIFY THE QUESTION TYPE QUESTIONS

1. D (*V*)
2. B (*V*)
3. A (*V*)

# Chapter 9: **Exam Part VII—Reading Comprehension**

- Test-Taking Strategies
- Reading Comprehension Practice Set
- Answer Key
- Answers and Explanations

### ⏱ Time Budget for Part VII: Approximately 50 minutes

In Part VII of the TOEIC exam, you will read a series of short passages in your test book. Each passage is followed by two to five questions. Each question has four answer choices. You must select the answer choice that best answers the question and mark it on your answer sheet.

Part VII begins with question 153 and ends with question 200. There are a total of 48 questions in Part VII. There are two kinds of reading passages in Part VII:

1. **Single Passage**—In this type of question set, there is one reading passage, followed by two to five questions. There are usually nine single-question passages. These are questions 153–184. Single passages make up more than half of Part VII (28 of 48 questions).
2. **Double Passages**—This type of question set has two related reading passages that are always followed by five questions. There are four sets of double passages. These are the last passages in Part VII (questions 185–200).

The passages are typically short news articles, advertisements, public notices, memos, email messages, letters, faxes and other business correspondence, instructions, and other kinds of everyday texts. They also include graphs, charts, tables, schedules, and other information of this kind.

The questions usually ask about details provided in the passage; inferences that can be made based on the information presented; and about the meaning of words as they are used in the passage. The questions generally ask about information in the order that it is presented in the passage. For the double passages, there is usually at least one question requiring you to use information found in both passages.

# TEST-TAKING STRATEGIES

## STRATEGY 1: KNOW THE DIRECTIONS

It is important to understand what you are being asked to do and to be sure that you know the directions before taking the test. The directions will look something like this:

> **Directions**: In this part, you will read a selection of text, such as magazine or newspaper articles, letters, or advertisements. Each text is followed by several questions. Select the best answer for each question and mark the letter on your answer sheet.

Here is an example of a Part VII single passage set:

Questions 153–155 refer to the following article.

---

**LOW CROP PRICES HURT FARMERS**

Unusually low prices for crops are causing hardships for farmers in Canada. Together with a strong Canadian dollar and rising costs, this has led to large-scale losses on many Canadian farms. The Canadian government forecasts net farm income (NFI) this year at $870 million, a significant decline from last year's $1.8 billion NFI.

NFI for the province of Saskatchewan is again likely to be negative this year at an estimated minus $207 million, compared with minus $77 million last year.

Manitoba, which is still recovering from floods earlier in the year, is also expected to fall behind expenses and is forecast to have an NFI deficit of $195 million.

Alberta, with its large-scale cattle industry, is generating more income than provinces where farming is based on grains. This year's NFI is forecast at $258 million.

Even at the current low prices, farmers in Saskatchewan and Manitoba are having a hard time selling their grains, due to this year's below-average-quality harvest.

Elsewhere, good returns on dairy, eggs, fruit, and poultry have boosted farm incomes.

---

153. What is expected for net farm income in Canada?

    (A) It will be much lower than the year before.

    (B) It will be about the same as the year before.

    (C) It will be higher than the original government forecasts.

    (D) It will be significantly lower than the original government forecasts.

154. According to the article, which Canadian farm product is selling poorly?

(A) Nuts

(B) Fruit

(C) Dairy

(D) Grains

155. Which of the following is *NOT* mentioned as a problem that Canadian farmers are facing?

(A) Floods

(B) Rising costs

(C) Low cattle prices

(D) Poor-quality crops

Here is an example of a Part VII double passage set:

Questions 181–185 refer to the following advertisement and registration form.

---

Revolutionize your investment strategies in as little as one hour!

Thursday, February 12 at 7:00 P.M.
Carlton Hotel, St. Morton, LA

We would like to invite you to join renowned investment expert Sandra Gellert for an exclusive free investment seminar.

Sandra is chief investment officer and portfolio manager of ALC Investments. She recognizes the strong economic environment in Louisiana right now and would like to help YOU with your investment strategy.

Three-time recipient of the coveted national Fund Manager of the Year award, Sandra brings vision as well as everyday good sense to strategic financial planning. She holds a bachelor of commerce degree, a master of business administration degree, a doctorate in finance, and is a chartered financial analyst. This education combined with a wealth of successful experience in managing financial portfolios means this seminar is an exciting opportunity for disciplined investment planning.

Topics to be covered:

- Wealth Creation
- Global Investment
- Financial Services
- Oil and Gas
- Pensions and Retirement Funds
- Foreign Exchange Markets
- Specific Company Suggestions

---

Seating at this event is limited. Please register for this exclusive free session online, or fill out the registration form on the back of this flyer and fax it to the number given below.

Register Online: *www.alcinvestments.com/seminar/registration.html*

Register by Fax: (456) 223-1232

This seminar with Sandra Gellert, one of the nation's most sought-after speakers on investments, is sponsored by Synergy Financial, St. Morton City Bank, and Integrated Wealth Services Inc.

(Registration form on back)

REGISTATION FORM

An Evening with Sandra Gellert

Thursday, February 12 at 7:00 P.M.
Carlton Hotel in St. Morton, LA

Limited Spaces—Register Now!

Name: Paolo Grazzi

Company: Consolidated Investments

Position in Organization: Senior Financial Advisor

Address: 125 67th Street, St. Morton, LA

Tel (work): 456-852-1386      Tel (evening): 456-852-7221

Email: paolog@consolidatedinvestments.com

No. of participants (max 3 per registration):  2

Name of additional participant: Michelle Dubois

Name of additional participant: N/A

Special interests: International investments, oil and gas, retirement funds

181. What is learned about Sandra Gellert?

  (A) She has taught at several universities.
  (B) She has won an award for her latest book.
  (C) She has several business-related degrees.
  (D) She has over 20 years' experience in the financial field.

182. Which of the following will *NOT* be discussed by Sandra Gellert?

   (A) Real estate
   (B) Currency trading
   (C) Retirement planning
   (D) Investing internationally

183. Who is said to be one of the seminar's sponsors?

   (A) Michelle Dubois
   (B) Consolidated Investments
   (C) The Morton Chamber of Commerce
   (D) Integrated Wealth Services Inc.

184. What is learned about Paolo Grazzi?

   (A) He has charged the registration to a credit card.
   (B) He is especially interested in technology stocks.
   (C) He will attend the presentation with one other person.
   (D) He is the chief investment officer for Consolidated Investments.

185. What will Paolo Grazzi probably do?

   (A) Fax his registration card.
   (B) Meet Sandra Gellert for lunch.
   (C) Go directly to the Carlton Hotel from the airport.
   (D) Discuss his investment strategy with Michelle Dubois.

## STRATEGY 2: KNOW THE QUESTION TYPES

The questions usually ask for information in the order that it is presented in the passage. For example, for a three-question passage, the first question will usually ask about information found near the beginning, the second question will ask about something found in the middle, and the third question will ask about something mentioned near the end.

There are four basic categories of questions for Part VII:

   1. **Gist**—Gist questions will ask what the main topic is, why the passage has been written, or what the passage's purpose is. Gist questions ask about the overall situation, rather than about specific details.

There is usually one Gist question per passage. Following are examples of Gist questions:

- *What is the article mainly about?*
- *Why has the bank written this letter?*
- *What is the main purpose of this email?*
- *What is learned about the company?*

2. **Detail**—Detail questions ask about information mentioned in the passage. They can ask about general information or very specific details. Examples of what Detail questions might ask about include what products or services a company provides; how much a product or service costs; when or where an action or event will take place; what role, function, or responsibility people will have; how a problem or situation is being handled; the order or manner in which things are to be done.

Examples of Detail questions include:

- *What service does Miller Consulting provide?*
- *How much are the XJ100s?*
- *Where will the meeting be held?*
- *When is the report due?*
- *What will Rob Dollison be responsible for doing?*
- *How should the filter be cared for?*

Some Detail questions are asked using *NOT*. For example:

- *What is NOT a service provided by Miller Consulting?*
- *What is NOT included on the meeting agenda?*
- *Which of the following is NOT on sale?*
- *Why will the goods NOT be shipped that day?*

For these questions, you must read the choices carefully. For the first example (*What is NOT a service provided by Miller Consulting?*), three of the four options will be services that *are* provided. You need to pick the one that is *NOT* provided. Be careful!

Detail questions are the most common Part VII questions. There is often more than one per passage.

3. **Implication/Inference questions**—Implication/Inference questions ask about things that are not stated directly in the passage. They often require you to make connections between information that has been presented in different parts of the passage. They may ask about

expectations, possibilities, or probable future actions; they can refer to people's emotions or feelings.

The following are examples of Implication/Inference questions:

- *Why were analysts surprised by the earnings announcement?*
- *What does Mr. Davis imply about the price of his products?*
- *Why does Mrs. Lopez mention April tenth in her email?*
- *What can be inferred about Tezla Corp.'s annual budget?*

There is usually one Implication/Inference question per passage.

At times, Implication/Inference questions and Gist questions may seem to be similar. For example, a Gist question that asks about the purpose of an email message might require drawing an inference; the message might provide enough information to make the purpose obvious, but that information might not be stated directly in the email.

Although some Gist questions require you to understand an implication or make an inference, their focus is on the larger picture or the overall situation. Implication/Inference questions tend to deal with implied details about the situation or context itself.

4. **Vocabulary**—Vocabulary questions ask you to identify the meaning of a word as it is used in the passage. They will refer to a specific line in a paragraph and will always have the same format. For example:

The word *coveted* in paragraph 2, line 4, is closest in meaning to

(A) devoted.

(B) desirable.

(C) fashionable.

(D) advantageous.

Vocabulary questions are not very common. There are usually no more than three on the entire test. They are usually found in the four-question and five-question passages and are usually the last questions in the set.

## STRATEGY 3: KNOW THE DISTRACTORS

All Part VII distractors must answer the question plausibly, that is, they must be possible answers to the question. When you read a Part VII question and the answer choices by themselves—without referring to the reading passage—each choice will answer the question in a logical and realistic way, and no choice can be eliminated using logic or common sense. Each answer choice will be a plausible answer to the question. There are no "impossible" answer choices.

Note that none of the Part VII questions is linked in any way—that is, the information contained in a set of question and answer choices will not help you to answer any other questions. Here is an example:

What is enclosed with the letter?

(A) A coupon

(B) A payment

(C) An invoice

(D) A brochure

Without reading the passage, none of the answer choices can be eliminated. Each option is a plausible answer to the question. There are no "impossible" answer choices.

The following are the basic types of distractors for Part VII questions:

1. **Not mentioned**—This type of distractor refers to things or ideas commonly associated with the passage content but that are not actually mentioned in the passage. The distractor answers the question plausibly, but it does not relate to the actual passage content.

2. **Repeated words**—This type of distractor uses a key word or phrase from the passage, but it is not true. The distractor answers the question plausibly but is incorrect.

3. **Incorrect paraphrase/misstatement**—This type of distractor uses specific language, facts, or ideas that are mentioned or implied in the passage, but it rephrases, paraphrases, and twists them so that they are not true. The distractor often contradicts or misstates the facts. Sometimes important information is omitted or new information is added. Most of the content of the distractor comes directly from the passage. The distractor answers the question plausibly, but it is incorrect.

   Incorrect choices for Vocabulary questions can all be considered "incorrect paraphrase/misstatement" distractors because they incorrectly paraphrase the vocabulary word being tested.

4. **Hybrid**—This is not actually a basic distractor type; it is a combination of two or more of the three basic types previously outlined.

A set of answer choices may use more than one type of distractor at a time. Each distractor type is discussed separately here.

Look at the Part VII single passage example again.

Questions 153–155 refer to the following article.

---

**LOW CROP PRICES HURT FARMERS**

Unusually low prices for crops are causing hardships for farmers in Canada. Together with a strong Canadian dollar and rising costs, this has led to large-scale losses on many Canadian farms. The Canadian government forecasts net farm income (NFI) this year at $870 million, a significant decline from last year's $1.8 billion NFI.

NFI for the province of Saskatchewan is again likely to be negative this year at an estimated minus $207 million, compared with minus $77 million last year. Manitoba, which is still recovering from floods earlier in the year, is also expected to fall behind expenses and is forecast to have an NFI deficit of $195 million.

Alberta, with its large-scale cattle industry, is generating more income than provinces where farming is based on grains. This year's NFI is forecast at $258 million.

Even at the current low prices, farmers in Saskatchewan and Manitoba are having a hard time selling their grains, due to this year's below-average-quality harvest.

Elsewhere, good returns on dairy, eggs, fruit, and poultry have boosted farm incomes.

---

153. What is expected for net farm income in Canada?

    (A) It will be much lower than the year before.

    (B) It will be about the same as the year before.

    (C) It will be higher than the original government forecasts.

    (D) It will be significantly lower than the original government forecasts.

This is a Detail question. The correct answer is choice (A). Choice (B) misstates the information presented in the first paragraph. This is an example of an incorrect paraphrase/misstatement distractor. Choice (C) contradicts the information in the first paragraph. This is an example of an incorrect paraphrase/misstatement distractor. Choice (D) repeats the words *significantly* and *government forecasts* from the first paragraph, but it twists the facts. It also refers to an "original" forecast that was not mentioned. This is an example of a hybrid distractor.

154. According to the article, which Canadian farm product is selling poorly?

    (A) Nuts

    (B) Fruit

    (C) Dairy

    (D) Grains

This is a Detail question. The correct answer is choice (D). Choice (A) is not mentioned in the passage. This is an example of a not mentioned distractor. Choices (B) and (C) are both words mentioned in the passage, but they are incorrect. These are examples of repeated words distractors.

155. Which of the following is *NOT* mentioned as a problem Canadian farmers are facing?

(A) Floods

(B) Rising costs

(C) Low cattle prices

(D) Poor-quality crops

This is a detail question using the NOT format. The correct answer is choice (C). Choices (A), (B), and (D) are all mentioned as being problems for Canadian farmers. Notice that for each of the questions, all the distractors are plausible answers and that none of the questions or answer choices are of any help in answering other questions.

## STRATEGY 4: KNOW HOW TO READ PASSAGES

Because you have a limited amount of time to read the passages and answer the questions, you must be an efficient reader. Reading every word of every passage is not reading efficiently. Efficient reading requires *skimming* and *scanning*, described here.

### Skim the Passage

*Skimming* a passage means reading it quickly to understand the main points. When you skim a passage, you are interested in identifying the main idea or main topic. Your goal is to answer the question "What is this passage mainly about?"

For the previous example passage, the answer to the question "What is the passage mainly about?" would be something like this: income from farming in Canada.

For the double passage example previously given, the answer to the question would be something like this: an upcoming investment seminar and the details of someone's registration for the seminar.

To skim a passage, begin at the top of the passage and read only the first few words of each sentence. This should be enough to give you a sense of what the passage is about. Look for and make note of words or phrases that are repeated throughout the passage—these are probably important.

You do not need to read every word of the passage to find the main idea. You are not interested in details—yet.

### Read the Questions

The passages contain more information than you need to answer the questions; there are things mentioned in the passage that are not tested. Your goal is *not* to read the entire passage. Your goal is only to answer the questions. The most efficient way to do this is to know what it is you are looking for *before* you read the passage in depth.

Read the questions—but not the answer choices—so that you know what information you will need to find when you read the passage.

### Answer Each Question

Read each question and predict the answer in your own words *before* reading the answer choices. If you understand the passage, you should be able to answer the questions in your own words. For each question, your predicted answer—or one very closely matching your predicted answer—should be among the answer choices.

Remember, there are no trick questions on the TOEIC exam. All the information needed to answer the questions is presented in the passage.

If you read the answer choices first—without answering the question in your own words—you are allowing the TOEIC exam writers to put ideas into your head. You will be tempted to make the answer one of the distractors. It is much better to have your own idea about the correct answer first, *before* looking at the answer choices.

### Scan the Passage

Once you know what information you need to find, you should scan the passage to find it. *Scanning* is the process of looking for the key words and phrases you need to answer the questions. Because you have read the questions and know what information to look for, you do not need to read every word in the passage. You only need to find the key words from the questions.

To scan a passage, start at the top and let your eyes go back and forth across the page; look for key words and phrases as you make your way to the bottom of the passage. You are looking only for the answers to the questions.

## STRATEGY 5: EVALUATE THE ANSWER CHOICES; MARK THE ANSWER

After you have scanned the passage to find the information you need, you will need to evaluate the answer choices. Find the answer choice that is the closest match to the answer you have been expecting and mark your answer sheet.

## STRATEGY 6: ELIMINATE ANSWER CHOICES

If none of the choices match your expected answer very well, you must eliminate as many choices as you can. Remember, because one question and answer choice set will not help you answer another, do not look at answer choices from one question for clues to answer another question.

If you must guess, eliminate any choices that do not use words and phrases from the passage—the not mentioned distracter type. The not mentioned distractors are often the easiest to eliminate.

If only one of the answer choices use words and phrases that you recognize from the passage, this is likely to be the correct one.

## STRATEGY 7: TACKLE SHORTER PASSAGES AND VOCABULARY QUESTIONS FIRST

This strategy is not for everyone. If you are the kind of person who is nervous about "breaking the rules," go ahead and answer the questions in the order in which they occur in your test book. There are some risks in tackling the shorter passages first. These will be explained later in this section.

In the Listening Comprehension Section, the order of the questions is controlled by the audio. In the Reading Comprehension Section, you are free to answer the questions in any order you choose. There is no rule that says you have to go through the passages in the order in which they are printed in your test book. Test writers would prefer that you answer the questions in the order they appear, but this does not mean you cannot answer them in another order.

The reading passages have between two and five questions each. Generally, passages with fewer questions are shorter and easier than passages with more questions. Therefore, you might consider tackling the short passages first. The basic idea is to answer all the two-question passages first, then the three-question passages, then the four-question passages, and so on.

The advantage to this approach is that you will probably answer more questions in a shorter amount of time, and more questions answered means a potentially higher score. If you answer the questions in the order they are presented, you may be slowed down by harder questions and run out of time, leaving easier questions you might have been able to answer unanswered. If you answer all the easy questions first, you are that much closer to being finished, and you can use your remaining time to work on the more difficult passages.

Some of the reading passages will have a question that asks about how a particular word is used in the passage. These are generally easy questions, and you should try to answer them first. If you are running out of time, look for these questions, scan the passage to find the word, and try to answer the question. Often, if you know the word being tested, you can eliminate one or two answer choices without even reading the passage.

The major disadvantage of answering the questions out of order is that you risk making careless mistakes on your answer sheet—marking the wrong oval or even missing an entire passage. If you make such a mistake, you could wind up with a lower score. If you decide to answer the questions out of order, make absolutely sure you are marking your answer sheet correctly. Double-check to be sure you have not accidentally filled in the wrong oval on your answer sheet. When the end of the test is near, check your answer sheet again to make sure you have not skipped any questions. If you are careful not to make mistakes, this strategy can be very effective.

## STRATEGY 8: MANAGE YOUR TIME

Everyone makes mistakes, especially when under pressure. If you finish the TOEIC exam before time is called, you should check your answer sheet to make sure you have not missed any questions or marked your answer sheet incorrectly in any way. Check your work for Parts V and VI, as well. If you find yourself running out of time, mark your answer sheet with your wild-guess letter. Do not leave any questions unanswered.

## STRATEGY SUMMARY

1. Know the directions.
2. Understand the question types and how the questions are ordered.
3. Understand the basic types of distractors.
4. Know how to read passages.
5. Evaluate the answer choices and mark the answer if you know it.
6. Eliminate answer choices that are wrong and select the best match from what is left.
7. Consider tackling the shorter passages and vocabulary questions first.
8. Manage your time and be sure to answer every question.

# READING COMPREHENSION PRACTICE SET

🕐 Time budget: 20 minutes for 26 questions

Questions 1–2 refer to the following weather forecast.

**This Week's Weather Forecast**

The weather forecast for Asia and Australia predicts warm temperatures for the next few days in Beijing; thundershowers on Wednesday could lead to cooler weather Thursday.

Episodes of rain in Shanghai this week, some possibly heavy.

Typically warm and muggy this week in Hong Kong and Singapore.

Windy and cool with showers in Melbourne Wednesday and Thursday, while Brisbane has sunshine every day this week.

1.  What is expected for Beijing on Wednesday?

    (A) Rain

    (B) Wind

    (C) Unusual warmth

    (D) Clear skies


2.  Where is sunny weather predicted?

    (A) Brisbane

    (B) Jakarta

    (C) Shanghai

    (D) Taipei

Questions 3–4 refer to the following email message.

| | |
|---|---|
| From: | Carlota Fernandez <c_fernandez@lgsystems.com> |
| To: | Staff Mailing List <staff@lgsystems.com> |
| Date: | May 15th 2010  10:38:42 A.M. |

Subject: Visit by Proplan, Inc.

Dear All,

This is to remind you that two representatives from Proplan, Inc. will be here on Friday, May 20, from 9 A.M. to 5 P.M. in the employee lounge. The Proplan representatives will be available to answer all questions regarding your health insurance policy, and to discuss how changes may affect you and your families. Please sign up for the 15-minute time slots. The sign-up sheet is in the lounge. I hope this is beneficial to you all.

Regards,
Carlota


3.  Why will the Proplan representatives visit?

    (A) To discuss health insurance

    (B) To provide medical examinations

    (C) To distribute health care policies

    (D) To sign up participants

4. What should interested employees do?

    (A) Talk to the benefits department.

    (B) Read the attached information.

    (C) Write down questions.

    (D) Sign up for appointments.

Questions 5–7 refer to the following letter.

---

Melissa Ketchem
1410 South Walnut Street
Bloomington, IN 47404

28 June 2010

Mr. Donald Baker
Personnel Director
The Asian Plaza Hotel
Tokyo, Japan

Dear Mr. Baker,

I am responding to your recent advertisement for a manager of programs and conventions on the hoteljobs.com website. Enclosed is my résumé, which outlines the considerable experience I have in the hotel management field.

My current position as assistant manager at the International Castle Hotel deals almost exclusively with booking and coordinating conventions. This, combined with a certificate from the Hotel School in Lausanne, Switzerland, makes me confident that I would be an asset to your staff.

I very much appreciate being considered for this position, and I would welcome the opportunity to meet with you at your earliest convenience.

Sincerely yours,
Melissa Ketchem

P.S. If you would like to speak with my current supervisor at the International Castle, please feel free to contact her without reservation.

---

5. What is Ms. Ketchem sending with this letter?

    (A) A résumé

    (B) A writing sample

    (C) A job description

    (D) A reference letter

6. How did Ms. Ketchem learn about the position?

   (A) From a friend

   (B) From a website

   (C) From a newspaper advertisement

   (D) From Mr. Baker

7. Which task is part of Ms. Ketchem's current job?

   (A) Handling conventions

   (B) Supervising staff

   (C) Coordinating food service

   (D) Registering guests

Questions 8–10 refer to the following letter.

Saysee Insurance Company
200 Wilshire Road
London, SW1

May 10, 2010

Mr. Franz Thurman
Polderstraaat 175
Brussels 1050, Belgium

Dear Mr. Thurman,

With this letter, we acknowledge receipt of your application materials for the position of claims manager at Saysee Insurance Company. Thank you for your interest. Due to the overwhelming response to our advertisement, we will conduct initial interviews over the telephone. Should a follow-up interview then be appropriate, we will ask that you come in to meet with us in person.

To better schedule the initial interview at a mutually convenient time, we are enclosing an Interview Schedule Card. Please complete this card and return it to us as soon as possible. Our schedule permits us to interview only those whose cards we receive prior to June 3rd.

Thank you once again for your interest. You appear to be a strong candidate, and we look forward to hearing from you soon.

Sincerely,

Marie Reilly
Personnel Manager

8. Who is Franz Thurman?

(A) An employee

(B) An interviewer

(C) An applicant

(D) A customer

9. What is the purpose of this letter?

(A) To schedule an appointment

(B) To make a job offer

(C) To reject a candidate

(D) To request information

10. What can be inferred about Saysee's advertisement?

(A) Many people replied to it.

(B) It was posted online.

(C) Few people read it.

(D) It ran for two weeks.

Questions 11–15 refer to the following article.

> HONG KONG—Four of the world's largest container shipping lines announced plans yesterday to form an alliance on routes linking Asia with Europe and North America. Negotiations between the companies are set to begin next month and, if successful, will gradually create an alliance over the next two years.
>
> (5) The four shipping lines, all among the top ten in the world, would share space on each other's vessels, so that maximum use can be made of new, faster ships now being built. This involves customers of one line having their containers put on a ship operated by another line in the alliance. The lines will not take equity stakes in each other.
>
> A spokesperson for one of the companies said the four hoped to agree on the specifics of (10) the plan within the next six to eight months.

11. What is the main idea of the article?

(A) A large trading block will be created.

(B) Cargo shipments are getting bigger.

(C) A transportation coalition will be formed.

(D) Air freight could become cheaper.

12. Who will participate in the alliance?

    (A) Four large shipping companies

    (B) Governments in Asia, Europe, and North America

    (C) A group of manufacturing companies

    (D) Several customer protection groups

13. How will members benefit from the alliance?

    (A) By sharing space on ships

    (B) Through reduced competition

    (C) By sharing port facilities

    (D) Through access to larger ships

14. The word *specifics* as used in line 9 is closest in meaning to

    (A) members.

    (B) costs.

    (C) details.

    (D) containers.

15. When will the alliance be created?

    (A) Immediately

    (B) At the end of the month

    (C) Within six to eight months

    (D) Over a two-year period

Questions 16–20 refer to the following report.

### The Chilean Commerce Service

Established to help Chilean firms compete more effectively in the global marketplace, the Chilean Commerce Service has a network of trade specialists located throughout Chile and 67 countries. Commerce Service offices provide information on foreign markets, agent/distributor location services, trade leads, financing aid, and counseling on business opportunities, barriers,
*(5)* and prospects abroad.

There are 15 offices throughout Chile, each headed by a director supported by trade specialists and other staff. Most offices maintain business libraries containing the latest reports from the Department of Commerce. Trade specialists can provide the business community with local export counseling and a variety of export programs and services, including one
*(10)* utilizing a computerized program to help firms determine their readiness to export. Specific recommendations are proposed to help strengthen and enhance a company's exporting ability.

Commercial Officers in the overseas posts gather information about trends and barriers to trade in their areas and seek out trade and investment opportunities to benefit Chile. They also provide a range of services to potential exporters traveling abroad, such as assisting
*(15)* with appointments with key buyers and government officials.

16. Why was the Commerce Service created?

   (A) To help Chilean companies import products
   (B) To aid Chilean companies working abroad
   (C) To educate international specialists
   (D) To counsel firms seeking to sell in Chile

17. What is likely to be found at a Commerce Service office?

   (A) A currency exchange facility
   (B) Conference rooms
   (C) Classrooms
   (D) A business library

18. What does the Commerce Service use to evaluate a firm's readiness to export?

   (A) A computer program
   (B) A questionnaire
   (C) An export analysis
   (D) A written survey

19. What would a Commercial Service office probably *NOT* do?

   (A) Introduce businesspeople to government contacts.
   (B) Look for investment opportunities.
   (C) Help a Chilean firm write a business plan.
   (D) Research local market trends.

20. The word *determine* in line 10 is closest in meaning to

   (A) evaluate.
   (B) improve.
   (C) allow.
   (D) start.

Questions 21–25 refer to the following invoice and email message.

---

Sunshine Medical Services

INVOICE No. 322

| | |
|---|---|
| Date: | August 5th, 2010 |
| Patient: | Barbara Yamada |
| Address: | 26 Whitworth Street, Manchester M24 OPJ |
| | |
| Details: | X-Ray Services |
| Amount: | £250 |
| Paid: | £100 |
| Payment: | Cash |
| Balance to pay: | £150 |

To: Mark Allen <m_allen@sunshinemedical.com>

From: David Simpson <d_simpson@sunshinemedical.com>

(5) Date: September 30, 2010 - 09:25:18 A.M.

Subject: Barbara Yamada's invoice

Attachments: invoice322.doc

Mark,

(10) Attached is a copy of Mrs. Yamada's invoice. This is still outstanding, so could you contact her please and ask her to settle the account? There's no telephone number on the invoice, but her contact details at home and work are on record. It might be best to call her on her cell phone if we have it, because she is usually out of her office most of the day. If you could you do this some time today, that would be great.

Many thanks,
David

---

21. What is the invoice for?

(A) Banking transactions

(B) Clothing purchases

(C) Accounting services

(D) Medical services

22. How was the first payment made?

    (A) By check
    (B) With a credit card
    (C) In cash
    (D) By bank transfer

23. How much is owed on the account?

    (A) £50
    (B) £100
    (C) £150
    (D) £200

24. The word *outstanding* in line 8 of the email is closest in meaning to

    (A) amazing.
    (B) noticeable.
    (C) exceptional.
    (D) overdue.

25. What does David imply about Mrs. Yamada?

    (A) Her home number is not on record.
    (B) Her cell phone number is not on record.
    (C) She may not be in her office.
    (D) She has moved to Manchester.

Questions 26–30 refer to the following note and advertisement.

---

Harriet

I came across this ad in an industry journal last week and immediately thought that it's just what we need. I've been looking through brochures for something similar, but haven't found anything that so closely matches what we need. All the others I've found are good for protecting paper files, but they wouldn't provide protection for our work. This one does, though. The only downside is that it's a bit pricier than other ones I've looked at. Still, I think it's worth the extra few dollars. Take a look and see what you think.

Bob

---

SURESAFE Media Protector

Do not let a fire destroy your business. Protect your priceless media and paper records in one compact unit with SURESAFE. Only 65 centimeters high, this safe fits conveniently under a desk or table. It features a three-number, changeable combination lock with a
(5)  concealed dial for security.

SURESAFE provides complete fire protection for electronic media. It also offers the extra heat/humidity protection that film records require. Paper records can withstand temperatures up to 175° C and high humidity, but a temperature of 55° C or a
(10) combination of 50° C and humidity greater than 85 percent will likely destroy film media. The heat/humidity protection of SURESAFE exceeds industry specifications.

26. How did Bob learn about the SURESAFE Media Protector?

(A) From an advertisement in a journal

(B) From Harriet

(C) From a SURESAFE brochure

(D) From a website review

27. What does Bob imply about the SURESAFE Media Protector?

(A) It is more expensive than similar items.

(B) It will not fit their needs.

(C) It is no longer available.

(D) It will take several weeks to be delivered.

28. What is *NOT* mentioned as being a feature of the SURESAFE Media Protector?

(A) Small size

(B) A changeable lock

(C) A hidden dial

(D) All-steel construction

29. The word *withstand* in line 7 of the advertisement is closest in meaning to

(A) burn.

(B) survive.

(C) increase.

(D) change.

30. What is claimed about the SURESAFE Media Protector?

    (A) It is guaranteed never to fail.

    (B) It is the strongest unit available at any price.

    (C) It cannot be opened by thieves or other criminals.

    (D) It protects against conditions of high heat and humidity.

## ANSWER KEY

| | | | |
|---|---|---|---|
| 1. | A | 16. | B |
| 2. | A | 17. | D |
| 3. | A | 18. | A |
| 4. | D | 19. | C |
| 5. | A | 20. | A |
| 6. | B | 21. | D |
| 7. | A | 22. | C |
| 8. | C | 23. | C |
| 9. | A | 24. | D |
| 10. | A | 25. | C |
| 11. | C | 26. | A |
| 12. | A | 27. | A |
| 13. | A | 28. | D |
| 14. | C | 29. | B |
| 15. | D | 30. | D |

## ANSWERS AND EXPLANATIONS

These are the explanations to the Reading Comprehension questions. Next to the answer choices for each question, we have explained in greater detail exactly why the wrong answer choices are incorrect.

For some questions, we have left the wrong-answer explanations blank so that you can fill them in. In the blanks next to the question, write the question type. In the blanks next to the answers, write a brief explanation of why the answer is incorrect. The more you can analyze and explain the errors in the wrong answer choices, the more skillful and efficient you will become at identifying, understanding, and eliminating incorrect choices, and selecting the correct ones.

Sample responses for these Identify the Error questions are included at the end of the Answers and Explanations section.

1. What is expected for Beijing on Wednesday? (Detail/*What*)

    (A) Rain CORRECT

    (B) Wind (Wind is predicted for Melbourne.)

    (C) Unusual warmth (This is not mentioned.)

    (D) Clear skies (This is not mentioned.)

2. Where is sunny weather predicted? (Detail/*Where*)

   (A) Brisbane CORRECT

   (B) Jakarta (This is not mentioned.)

   (C) Shanghai (This repeats the word *Shanghai*.)

   (D) Taipei (This is not mentioned.)

3. Why will the Proplan representatives visit? (Gist/*Why*)

   (A) To discuss health insurance CORRECT

   (B) To provide medical examinations (This plays on the health topic.)

   (C) To distribute health care policies (This repeats the words *health care policy*.)

   (D) To sign up participants (This may be a possible reason, but it is not mentioned.)

4. What should interested employees do? (Detail/*What*)

   (A) Talk to the benefits department. (No, the memo is from the benefits department.)

   (B) Read the attached information. (This is not mentioned.)

   (C) Write down questions. (This plays on the words *answer questions*.)

   (D) Sign up for appointments. CORRECT

5. What is Ms. Ketchem sending with this letter? (Detail/*What*)

   (A) A résumé CORRECT

   (B) A writing sample (This is not mentioned.)

   (C) A job description (This is not mentioned.)

   (D) A reference letter (This is not mentioned.)

6. How did Ms. Ketchem learn about the position? (Detail/*How*)

   (A) From a friend (This is not mentioned.)

   (B) From a website CORRECT

   (C) From a newspaper advertisement (No, she saw the position advertised online.)

   (D) From Mr. Baker (This repeats the words *Mr. Baker.*)

7. Which task is part of Ms. Ketchem's current job? (Detail/*What*)

   (A) Handling conventions CORRECT

   (B) Supervising staff (This is not mentioned; it simply repeats the word *staff.*)

   (C) Coordinating food service (This is not mentioned.)

   (D) Registering guests (This is not mentioned.)

**KAPLAN**

8. Who is Franz Thurman? (Detail/*Who*)

    (A) An employee (No, he would like to be an employee.)

    (B) An interviewer (He will be the interviewee.)

    (C) An applicant CORRECT

    (D) A customer (This is not mentioned.)

9. What is the purpose of this letter? (Gist/*What*)

    (A) To schedule an appointment CORRECT

    (B) To make a job offer (A job offer would come after the interview.)

    (C) To reject a candidate (The company wants to interview the candidate by telephone.)

    (D) To request information (No information is being requested.)

10. What can be inferred about Saysee's advertisement? (Detail/*What*)

    (A) Many people replied to it. CORRECT

    (B) It was posted online. (This is not mentioned. Also, we do not know where it was posted.)

    (C) Few people read it. (No, the response was overwhelming, meaning many people applied.)

    (D) It ran for two weeks. (This is not mentioned.)

11. What is the main idea of the article? (Gist/*What*)

    (A) A large trading block will be created. (A trading block is not being created.)

    (B) Cargo shipments are getting bigger. (Possibly, but this is not mentioned.)

    (C) A transportation coalition will be formed. CORRECT

    (D) Air freight could become cheaper. (This is not mentioned.)

12. Who will participate in the alliance? (Gist/*Who*)

    (A) Four large shipping companies CORRECT

    (B) Governments in Asia, Europe, and North America (These are the shipping routes that will be "linked.")

    (C) A group of manufacturing companies (These are not manufacturing companies.)

    (D) Several customer protection groups (This is not mentioned.)

13. How will members benefit from the alliance? (Detail/*How*)

    (A) By sharing space on ships CORRECT

    (B) Through reduced competition (This is possible, but is not mentioned.)

    (C) By sharing port facilities (This is possible, but is not mentioned.)

    (D) Through access to larger ships (No, the passage says to *maximize use ... of faster ships*.)

14. The word *specifics* as used in line 9 is closest in meaning to (Vocabulary)

    (A) members.

    (B) costs.

    (C) details. CORRECT

    (D) containers.

15. When will the alliance be created? (Detail/*When*)

    (A) Immediately (This is not mentioned.)

    (B) At the end of the month (Negotiations will begin next month.)

    (C) Within six to eight months (This is not mentioned.)

    (D) Over a two-year period CORRECT

16. Why was the Commerce Service created? (Gist/*Why*)

    (A) To help Chilean companies import products (The emphasis is on exporting Chilean products.)

    (B) To aid Chilean companies working abroad CORRECT

    (C) To educate international specialists (Each office already has a trade specialist.)

    (D) To counsel firms seeking to sell in Chile (This is not mentioned.)

17. What is likely to be found at a Commerce Service office? (Detail/*What*)

    (A) A currency exchange facility (This is not mentioned.)

    (B) Conference rooms (This is not mentioned.)

    (C) Classrooms (This is not mentioned.)

    (D) A business library CORRECT

18. What does the Commerce Service use to evaluate a firm's readiness to export? (Detail/*What*)

   (A) A computer program CORRECT

   (B) A questionnaire (This is not mentioned.)

   (C) An export analysis (This is not mentioned.)

   (D) A written survey (This is not mentioned.)

19. What would a Commercial Service office probably *NOT* do? (Detail/*What*)

   (A) Introduce businesspeople to government contacts. (They assist *with* appointments with key buyers and government officials.)

   (B) Look for investment opportunities. (They seek out trade and investment opportunities.)

   (C) Help a Chilean firm write a business plan. CORRECT

   (D) Research local market trends. (They gather information about trends.)

20. The word *determine* in line 10 is closest in meaning to (Vocabulary)

   (A) evaluate. CORRECT

   (B) improve.

   (C) allow.

   (D) start.

21. What is the invoice for? (Gist/*What*)

   (A) Banking transactions (This plays on the topic of account information.)

   (B) Clothing purchases (This is not mentioned.)

   (C) Accounting services (This plays on the topic of account information.)

   (D) Medical services CORRECT

22. How was the first payment made? (Detail/*How*)

   (A) By check (This is not mentioned.)

   (B) With a credit card (This is not mentioned.)

   (C) In cash CORRECT

   (D) By bank transfer (This is not mentioned.)

23. How much is owed on the account? (Detail/*How*)

    (A) £50 (This is not mentioned.)

    (B) £100 (This is what has been paid.)

    (C) £150 CORRECT

    (D) £200 (This is not mentioned.)

24. The word *outstanding* in line 8 of the email is closest in meaning to (Vocabulary)

    (A) amazing.

    (B) noticeable.

    (C) exceptional.

    (D) overdue. CORRECT

25. What does David imply about Mrs. Yamanda? (Detail/*What*)

    (A) Her home number is not on record. (It is on record.)

    (B) Her cell phone number is not on record. (It is on record.)

    (C) She may not be in her office. CORRECT

    (D) She has moved to Manchester. (This uses Manchester from the address on the invoice.)

26. How did Bob learn about the SURESAFE Media Protector? _____
    _____

    (A) From an advertisement in a journal CORRECT

    (B) From Harriet _____

    (C) From a SURESAFE brochure _____

    (D) From a website review _____

27. What does Bob imply about the SURESAFE Media Protector? _____
    _____

    (A) It is more expensive than similar items. CORRECT

    (B) It will not fit their needs. _____

    (C) It is no longer available. _____

    (D) It will take several weeks to be delivered. _____

28. What is NOT mentioned as being a feature of the SURESAFE Media Protector? _____
    _____

    (A) Small size _____

    (B) A changeable lock _____

    (C) A hidden dial _____

    (D) All-steel construction CORRECT

29. The word *withstand* in line 7 of the advertisement is closest in meaning to (Vocabulary)

    (A) burn.

    (B) survive. CORRECT

    (C) increase.

    (D) change.

30. What is claimed about the SURESAFE Media Protector? (Detail/*What*)

    (A) It is guaranteed never to fail. (This is not mentioned.)

    (B) It is the strongest unit available at any price. (This is not mentioned.)

    (C) It cannot be opened by thieves or other criminals. (This is not mentioned.)

    (D) It protects against conditions of high heat and humidity. CORRECT

## Answers for the Identify the Error Questions

26. How did Bob learn about the SURESAFE Media Protector? (*Detail/How*)

    (A) From an advertisement in a journal CORRECT

    (B) From Harriet (*Bob is informing Harriet about the product.*)

    (C) From a SURESAFE brochure (*Brochures are mentioned, but this is not how Bob learns about the product.*)

    (D) From a website review (*This is not mentioned.*)

27. What does Bob imply about the SURESAFE Media Protector? (*Detail/What*)

    (A) It is more expensive than similar items. CORRECT

    (B) It will not fit their needs. (*He says it's just what we need.*)

    (C) It is no longer available. (*This is not mentioned.*)

    (D) It will take several weeks to be delivered. (*This is not mentioned.*)

28. What is *NOT* mentioned as being a feature of the SURESAFE Media Protector? (Detail/*What*)

    (A) Small size (*An entire sentence describes the advantages of its small size.*)

    (B) A changeable lock (*It has a three-number changeable combination lock.*)

    (C) A hidden dial (*The dial is concealed for security.*)

    (D) All-steel construction CORRECT

# PART FOUR

# Vocabulary Builders

# Chapter 10: **Vocabulary-Building Exercises**

- Vocabulary Lists
- Vocabulary Exercises
- Vocabulary and Grammar Exercises for Part V
- Vocabulary and Grammar Exercises for Part VI
- Glossary

There is no better way to boost your TOEIC exam score than to boost your vocabulary. Therefore, in addition to learning Kaplan's test-taking strategies and practicing the different types of TOEIC exam questions, review the list of words included in this chapter. Nevertheless, it is not enough to know a word's meaning; you have to be able to understand the word when you hear or see it in different contexts and know how to use the word yourself. That is where the vocabulary exercises come in. They will help you put your newly acquired vocabulary into action.

The five word lists that follow each include ten of the most common word families you will find on the TOEIC exam. They are grouped in word families because we have found that students learn more words more efficiently when the words are grouped together. In fact, anytime you come across a new word—in this book or any reading material—it is a good idea to study the other words within the same family.

You will find this especially helpful for Part V Incomplete Sentences because you must often distinguish between the different forms of a particular word. The vocabulary and grammar exercises also provide additional focused review for the types of questions you'll encounter in Part V.

For even more vocabulary-building, read as much material in English as you can. Many English-language newspapers and magazines are available for free online; for example, you can read the *Washington Post* daily newspaper online at *www.washingtonpost.com.*

In addition, write each new word you encounter and its sentence in a notebook. Writing down new words helps you to remember them. You should also make note of new uses of words you already know, and review your notebook often.

 **WORDS YOU NEED TO KNOW**

The words in these lists appear frequently on the TOEIC exam—and they are commonly used in business situations. Mastering these words can help you on the TOEIC exam and in your career.

Remember: You cannot learn all these words in a day—or even in a week for that matter! Instead, work with the lists and exercises little by little each day that you study.

1. Look up all the words on a list in the glossary on page **227**.
2. Listen to the list on the audio CD.
3. Try the exercises for that list.
4. Check your answers using the answer key at the end of this chapter.

 To help you learn the correct pronunciation of these words, we have included them on the audio CD.

1. To hear List 1, play track 1 on Audio CD 2.
2. To hear List 2, play track 2 on Audio CD 2.
3. To hear List 3, play track 3 on Audio CD 2.
4. To hear List 4, play track 4 on Audio CD 2.
5. To hear List 5, play track 5 on Audio CD 2.

## VOCABULARY LISTS

| List 1 | List 2 |
| --- | --- |
| ad *noun* | accept *verb* |
| advertise *verb* | acceptable *adjective* |
| advertisement *noun* | acceptance *noun* |
| applicant *noun* | accepting *adjective* |
| application *noun* | attend *verb* |
| apply *verb* | attendance *noun* |
| beneficent *adjective* | attendant *noun* |
| beneficial *adjective* | attention *noun* |
| beneficially *adverb* | develop *verb* |
| beneficiary *noun* | developers *noun* |
| benefit *noun, verb* | development *noun* |
| confide *verb* | expect *verb* |
| confidence *noun* | expectation *noun* |
| confident *adjective* | expecting *verb* |

confidential *adjective*

employ *verb*

employee *noun*

employer *noun*

employment *noun*

experience *noun, verb*

interview *noun, verb*

interviewee *noun*

interviewer *noun*

person *noun*

personal *adjective*

personalized *adjective*

personnel *noun*

position *noun, verb*

train *verb*

trainee *noun*

trainer *noun*

training *noun*

facilitate *verb*

facility/facilities *noun*

form/forms *noun*

form/forms *verb*

format *noun*

network *noun, verb*

networking *noun, adjective*

procedure/procedures *noun*

proceed *verb*

proceeding *noun*

process *noun, verb*

processing *noun*

specific *adjective*

specifically *adverb*

specification *noun*

specifics *noun*

specify *verb*

| List 3 | List 4 |
|---|---|
| account *noun, verb* | arrange *verb* |
| accountant *noun* | arrangement *noun* |
| accounting *noun* | brochure *noun* |
| budget *noun, verb* | complete *adjective, verb* |
| consult *verb* | completion *noun* |
| consultant *noun* | manage *verb* |
| consulting *adjective* | management *noun* |
| document *noun, verb* | manager *noun* |
| documentation *noun* | managerial *adjective* |
| firm *adjective, noun* | operate *verb* |
| interest *noun, verb* | operation *noun* |
| interested *adjective* | operational *adjective* |
| interesting *adjective* | operator *noun* |
| inventory *noun* | policy *noun* |
| organization *noun* | post *verb* |
| organize *verb* | postage *noun* |
| pay *noun, verb* | postal *adjective* |

payable *adjective*

payment *noun*

profit *noun, verb*

profitability *noun*

profitable *adjective*

proposal *noun*

supervise *verb*

postmaster *noun*

present *adjective*

present *noun*

present *verb*

presentation *noun*

propose *verb*

supervisor *noun*

---

### List 5

commerce *noun*

commercial *adjective, noun*

compete *verb*

competent *adjective*

competition *noun*

competitive *adjective*

competitor *noun*

export *noun, verb*

exporter *noun*

global *adjective*

industrial *adjective*

industrialize *verb*

industry *noun*

international *adjective*

internationalize *verb*

market *noun, verb*

marketing plan *noun*

negotiate *verb*

negotiations *noun*

negotiator *noun*

promote *verb*

promotion *noun*

promotional *adjective*

trade *noun, verb*

---

# VOCABULARY EXERCISES FOR LIST 1

## EXERCISE 1

**Directions:** Give the verb form for each of the following nouns in the space provided.

| Noun | Verb |
|------|------|
| 1. ad | |
| 2. application | |
| 3. beneficiary | |
| 4. confidence | |
| 5. employer | |
| 6. trainee | |

## Exercise 2

**Directions**: Replace the underlined words or phrases with a word from the following list that has a similar meaning. Use each word only once.

question

beneficiary

position

trainee

personal

profit

experience

employ

advertisement

confidential

1. George did not know about the concert until he saw the <u>poster</u> about it. _____

2. The company expects to <u>benefit</u> a great deal from the new trade agreement between the United States and Mexico. _____

3. I would like for these discussions regarding our dealings with Cedar Industries to be <u>secret</u>.

   _____

4. Jorge's grandmother named him in her will as the <u>recipient</u> of her home and all its furnishings.

   _____

5. Mariko's <u>background</u> in the publishing industry was rather limited, but the manager liked her enthusiasm and willingness to learn. _____

6. During the busy holiday season, many retailers <u>use</u> temporary help. _____

7. Martha received a promotion and she now has a new <u>job</u> in the international marketing department. _____

8. Everyone passed the course, except one <u>new employee</u>. _____

9. The reporter wanted to <u>interview</u> the company president about his plans to expand operations to Vietnam. _____

10. I considered some of the employer's questions <u>private</u> and answered them reluctantly.

    _____

## Exercise 3

**Directions**: Complete the sentences with the correct form of the underlined word.

1. If you are interested in <u>applying</u> for the job, you should fill out an _____.

2. The <u>interviewee</u> seemed uncomfortable during the _____ and only responded in short answers.

3. An <u>advertising</u> campaign is being developed to _____ our new soft drink to teenagers.

4. The message was very _____, so I decided to deliver it in <u>person</u>.

5. Per the terms of the new labor agreement, the company needs to <u>employ</u> ten new _____ by the end of the month.

6. The <u>benefit</u> for the Children's Food Bank raised a lot of money, proving once again how _____ these types of events are.

## EXERCISE 4

**Directions**: Match the word in column A with its definition in column B.

| Column A | Column B |
| --- | --- |
| 1. trainee | a. a person who gives a job to someone |
| 2. applicant | b. someone who will inherit some money |
| 3. employer | c. someone learning a new trade |
| 4. interviewer | d. a candidate for a job |
| 5. person | e. someone asking another person questions |
| 6. beneficiary | f. an individual |

## EXERCISE 5

**Directions**: Complete the sentences by filling the blank with the correct word from the list. Use each word only once.

beneficially
confided
personalized
positions
employment
training

1. Many graduates will be seeking permanent _____ in July.

2. If Joyce loses any of her _____ pens, she knows someone will recognize her initials.

3. Very few people lost their _____ despite the company's restructuring program.

4. I have two weeks of _____ before I actually start my new job.

5. Mr. LaRue _____ in his employees that the company was seeking bankruptcy.

6. Leigh Ann tries to act _____ toward many causes.

# VOCABULARY EXERCISES FOR LIST 2

## EXERCISE 1

**Directions**: Form nouns from these verbs by adding *-ance, -ation,* or *-ment.*

| Verb Form | Noun Form |
|---|---|
| 1. to develop | _____ |
| 2. to specify | _____ |
| 3. to accept | _____ |
| 4. to attend | _____ |
| 5. to expect | _____ |

## EXERCISE 2

**Directions**: Fill the blanks with the correct preposition in parentheses.

1. Attendance _____ (at, in) the play had dropped, so they decided to cancel the remaining shows.
2. The speaker was frustrated because no one seemed to be paying attention _____ (with, to) him.
3. The process _____ (for, to) recycling many of our household items is not as difficult as many people think.
4. Networking all computers would facilitate the sales team _____ (on, with) their work.
5. The president wanted a status report on the development _____ (of, for) the new software program.
6. The attendant was very polite and helpful _____ (to, at) the customers and received many compliments.
7. Thomas was unable to attend the awards banquet, so Mark accepted the award _____ (for, with) him.
8. The workers formed a circle _____ (around, through) Mr. Martini's desk and sang "Happy Birthday" to him.

## EXERCISE 3

**Directions**: Complete these sentences by filling the blanks with the correct word in parentheses.

1. Because they did not _____ (specific, specifically) say the meeting would start at noon, no one knew when to arrive.
2. The food _____ (process, processing) plant had to close down because of a labor dispute.

3. Some wealthy _____ (developers, developing) are hoping to build a resort along the coast.

4. David is not very _____ (acceptable, accepting) of changes in the office.

5. _____ (Attendance, Attending) at today's staff meeting is required.

6. The _____ (attendant, attending) physician had to call a specialist to help with this case.

7. Many professionals join organizations because they are often a good _____ (network, networking) source.

8. Two workers were fined for not following the correct _____ (procedures, proceedings).

## EXERCISE 4

**Directions**: Complete this paragraph by filling the blanks with the correct word from the list. Use each word once.

| | | |
|---|---|---|
| form | acceptable | networks |
| format | processing | specifications |
| attendance | developing | forms |
| expected | facilitate | |

At the beginning of the new season, the television (1) _____ mailed out viewer response (2) _____ to get feedback on their new shows. After (3) _____ and evaluating the completed cards, it became apparent that most viewers did not like the violent (4) _____ of many shows. Violent TV shows were no longer (5) _____ to most viewers. The television producers had not (6) _____ such a negative response to their shows. They decided to (7) _____ a committee of viewers and writers to establish some (8) _____ for (9) _____ a new television show. One producer was selected to (10) _____ the meetings, and all those in (11) _____ said that much was accomplished.

# VOCABULARY EXERCISES FOR LIST 3

## EXERCISE 1

**Directions**: Complete these sentences by filling in the blanks with the correct form of the underlined word.

1. I have hired an _____ to take care of all my <u>accounts</u>.

2. We probably won't use those <u>consultants</u> again, because their _____ fee was very high.

3. Sally had to get the original <u>documents</u> from the shipping company, because customs would not release the package without proper _____.

4. A smart consumer should <u>be interested</u> in the _____ rates that banks charge on credit cards.

5. Those in the advertising field are <u>organizing</u> an advertising _____ that would cater to new graduates.

6. The department store claimed that he had failed to <u>pay</u> his last bill, but according to his records, he had sent a _____ three weeks ago.

7. Peter was convinced that his new venture would be _____, and he predicted that they would see <u>profits</u> within the year.

8. The law _____ stood <u>firmly</u> behind its decision to represent the oil company.

# EXERCISE 2

**Directions**: Underline the two words in column B that are associated with the word in column A.

| Column A | Column B |
|---|---|
| 1. payable | due, free, owing, trade |
| 2. payment | crime, service, cash, check |
| 3. budget | economize, unorganized, plan, start |
| 4. interest | savings, loan, loss, purchase |
| 5. organization | business, individual, profit, foundation |
| 6. document | verbal, painting, paper, birth certificate |
| 7. consultant | advisor, conference, mentor, distributor |

# EXERCISE 3

**Directions**: Fill the blanks with the correct word from the list. Use each word once.

| paid | documented | budget | inventory | organize |
|---|---|---|---|---|
| firm | profitable | account | consult | interests |

1. The company appeared to be _____, so the business community was surprised when it filed for bankruptcy.

2. The invoice had been incorrectly marked _____, so a past due notice was never mailed to the customer.

3. The union tried to _____ its members to vote against the new contract.

4. Our _____ of women's shoes needs to be updated with new styles.

5. The idea _____ me, but I need about a week to think it over.

6. Management was _____ about its decision to penalize employees for being late.

7. The police officer _____ what each witness had to say about the accident.

8. Unsure of the import-export laws of Brazil, Auto Components, Inc. decided to _____ with a trade expert.

9. Peggy finds that she needs to _____ her time if she wants to get everything done.

10. The witness gave a detailed _____ of the accident to the police officer.

## EXERCISE 4

**Directions:** Fill the blanks with the correct form of the word in parentheses.

1. That idea sounds _____ (interested, interesting) to me; I'd like to see some further research.

2. The bill was marked _____ (paid, payable), so I mailed a check the next day.

3. After several years of struggling, the company is finally showing signs of _____ (profitable, profitability).

4. Edward goes to all the shareholders' meetings because he has an _____ (interest, interesting) in the company.

5. International travelers should be careful to keep all _____ (document, documentation) of items purchased on a trip.

6. The hotel manager was unable to _____ (account, accounting) for the drop in hotel guests.

7. I'm thinking of leaving the company and becoming an independent _____ (consulting, consultant).

## VOCABULARY EXERCISES FOR LIST 4

## EXERCISE 1

**Directions:** Underline the word in the sentence that is closest in meaning to the word in parentheses.

1. (placement)    The president did not like the arrangement of the chairs at the head table of the banquet.

2. (booklet)    The museum decided to add colored photos to its brochure, and everyone seemed to be pleased with the result.

3. (fully)    Ms. Abrams was not completely convinced of the need to hire a part-time receptionist.

4. (completion)    The fulfillment of this contract certainly calls for a celebration, as everyone worked so hard on it.

5. (governing)    Carlos was hired for his excellent managerial skills, and the board is counting on him to organize the various departments.

6. (operating)    The company decided to lower its overhead expenses and move to a less expensive building.

7. (policy)    Many companies have initiated a no-smoking rule inside the office; smokers now have to go outside.

8. (postage)    I didn't put enough stamps on my letter, so it was returned to me.

9. (present)    The board of directors awarded the retiring vice president with a commemorative gift for his 35 years of service to the company.

10. (suggest)    I propose that we discuss this matter over lunch.

## EXERCISE 2

**Directions**: Match the words in column B that have the opposite meaning to the words in column A.

| Column A | Column B |
| --- | --- |
| 1. arrange | a. out of order |
| 2. complete | b. absent |
| 3. operational | c. subordinate |
| 4. to post | d. partial |
| 5. present | e. disorganize |
| 6. supervisor | f. to remove |

## EXERCISE 3

**Directions**: Complete the sentences with the correct word from the list. Use each word once.

| policy | management | supervises |
| --- | --- | --- |
| operating | arranged | posted |
| brochure | complete | managerial |

1. Anyone _____ heavy machinery should not take medications.

2. The homeowner _____ a sign warning trespassers to stay off his property.

3. The trading partners of the developing country have complained about what they consider to be an overly restrictive trade _____.

4. The company will be laying off some employees, and some of those positions are in _____.

5. Alice wanted to purchase the _____ works of her husband's favorite composer for his birthday.

6. Shawn looked through the Help Wanted ads for any _____ positions, but he only found a few entry-level positions in the fields that interested him.

7. According to this _____, there is a scenic highway that goes all the way to the coast.

8. The receptionist did not like the way the temporary help had _____ her desk.

9. David received a promotion, and now he _____ four other employees.

## EXERCISE 4

**Directions**: Match each sentence part in column A with its correct completion in column B.

| Column A | Column B |
|---|---|
| 1. Once the fan belt had been fixed | a. after two accidents in one year. |
| 2. A complete audit was requested | b. for organizing the next day's operations. |
| 3. The cruise line had trouble renewing its insurance policy | c. the machine was operational. |
| 4. The proposal to raise room rates | d. but only a partial one was approved. |
| 5. The evening supervisor is responsible | e. was approved by hotel management. |

# VOCABULARY EXERCISES FOR LIST 5

## EXERCISE 1

**Directions**: Match the words in column B that have the opposite meaning to the words in column A.

| Column A | Column B |
|---|---|
| 1. export | a. closed to debate |
| 2. competitor | b. internal |
| 3. global | c. import |
| 4. negotiate | d. colleague |
| 5. promote | e. downplay |

# EXERCISE 2

**Directions**: Circle the word in the list that does not belong with the others.

1. international, foreign, domestic, global, intercontinental
2. market, farm, shop, retail store, bazaar
3. bargain, stall, negotiate, compromise, talk over
4. criticize, promote, advertise, market, build up
5. competitor, challenger, rival, adversary, loser

# EXERCISE 3

**Directions**: Match each sentence part in column A with its correct completion in column B.

| Column A | Column B |
|---|---|
| 1. Dan received a promotion | a. because the exchange rate is much higher. |
| 2. Some people change currency | b. because it is unable to compete on the black market with the international firms. |
| 3. The negotiations to lease the building | c. after being with the company for seven years. |
| 4. I'm sure that Mary is a competent worker | d. apply for a job at an ad agency. |
| 5. After graduating in marketing, Elaine decided to | e. because her references say that she is capable of handling most situations. |
| 6. The clothing industry is not doing well here | f. came to a halt when one of the attorneys became ill. |

# EXERCISE 4

**Directions**: Complete the dialog by filling in the blanks with the correct word from the list. Use each word once.

| | | |
|---|---|---|
| Industrial | promotional | compete |
| promoting | industries | internationally |
| market | commercials | negotiated |

A: How did the viewers like the new movie?

B: It hasn't come out yet. We have just started (1) _____ it.

A: What's the movie about again?

B: It takes place during the (2) _____ Revolution and features workers in various (3) _____.

A: How do you plan to (4) _____ it?

B: Well, we have (5) _____ with several theaters around the country and they'll all begin showing it next month. We also hope it will be shown (6) _____.

A: Do you think it will (7) _____ well with the action movies?

B: It should. We need to run some (8) _____ on television and develop more (9) _____ materials.

## EXERCISE 5

**Directions**: Complete each sentence with the correct form of the verb in parentheses.

1. Two local companies _____ (compete) last year for the government contract to build a federal building.

2. The company is planning on _____ (export) its laser printers to Europe next year.

3. Developing countries are working hard to become _____ (industrialize) in order to improve their economies.

4. Rolf should be a good addition to the sales team; his experience is extensive and he _____ (market) automobile parts for five years now.

5. William _____ (negotiate) the sale of timber products to a foreign country and received a promotion from his employer in the timber industry.

6. Once the trade ban is lifted, our company will be free _____ (trade) with that country again.

## VOCABULARY AND GRAMMAR EXERCISES FOR PART V

For Vocabulary questions in Part V, all four possible answers will be the same part of speech. That is, they will all either be verbs, nouns, modifiers (adjectives and adverbs), conjunctions (*and*, *but*, *either*, etc.), or prepositions. Focus on the context of the sentence and your knowledge of vocabulary to identify the correct answer. Make sure you read the entire sentence so that you get the full context of the sentence before trying to complete it.

For the Grammar questions in Part V, all four possible answers share a common root but are different parts of speech. The possible answers will be a variety of verbs, nouns, modifiers (adjectives and adverbs), and pronouns. Because the answer choices are usually different forms of the same word, your task is to select the form of the word that is grammatically correct. To start, read the entire sentence to get its full context; then, focus on the words on either side of the missing word. These often provide clues as to which part of speech is required. For example, the article *the* or *a* in front of the blank tells you a noun is missing.

The vocabulary tested on the TOEIC exam is the kind that you would expect to see in business reports, newspaper or magazine articles, advertisements, public notices, and other types of everyday written contexts. The TOEIC exam tests a wide variety of grammar points. At a minimum, you should be familiar with the following:

- **PRONOUNS**
  - Possessive pronouns (*mine, yours, his, hers, its, ours, theirs*)
  - Subject pronouns (*I, you, he, she, it, we, they*)
  - Object pronouns (*me, you, him, her, it, us, them*)
  - Reflexive pronouns (*myself, yourself, himself, herself, itself, ourselves, yourselves, themselves*)
  - Relative pronouns (*who, which, what, that*)
  - Interrogative pronouns (*who, which, what*)
  - Demonstrative pronouns (*this, that, these, those*)

- **VERBS**
  - Tenses and their usage
  - When to use *-ing* forms
  - Infinitives with and without *to*
  - Common irregular verbs and their forms
  - Irregular past participles
  - Subject-verb agreement

- **ADJECTIVES and ADVERBS**
  - Differences between adjectives and adverbs
  - Use of adjectives, including nouns as adjectives
  - Use and forms of comparatives and superlatives
  - Use of adverbs

- **PREPOSITIONS and PHRASAL VERBS**
  - Common prepositions (*to, on, in, at, from…*)
  - Common prepositional phrases (*look up, go over, turn on…*)

- **CONJUNCTIONS**
  - Common conjunctions and their uses (*but, however, although, yet, so, despite…*)

## VOCABULARY AND GRAMMAR PRACTICE EXERCISES

1. We _____ credit cards, checks, or money orders for payment.

   (A) accept

   (B) exist

   (C) pay

   (D) are

2. Due to decreasing sales, major automobile manufacturers are _____ customer rebates.

   (A) asking

   (B) offering

   (C) showing

   (D) taking

3. Sales have improved since we changed the way _____ is displayed in the window.

   (A) mechanic

   (B) management

   (C) merchandise

   (D) mask

4. Susan went _____ early on Friday because she was ill.

   (A) town

   (B) home

   (C) house

   (D) place

5. We have arranged for an _____ flight on Tuesday.

   (A) early

   (B) angry

   (C) ugly

   (D) eager

6. Passengers are able to travel _____ and inexpensively by train.

    (A) frankly
    (B) perfectly
    (C) shortly
    (D) comfortably

7. Both President Scarpati _____ Chairman Green spoke at the national meeting.

    (A) or
    (B) and
    (C) but
    (D) yet

8. Mr. Lipton was in good spirits and reported that he was neither tired _____ hungry after his flight from Sydney.

    (A) nor
    (B) either
    (C) and
    (D) but

9. Please have the attached documents sent out _____ express mail service.

    (A) of
    (B) at
    (C) to
    (D) by

10. Ms. Roswell was transferred from Mexico City _____ Los Angeles in April.

    (A) by
    (B) to
    (C) through
    (D) with

11. They _____ the brochure before we could make the changes.

    (A) printed
    (B) printing
    (C) printers
    (D) prints

12. The memorandum was _____ through via mail.

    (A) sending
    (B) sends
    (C) sender
    (D) sent

13. Because the _____ was broken, the equipment had to be brought up the stairs.

    (A) elevation
    (B) elevator
    (C) elevate
    (D) elevated

14. If full payment is not received within 30 days, _____ will be charged on the amount due.

    (A) interesting
    (B) interest
    (C) interested
    (D) interests

15. After months of negotiations, we were _____ awarded the Gibbson account.

    (A) final
    (B) finalized
    (C) finally
    (D) finality

16. The convention provides a chance to meet _____ distributors and representatives without leaving the country.

    (A) international
    (B) internationalize
    (C) internationally
    (D) internationalized

17. On behalf of the social services committee, _____ have the honor of inviting you to the Annual Spring Fashion Show.

    (A) you
    (B) our
    (C) we
    (D) me

18. Ms. Wilson says the hardest part of _____ job is setting priorities.

    (A) she
    (B) herself
    (C) hers
    (D) her

## ANSWER KEY

1. A
2. B
3. C
4. B
5. A
6. D
7. B
8. A
9. D

10. B
11. A
12. D
13. B
14. B
15. C
16. A
17. C
18. D

## VOCABULARY AND GRAMMAR REVIEW FOR PART VI

On Part VI of the TOEIC exam, you will be making use of strategies very similar to those you used for Part V. This is because, essentially, Part VI is a variation of Part V that uses whole texts instead of individual sentences. The missing words and phrases fall into the two categories we discussed in chapter 7: those that test your knowledge of vocabulary and those that test your knowledge of grammar. Your first strategy, therefore, is to identify which type of incomplete sentence you are completing.

However, there is one important difference between the Part V and Part VI. In Part VI, you are given full texts, not single sentences, so some of the missing words are cohesive devices. These are words that hold the text together, or organize it. Examples of cohesive devices are:

- Pronouns (*he, she, him, them*)
- Possessive adjectives (*his, her, your*)
- Conjunctions (*because, but, however, whereas*)

Sometimes these are used to refer back or forward to things mentioned in the text. Other times they are used to join thoughts or ideas together.

## Practice 1

Questions 1–3 refer to the following letter.

Dear Mr. Jones,

As a valued _____ to *Coffee Aficionado* magazine, we thought you ought to be the first to know of a

1. (A) subscriber
   (B) buyer
   (C) member
   (D) associate

very special offer we are making beginning next month. Now that you've been receiving *Coffee Aficionado* for some time, you'll no doubt have gotten used to our first-class reporting of all the latest industry news. You'll also have realized that there is no other _____ currently available that gives the

2. (A) reporter
   (B) coffee
   (C) pamphlet
   (D) publication

depth and _____ of information you expect to find on all things coffee. And certainly you'll have

3. (A) size
   (B) width
   (C) breadth
   (D) height

understood that from our team of experts and specialists in the field, you are getting the most informed opinions available. And things just got better! We're making you this very special offer: a two-year subscription to *Coffee Aficionado* for only $32.95.

**Practice 2**

Questions 4–6 refer to the following passage.

---

**White Noise Is Good Noise**

We live in an _____ noisy world. Heavy traffic, barking dogs, and loud music from our

4. (A) increase
   (B) increased
   (C) increasingly
   (D) increasing

neighbors are all examples of the kind of noise pollution that many people find unbearable. Doctors now cite noise disturbance as one of the most common causes of anxiety and depression in their patients. One way to reduce _____ impact is the use of a white noise generator in the home or office. White noise

5. (A) its
   (B) their
   (C) your
   (D) our

is sound at a certain frequency that effectively blocks out or neutralizes other sounds. White noise actually occurs often in nature: pouring rain, waterfalls, or surf crashing on the beach are all examples. Some units simply reproduce recordings of these sounds, _____ other more sophisticated units generate

6. (A) when
   (B) nevertheless
   (C) likewise
   (D) whereas

white noise electronically.

---

# ANSWER KEY

1. A
2. D
3. C
4. C
5. A
6. D

# GLOSSARY

The following is a glossary for the words in all five lists.

### List 1

| | |
|---|---|
| ad *noun* | advertisement |
| advertise *verb* | to show that something is for sale/that you want something |
| advertisement *noun* | notice which shows that something is for sale/that you want something |
| applicant *noun* | a person who applies, as for employment |
| application *noun* | asking for a job; a request, or a form filled out in making one; any thing applied, as a remedy |
| apply *verb* | to ask for a job; to refer to; to make a request; to put or spread on |
| beneficent *adjective* | doing or resulting in good |
| beneficial *adjective* | producing benefits; advantageous; favorable |
| beneficially *adverb* | producing benefits; advantageous; favorable |
| beneficiary *noun* | anyone receiving or to receive benefit, as funds from a will, an insurance policy, etc. |
| benefit *noun* | anything contributing to improvement; advantage; payments made by an insurance company, public agency; a public performance, bazaar, etc. with the proceeds going to help some person or cause |
| benefit *verb* | to receive advantage; to profit |
| confide *verb* | to trust (in someone), especially by sharing secrets |
| confidence *noun* | trust; assurance; belief in one's ability |
| confident *adjective* | full of confidence; certain; sure of oneself |
| confidential *adjective* | secret; entrusted with private matters |
| employ *verb* | to give work to someone, usually for payment; to use |
| employee *noun* | a person who is employed by an employer; one who works for another |
| employer *noun* | a person who hires workers and pays them for their work |

| | |
|---|---|
| employment *noun* | working; a job |
| experience *noun* | something that happens to you; knowledge of something because you have seen it or done it |
| experience *verb* | to have experience of; to undergo |
| interview *noun* | a talk with someone, often broadcast or reported in a newspaper |
| interview *verb* | to talk with someone; to ask questions of someone |
| interviewee *noun* | the person being interviewed |
| interviewer *noun* | the person conducting the interview; a person asking someone questions |
| person *noun* | a human being |
| personal *adjective* | private, individual; belonging to one person |
| personalized *adjective* | made personal; marked with one's name, etc. |
| personnel *noun* | persons employed in any work, enterprise, service, etc.; a department for hiring employees, etc. |
| position *noun* | the way in which a person or thing is placed or arranged; one's attitude or opinion; rank; employment, job |
| position *verb* | to put in a certain position |
| train *verb* | to teach someone or an animal how to do something; to practice for a sport |
| trainee *noun* | a person being trained |
| trainer *noun* | a person who trains others |
| training *noun* | instruction, practice |

## List 2

| | |
|---|---|
| accept *verb* | to agree to receive something; to agree to something |
| acceptable *adjective* | worth accepting; satisfactory |
| acceptance *noun* | the act of receiving something; an approval |
| accepting *adjective* | a willingness to accept |
| attend *verb* | to take care of; to go with; to be present at |
| attendance *noun* | the number of persons attending |
| attendant *noun* | one who attends or serves |
| attention *noun* | mental concentration or readiness; notice or observation; care or consideration |
| develop *verb* | to grow or make grow; to use for a better purpose; to start to get |
| developers *noun* | those who develop things, especially real estate and projects |
| development *noun* | thing that develops; being developed; area where new houses are built |

| | |
|---|---|
| expect *verb* | to think/to hope that something is going to happen or is true |
| expectation *noun* | anticipation; a thing looked forward to |
| expecting *verb* | anticipating |
| facilitate *verb* | to make easy or easier, to assist |
| facility/facilities *noun* | skill; dexterity; a building that facilitates some activity |
| form/forms *noun* | shape; paper with blank spaces that you have to write in; state/condition |
| format *noun* | the shape, size, and arrangement of something such as a book; the arrangement or plan of a presentation |
| form *verb* | to shape, to make |
| network *noun* | an arrangement of parallel wires; a system of interconnected roads, individuals; a chain of transmitting radio and TV stations |
| network *verb* | to connect; to interconnect wires, roads, individuals |
| networking *noun* | the making of contacts and trading of information; the interconnection of computer systems |
| procedure/procedures *noun* | the act or method of proceeding in an action; a series of steps taken to accomplish an end; a guideline |
| proceed *verb* | to go on; to carry on some action; to take legal action |
| proceeding *noun* | a going on with what one has been doing; a course of action; a record of transactions |
| process *noun* | the course of being done; course of time, etc.; method of doing something, with all the steps involved |
| process *verb* | to prepare by or subject to a special process |
| processing *noun* | preparation by a special process |
| specific *adjective* | definite; peculiar to or characteristic of something; of a particular kind |
| specifically *adverb* | definite, peculiar with respect to a particular action |
| specification *noun* | a list of particulars, as to size, quality, etc.; something specified |
| specifics *noun* | specified details, particulars |
| specify *verb* | to describe details |

## List 3

| | |
|---|---|
| account *noun* | a counting; a record of business transactions, bank/charge account; a credit customer; an explanation, report |
| account *verb* | to give a financial reckoning; to give reasons |
| accountant *noun* | one whose work is accounting |
| accounting *noun* | the figuring and recording of financial accounts |
| budget *noun* | a stock of items; a plan adjusting expenses to income; estimated cost of living, operating |
| budget *verb* | to put on a budget; to plan (your time) |

| | |
|---|---|
| consult *verb* | to talk things over; to seek information or instruction from; to consider |
| consultant *noun* | a person who consults another; a person who gives professional or technical advice |
| consulting *adjective* | advising |
| document *noun* | anything printed, written, etc. that may be used to record or prove something |
| document *verb* | to provide with or support by documents |
| documentation *noun* | being documented or having documents |
| firm *adjective* | solid, hard; showing determination; strong, certain |
| firm *noun* | a business company |
| interest *noun* | a right to, or share in something; advantage; a feeling of curiosity, concern about something; money paid for the use of money |
| interest *verb* | to involve or excite the interest or attention of; to cause to have an interest, share in |
| interested *adjective* | having an interest or share; feeling or showing interest |
| interesting *adjective* | exciting curiosity or attention; of interest |
| inventory *noun* | an itemized list of goods, property, etc., as of business; the store of goods for such listing, stock |
| organization *noun* | an organizing or being organized; any organized group, as a club |
| organize *verb* | to arrange for; to establish; to persuade to join a cause, group |
| pay *noun* | money paid, wages, salary |
| pay *verb* | to give what is due; to settle; to give (a compliment, attention, etc.); to be profitable |
| payable *adjective* | that can be paid; due to be paid |
| payment *noun* | a paying or being paid; something paid |
| profit *noun* | advantage, gain; financial gain, the sum remaining after deducting costs |
| profit *verb* | to gain financially; to benefit; to be of advantage |
| profitability *noun* | having profit, capability to gain profit |
| profitable *adjective* | having profit, advantageous |

**List 4**

| | |
|---|---|
| arrange *verb* | to put in the correct order; to classify; to prepare or plan |
| arrangement *noun* | an arranging; a plan; a settlement |
| brochure *noun* | a short printed document for informational or promotional purposes, a pamphlet |
| complete *adjective* | whole; entire; thorough |
| complete *verb* | to finish; to make whole or perfect |
| completion *noun* | the finishing/end of something |
| manage *verb* | to control the movement or behavior of; to have charge of; direct |

| | |
|---|---|
| management *noun* | a managing or being managed; the person managing a business, institution, etc. |
| manager *noun* | one who manages |
| managerial *adjective* | of a manager or management |
| operate *verb* | to be in action; act; work |
| operation *noun* | the act or method of operating; any of a series of procedures in some work or plan as in industry or warfare; any surgical procedure |
| operational *adjective* | having to do with the operation of a device, system; that can be used; in use |
| operator *noun* | a person who operates a machine (a telephone operator); a person engaged in business or industrial operations |
| policy *noun* | wise management; principle, plan; a written insurance contract |
| post *verb* | to put up; to announce/warn by posting notices; to mail |
| postage *noun* | the amount charged for mailing something |
| postal *adjective* | of mail or post offices |
| postmaster *noun* | a manager of a post office |
| present *adjective* | being at a specified place; the present time or occasion |
| present *noun* | the present time or occasion; a gift |
| present *verb* | to introduce (a person); to exhibit, show; to give a gift |
| presentation *noun* | a presenting or being presented; something presented |
| proposal *noun* | a proposing; a proposed plan; an offer of marriage |
| propose *verb* | to put forth for consideration, approval; to plan or intend |
| supervise *verb* | to oversee or direct |
| supervisor *noun* | one who oversees or directs |

## List 5

| | |
|---|---|
| commerce *noun* | trade on a large scale, as between countries |
| commercial *adjective* | of commerce or business; made or done for profit |
| commercial *noun* | a paid advertisement, often on television or radio |
| compete *verb* | to be in rivalry; contend |
| competent *adjective* | capable, fit; sufficient |
| competition *noun* | a contest, match |
| competitive *adjective* | liking competition |
| competitor *noun* | one who competes |
| export *noun* | anything exported |
| export *verb* | to send to another country or region for sale |
| exporter *noun* | one who exports |
| global *adjective* | worldwide |
| industrial *adjective* | having to do with industries or with the people working in industries |

| industrialize *verb* | to establish or develop industrialism; organize as an industry |
| industry *noun* | steady effort; any branch of productive, manufacturing enterprise; any large-scale business activity; the owners and managers of industry |
| international *adjective* | between or among nations; concerned with the relations between nations; of or for people in various nations |
| internationalize *verb* | to become international, develop international relations |
| market *noun* | a gathering of people for buying and selling things; a place where goods are sold; trade; demand (for goods, etc.) |
| market *verb* | to offer for sale; to sell |
| marketing plan *noun* | a plan to sell/promote goods |
| negotiate *verb* | to settle a transaction; to discuss with view a to reaching an agreement |
| negotiations *noun* | discussions toward an agreement |
| negotiator *noun* | one who negotiates agreements |
| promote *verb* | to raise to a higher rank or position; to further growth |
| promotion *noun* | a raise; increase in rank or position |
| promotional *adjective* | of or for growth in sales |
| trade *noun* | an occupation, skilled work; buying and selling; commerce |
| trade *verb* | to carry on a business; to exchange; barter |

# VOCABULARY EXERCISES ANSWERS

## LIST 1

| Exercise 1 | Exercise 2 | Exercise 3 | Exercise 4 | Exercise 5 |
|---|---|---|---|---|
| 1. advertise | 1. advertisement | 1. application | 1. c | 1. employment |
| 2. apply | 2. profit | 2. interview | 2. d | 2. personalized |
| 3. benefit | 3. confidential | 3. advertise | 3. a | 3. positions |
| 4. confide | 4. beneficiary | 4. personal | 4. e | 4. training |
| 5. employ | 5. experience | 5. employees | 5. f | 5. confided |
| 6. train | 6. employ | 6. beneficial | 6. b | 6. beneficially |
| | 7. position | | | |
| | 8. trainee | | | |
| | 9. question | | | |
| | 10. personal | | | |

## LIST 2

| Exercise 1 | Exercise 2 | Exercise 3 | Exercise 4 |
|---|---|---|---|
| 1. development | 1. at | 1. specifically | 1. networks |
| 2. specification | 2. to | 2. processing | 2. forms |
| 3. acceptance | 3. for | 3. developers | 3. processing |
| 4. attendance | 4. with | 4. accepting | 4. format |
| 5. expectation | 5. of | 5. attendance | 5. acceptable |
| | 6. to | 6. attending | 6. expected |
| | 7. for | 7. networking | 7. form |
| | 8. around | 8. procedures | 8. specifications |
| | | | 9. developing |
| | | | 10. facilitate |
| | | | 11. attendance |

## LIST 3

| Exercise 1 | Exercise 2 | Exercise 3 | Exercise 4 |
|---|---|---|---|
| 1. accountant | 1. due/owing | 1. profitable | 1. interesting |
| 2. consulting | 2. cash/check | 2. paid | 2. payable |
| 3. documentation | 3. economize/plan | 3. organize | 3. profitability |

4. interest
5. organization
6. payment
7. profitable
8. firm

4. savings/loan
5. business/foundation
6. paper/birth certificate
7. advisor/mentor

4. inventory
5. interests
6. firm
7. documented
8. consult
9. budget
10. account

4. interest
5. documentation
6. account
7. consultant

## List 4

**Exercise 1**
1. arrangement
2. brochure
3. completely
4. fulfillment
5. managerial
6. overhead
7. rule
8. stamps
9. gift
10. propose

**Exercise 2**
1. e
2. d
3. a
4. f
5. b
6. c

**Exercise 3**
1. operating
2. posted
3. policy
4. management
5. complete
6. managerial
7. brochure
8. arranged
9. supervises

**Exercise 4**
1. c
2. d
3. a
4. e
5. b

## List 5

**Exercise 1**
1. c
2. d
3. b
4. a
5. e

**Exercise 2**
1. domestic
2. farm
3. stall
4. criticize
5. loser

**Exercise 3**
1. c
2. a
3. f
4. e
5. d
6. b

**Exercise 4**
1. promoting
2. Industrial
3. industries
4. market
5. negotiated
6. internationally
7. compete
8. commercials
9. promotional

**Exercise 5**
1. competed
2. exporting
3. industrialized
4. has marketed
5. negotiated
6. to trade

# PART FIVE

# Practice Test

# HOW TO TAKE THIS PRACTICE TEST

To get the most out of this Practice Test, try taking it under conditions that are similar to what you will face on Test Day. Find a quiet place where you can work uninterrupted for approximately two hours. Time yourself according to the actual TOEIC exam time limits—give yourself 45 minutes to complete the Listening Comprehension Section and 75 minutes to complete the Reading Comprehension Section. Make sure you have a comfortable desk, your audio CD, and several No. 2 pencils. Use the answer grid on page 238 to record your answers.

You will find prompts throughout the Listening Comprehension Section (Parts I–IV), indicating which tracks to play on the audio CD.

Remember, you can review any question within a section, but once you start the Reading Comprehension Section, do not go back to any questions from the Listening Comprehension Section. You will not be able to do that on the real test.

You will find the answer key, scoring information, and explanations following the test. A transcript of the Listening Comprehension Section can be found in Part 6 of this book.

Good luck!

## IMPORTANT INFORMATION

- Use only a No. 2 or HB pencil to complete this answer sheet. Do not use ink.
- Mark one—and only one—answer to each question. Be sure to fill in completely the space for your intended answer choice. If you erase, do so completely. Mark no stray marks.

Right Mark: ⬤

Wrong Marks: ☑ ☒ ◉

| LISTENING SECTION | | READING SECTION | |
|---|---|---|---|
| 1 Ⓐ Ⓑ Ⓒ Ⓓ | 51 Ⓐ Ⓑ Ⓒ Ⓓ | 101 Ⓐ Ⓑ Ⓒ Ⓓ | 151 Ⓐ Ⓑ Ⓒ Ⓓ |
| 2 Ⓐ Ⓑ Ⓒ Ⓓ | 52 Ⓐ Ⓑ Ⓒ Ⓓ | 102 Ⓐ Ⓑ Ⓒ Ⓓ | 152 Ⓐ Ⓑ Ⓒ Ⓓ |
| 3 Ⓐ Ⓑ Ⓒ Ⓓ | 53 Ⓐ Ⓑ Ⓒ Ⓓ | 103 Ⓐ Ⓑ Ⓒ Ⓓ | 153 Ⓐ Ⓑ Ⓒ Ⓓ |
| 4 Ⓐ Ⓑ Ⓒ Ⓓ | 54 Ⓐ Ⓑ Ⓒ Ⓓ | 104 Ⓐ Ⓑ Ⓒ Ⓓ | 154 Ⓐ Ⓑ Ⓒ Ⓓ |
| 5 Ⓐ Ⓑ Ⓒ Ⓓ | 55 Ⓐ Ⓑ Ⓒ Ⓓ | 105 Ⓐ Ⓑ Ⓒ Ⓓ | 155 Ⓐ Ⓑ Ⓒ Ⓓ |
| 6 Ⓐ Ⓑ Ⓒ Ⓓ | 56 Ⓐ Ⓑ Ⓒ Ⓓ | 106 Ⓐ Ⓑ Ⓒ Ⓓ | 156 Ⓐ Ⓑ Ⓒ Ⓓ |
| 7 Ⓐ Ⓑ Ⓒ Ⓓ | 57 Ⓐ Ⓑ Ⓒ Ⓓ | 107 Ⓐ Ⓑ Ⓒ Ⓓ | 157 Ⓐ Ⓑ Ⓒ Ⓓ |
| 8 Ⓐ Ⓑ Ⓒ Ⓓ | 58 Ⓐ Ⓑ Ⓒ Ⓓ | 108 Ⓐ Ⓑ Ⓒ Ⓓ | 158 Ⓐ Ⓑ Ⓒ Ⓓ |
| 9 Ⓐ Ⓑ Ⓒ Ⓓ | 59 Ⓐ Ⓑ Ⓒ Ⓓ | 109 Ⓐ Ⓑ Ⓒ Ⓓ | 159 Ⓐ Ⓑ Ⓒ Ⓓ |
| 10 Ⓐ Ⓑ Ⓒ Ⓓ | 60 Ⓐ Ⓑ Ⓒ Ⓓ | 110 Ⓐ Ⓑ Ⓒ Ⓓ | 160 Ⓐ Ⓑ Ⓒ Ⓓ |
| 11 Ⓐ Ⓑ Ⓒ Ⓓ | 61 Ⓐ Ⓑ Ⓒ Ⓓ | 111 Ⓐ Ⓑ Ⓒ Ⓓ | 161 Ⓐ Ⓑ Ⓒ Ⓓ |
| 12 Ⓐ Ⓑ Ⓒ Ⓓ | 62 Ⓐ Ⓑ Ⓒ Ⓓ | 112 Ⓐ Ⓑ Ⓒ Ⓓ | 162 Ⓐ Ⓑ Ⓒ Ⓓ |
| 13 Ⓐ Ⓑ Ⓒ Ⓓ | 63 Ⓐ Ⓑ Ⓒ Ⓓ | 113 Ⓐ Ⓑ Ⓒ Ⓓ | 163 Ⓐ Ⓑ Ⓒ Ⓓ |
| 14 Ⓐ Ⓑ Ⓒ Ⓓ | 64 Ⓐ Ⓑ Ⓒ Ⓓ | 114 Ⓐ Ⓑ Ⓒ Ⓓ | 164 Ⓐ Ⓑ Ⓒ Ⓓ |
| 15 Ⓐ Ⓑ Ⓒ Ⓓ | 65 Ⓐ Ⓑ Ⓒ Ⓓ | 115 Ⓐ Ⓑ Ⓒ Ⓓ | 165 Ⓐ Ⓑ Ⓒ Ⓓ |
| 16 Ⓐ Ⓑ Ⓒ Ⓓ | 66 Ⓐ Ⓑ Ⓒ Ⓓ | 116 Ⓐ Ⓑ Ⓒ Ⓓ | 166 Ⓐ Ⓑ Ⓒ Ⓓ |
| 17 Ⓐ Ⓑ Ⓒ Ⓓ | 67 Ⓐ Ⓑ Ⓒ Ⓓ | 117 Ⓐ Ⓑ Ⓒ Ⓓ | 167 Ⓐ Ⓑ Ⓒ Ⓓ |
| 18 Ⓐ Ⓑ Ⓒ Ⓓ | 68 Ⓐ Ⓑ Ⓒ Ⓓ | 118 Ⓐ Ⓑ Ⓒ Ⓓ | 168 Ⓐ Ⓑ Ⓒ Ⓓ |
| 19 Ⓐ Ⓑ Ⓒ Ⓓ | 69 Ⓐ Ⓑ Ⓒ Ⓓ | 119 Ⓐ Ⓑ Ⓒ Ⓓ | 169 Ⓐ Ⓑ Ⓒ Ⓓ |
| 20 Ⓐ Ⓑ Ⓒ Ⓓ | 70 Ⓐ Ⓑ Ⓒ Ⓓ | 120 Ⓐ Ⓑ Ⓒ Ⓓ | 170 Ⓐ Ⓑ Ⓒ Ⓓ |
| 21 Ⓐ Ⓑ Ⓒ Ⓓ | 71 Ⓐ Ⓑ Ⓒ Ⓓ | 121 Ⓐ Ⓑ Ⓒ Ⓓ | 171 Ⓐ Ⓑ Ⓒ Ⓓ |
| 22 Ⓐ Ⓑ Ⓒ Ⓓ | 72 Ⓐ Ⓑ Ⓒ Ⓓ | 122 Ⓐ Ⓑ Ⓒ Ⓓ | 172 Ⓐ Ⓑ Ⓒ Ⓓ |
| 23 Ⓐ Ⓑ Ⓒ Ⓓ | 73 Ⓐ Ⓑ Ⓒ Ⓓ | 123 Ⓐ Ⓑ Ⓒ Ⓓ | 173 Ⓐ Ⓑ Ⓒ Ⓓ |
| 24 Ⓐ Ⓑ Ⓒ Ⓓ | 74 Ⓐ Ⓑ Ⓒ Ⓓ | 124 Ⓐ Ⓑ Ⓒ Ⓓ | 174 Ⓐ Ⓑ Ⓒ Ⓓ |
| 25 Ⓐ Ⓑ Ⓒ Ⓓ | 75 Ⓐ Ⓑ Ⓒ Ⓓ | 125 Ⓐ Ⓑ Ⓒ Ⓓ | 175 Ⓐ Ⓑ Ⓒ Ⓓ |
| 26 Ⓐ Ⓑ Ⓒ Ⓓ | 76 Ⓐ Ⓑ Ⓒ Ⓓ | 126 Ⓐ Ⓑ Ⓒ Ⓓ | 176 Ⓐ Ⓑ Ⓒ Ⓓ |
| 27 Ⓐ Ⓑ Ⓒ Ⓓ | 77 Ⓐ Ⓑ Ⓒ Ⓓ | 127 Ⓐ Ⓑ Ⓒ Ⓓ | 177 Ⓐ Ⓑ Ⓒ Ⓓ |
| 28 Ⓐ Ⓑ Ⓒ Ⓓ | 78 Ⓐ Ⓑ Ⓒ Ⓓ | 128 Ⓐ Ⓑ Ⓒ Ⓓ | 178 Ⓐ Ⓑ Ⓒ Ⓓ |
| 29 Ⓐ Ⓑ Ⓒ Ⓓ | 79 Ⓐ Ⓑ Ⓒ Ⓓ | 129 Ⓐ Ⓑ Ⓒ Ⓓ | 179 Ⓐ Ⓑ Ⓒ Ⓓ |
| 30 Ⓐ Ⓑ Ⓒ Ⓓ | 80 Ⓐ Ⓑ Ⓒ Ⓓ | 130 Ⓐ Ⓑ Ⓒ Ⓓ | 180 Ⓐ Ⓑ Ⓒ Ⓓ |
| 31 Ⓐ Ⓑ Ⓒ Ⓓ | 81 Ⓐ Ⓑ Ⓒ Ⓓ | 131 Ⓐ Ⓑ Ⓒ Ⓓ | 181 Ⓐ Ⓑ Ⓒ Ⓓ |
| 32 Ⓐ Ⓑ Ⓒ Ⓓ | 82 Ⓐ Ⓑ Ⓒ Ⓓ | 132 Ⓐ Ⓑ Ⓒ Ⓓ | 182 Ⓐ Ⓑ Ⓒ Ⓓ |
| 33 Ⓐ Ⓑ Ⓒ Ⓓ | 83 Ⓐ Ⓑ Ⓒ Ⓓ | 133 Ⓐ Ⓑ Ⓒ Ⓓ | 183 Ⓐ Ⓑ Ⓒ Ⓓ |
| 34 Ⓐ Ⓑ Ⓒ Ⓓ | 84 Ⓐ Ⓑ Ⓒ Ⓓ | 134 Ⓐ Ⓑ Ⓒ Ⓓ | 184 Ⓐ Ⓑ Ⓒ Ⓓ |
| 35 Ⓐ Ⓑ Ⓒ Ⓓ | 85 Ⓐ Ⓑ Ⓒ Ⓓ | 135 Ⓐ Ⓑ Ⓒ Ⓓ | 185 Ⓐ Ⓑ Ⓒ Ⓓ |
| 36 Ⓐ Ⓑ Ⓒ Ⓓ | 86 Ⓐ Ⓑ Ⓒ Ⓓ | 136 Ⓐ Ⓑ Ⓒ Ⓓ | 186 Ⓐ Ⓑ Ⓒ Ⓓ |
| 37 Ⓐ Ⓑ Ⓒ Ⓓ | 87 Ⓐ Ⓑ Ⓒ Ⓓ | 137 Ⓐ Ⓑ Ⓒ Ⓓ | 187 Ⓐ Ⓑ Ⓒ Ⓓ |
| 38 Ⓐ Ⓑ Ⓒ Ⓓ | 88 Ⓐ Ⓑ Ⓒ Ⓓ | 138 Ⓐ Ⓑ Ⓒ Ⓓ | 188 Ⓐ Ⓑ Ⓒ Ⓓ |
| 39 Ⓐ Ⓑ Ⓒ Ⓓ | 89 Ⓐ Ⓑ Ⓒ Ⓓ | 139 Ⓐ Ⓑ Ⓒ Ⓓ | 189 Ⓐ Ⓑ Ⓒ Ⓓ |
| 40 Ⓐ Ⓑ Ⓒ Ⓓ | 90 Ⓐ Ⓑ Ⓒ Ⓓ | 140 Ⓐ Ⓑ Ⓒ Ⓓ | 190 Ⓐ Ⓑ Ⓒ Ⓓ |
| 41 Ⓐ Ⓑ Ⓒ Ⓓ | 91 Ⓐ Ⓑ Ⓒ Ⓓ | 141 Ⓐ Ⓑ Ⓒ Ⓓ | 191 Ⓐ Ⓑ Ⓒ Ⓓ |
| 42 Ⓐ Ⓑ Ⓒ Ⓓ | 92 Ⓐ Ⓑ Ⓒ Ⓓ | 142 Ⓐ Ⓑ Ⓒ Ⓓ | 192 Ⓐ Ⓑ Ⓒ Ⓓ |
| 43 Ⓐ Ⓑ Ⓒ Ⓓ | 93 Ⓐ Ⓑ Ⓒ Ⓓ | 143 Ⓐ Ⓑ Ⓒ Ⓓ | 193 Ⓐ Ⓑ Ⓒ Ⓓ |
| 44 Ⓐ Ⓑ Ⓒ Ⓓ | 94 Ⓐ Ⓑ Ⓒ Ⓓ | 144 Ⓐ Ⓑ Ⓒ Ⓓ | 194 Ⓐ Ⓑ Ⓒ Ⓓ |
| 45 Ⓐ Ⓑ Ⓒ Ⓓ | 95 Ⓐ Ⓑ Ⓒ Ⓓ | 145 Ⓐ Ⓑ Ⓒ Ⓓ | 195 Ⓐ Ⓑ Ⓒ Ⓓ |
| 46 Ⓐ Ⓑ Ⓒ Ⓓ | 96 Ⓐ Ⓑ Ⓒ Ⓓ | 146 Ⓐ Ⓑ Ⓒ Ⓓ | 196 Ⓐ Ⓑ Ⓒ Ⓓ |
| 47 Ⓐ Ⓑ Ⓒ Ⓓ | 97 Ⓐ Ⓑ Ⓒ Ⓓ | 147 Ⓐ Ⓑ Ⓒ Ⓓ | 197 Ⓐ Ⓑ Ⓒ Ⓓ |
| 48 Ⓐ Ⓑ Ⓒ Ⓓ | 98 Ⓐ Ⓑ Ⓒ Ⓓ | 148 Ⓐ Ⓑ Ⓒ Ⓓ | 198 Ⓐ Ⓑ Ⓒ Ⓓ |
| 49 Ⓐ Ⓑ Ⓒ Ⓓ | 99 Ⓐ Ⓑ Ⓒ Ⓓ | 149 Ⓐ Ⓑ Ⓒ Ⓓ | 199 Ⓐ Ⓑ Ⓒ Ⓓ |
| 50 Ⓐ Ⓑ Ⓒ Ⓓ | 100 Ⓐ Ⓑ Ⓒ Ⓓ | 150 Ⓐ Ⓑ Ⓒ Ⓓ | 200 Ⓐ Ⓑ Ⓒ Ⓓ |

To hear the audio portion for Part I, play track 6 on Audio CD 2.

# SECTION 1—LISTENING COMPREHENSION SECTION

In the Listening Comprehension Section, you will have the chance to demonstrate how well you understand spoken English. The Listening Comprehension Section will take approximately 45 minutes. There are four parts, and directions are given for each part. You must mark your answers on the answer sheet. Do not write them in the test book.

# PART I: PHOTOGRAPHS

**Directions**: For each question, you will hear four statements about the photograph in your test book. When you hear the statements, choose the one statement that best describes what you see in the photograph. Then, find the number of the question on your answer sheet and mark your answer. The statements will not be written in your test book and will be spoken just once.

Now, listen to the four statements.

Statement (B), *They're gathered around the table*, best describes what is in the photograph. Therefore, you should fill in choice (B) in your answer sheet.

1.

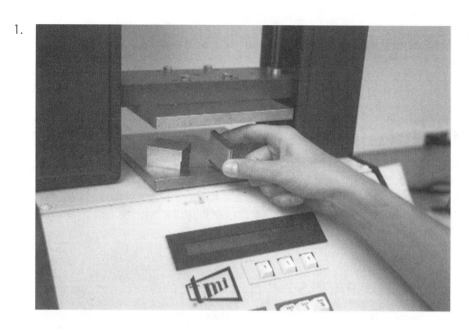

2.

3.

4.

5.

6.

7.

8.

9.

10.

To hear the audio portion for Part II, play track 7 on Audio CD 2.

# PART II: QUESTION-RESPONSE

**Directions**: You will hear a question or statement and three responses spoken in English. They will be spoken only once and will not be printed in your test book. Choose the best response to the question or statement and mark the letter on your answer sheet.

Listen to a sample question:

Sample Answer

Choice (B), *It's the second room on the left,* is the best response to the question. Therefore, you should fill in choice (B) in your answer sheet.

11. Mark your answer on your answer sheet.

12. Mark your answer on your answer sheet.

13. Mark your answer on your answer sheet.

14. Mark your answer on your answer sheet.

15. Mark your answer on your answer sheet.

16. Mark your answer on your answer sheet.

17. Mark your answer on your answer sheet.

18. Mark your answer on your answer sheet.

19. Mark your answer on your answer sheet.

20. Mark your answer on your answer sheet.

21. Mark your answer on your answer sheet.

22. Mark your answer on your answer sheet.

23. Mark your answer on your answer sheet.

24. Mark your answer on your answer sheet.

25. Mark your answer on your answer sheet.

26. Mark your answer on your answer sheet.

27. Mark your answer on your answer sheet.

28. Mark your answer on your answer sheet.

29. Mark your answer on your answer sheet.

30. Mark your answer on your answer sheet.

31. Mark your answer on your answer sheet.

32. Mark your answer on your answer sheet.

33. Mark your answer on your answer sheet.

34. Mark your answer on your answer sheet.

35. Mark your answer on your answer sheet.

36. Mark your answer on your answer sheet.

37. Mark your answer on your answer sheet.

38. Mark your answer on your answer sheet.

39. Mark your answer on your answer sheet.

40. Mark your answer on your answer sheet.

To hear the audio portion for Part III, play track 8 on Audio CD 2.

# PART III: SHORT CONVERSATIONS

**Directions**: You will now hear a number of conversations between two people. You will be asked to answer three questions about what the speakers say. Select the best response to each question and mark the letter on your answer sheet. The conversations will be spoken only once and will not be printed in your test book.

41. What are the speakers planning?

   (A) A luncheon
   (B) A conference
   (C) A seminar
   (D) A dinner

42. How many people are expected to attend?

   (A) 50
   (B) 55
   (C) 60
   (D) 65

43. What has changed?

   (A) The time
   (B) The number of people
   (C) The venue
   (D) The catering company

44. What are the speakers talking about?

   (A) A conference
   (B) A job interview
   (C) A project meeting
   (D) A presentation

45. Who asked questions?

    (A) The personnel director

    (B) A researcher

    (C) The office manager

    (D) A client

46. How does the man feel?

    (A) Pleased

    (B) Disappointed

    (C) Worried

    (D) Surprised

47. What has Mr. Jansen called about?

    (A) Air tickets

    (B) Travel insurance

    (C) A meeting confirmation

    (D) A hotel reservation

48. Where is Ms. Brody?

    (A) Traveling abroad

    (B) At the travel agency

    (C) At home

    (D) In a meeting

49. What does Mr. Jansen need to know regarding Ms. Brody's trip?

    (A) Where she plans to travel

    (B) When she will arrive

    (C) Which airline she is traveling with

    (D) What she will be presenting

50. Who is the man?

    (A) A job applicant
    (B) An employee
    (C) A government official
    (D) A customer

51. Where will the speakers go?

    (A) A factory
    (B) A government office
    (C) A conference
    (D) A restaurant

52. What will the man need to wear?

    (A) A suit and tie
    (B) Safety equipment
    (C) An ID badge
    (D) A microphone

53. Who are the speakers talking about?

    (A) A painter
    (B) A writer
    (C) A sculptor
    (D) An actor

54. Where are the speakers?

    (A) New York
    (B) London
    (C) Paris
    (D) Glasgow

55. What event do the speakers refer to?

    (A) An exhibition
    (B) A dinner
    (C) A conference
    (D) A play

56. Who are the men?

    (A) Electricians
    (B) Plumbers
    (C) Movers
    (D) Decorators

57. Where is the blue box?

    (A) In the office
    (B) In the kitchen
    (C) In the bedroom
    (D) In the truck

58. Where are the men working?

    (A) In an office block
    (B) In a factory
    (C) In a house
    (D) In a school

59. Where are the speakers?

    (A) At a cafe
    (B) In a supermarket
    (C) In an office
    (D) At home

60. Where is the man going?

    (A) To a bank
    (B) To the marketing department
    (C) To the post office
    (D) To a bookstore

61. What does the woman want?

    (A) A copy of a report
    (B) Some food
    (C) A book
    (D) Some stamps

62. Why is Colleen Rankin in Australia?

    (A) She works there.
    (B) She is on vacation there.
    (C) She is on a business trip there.
    (D) She has retired there.

63. When will the woman return from Australia?

    (A) Thursday
    (B) Friday
    (C) Saturday
    (D) Sunday

64. Who is the man in relation to the woman?

    (A) Her boss
    (B) Her employee
    (C) Her customer
    (D) Her travel agent

65.  What goods are the speakers talking about?

   (A) Newspapers

   (B) Office equipment

   (C) Clothes

   (D) Electrical appliances

66.  Where has the shipment come from?

   (A) Shanghai

   (B) Dublin

   (C) Dubai

   (D) Hong Kong

67.  What has caused the delay?

   (A) Payment problems

   (B) Bad weather

   (C) Customs issues

   (D) Manufacturing problems

68.  What are the speakers talking about?

   (A) A desktop computer

   (B) A printer

   (C) A laptop computer

   (D) A scanner

69.  What does the special offer include?

   (A) A rebate

   (B) Extra user support

   (C) An extended warranty

   (D) Extra equipment

70.  What does the man ask for?

   (A) A reduction in price

   (B) A catalog

   (C) A product demonstration

   (D) A business card

To hear the audio portion for Part IV, play track 9 on Audio CD 2.

# PART IV: SHORT TALKS

**Directions**: You will now hear short talks given by a single speaker. You will be asked to answer three questions about what the speaker says. Select the best response to each question and mark the letter on your answer sheet. The talks will be spoken only once and will not be printed in your test book.

71. What event will occur on May 28?

(A) A speech

(B) A play

(C) A ballet

(D) A concert

72. How much is the cheapest ticket without the discount?

(A) $3

(B) $8

(C) $13

(D) $18

73. Where can people buy tickets?

(A) In local stores

(B) At the student union office

(C) On the Internet

(D) From the speaker

74. What is Mr. Park's title?

(A) Head chef

(B) Head waiter

(C) Vice president

(D) Customer service representative

75. What will Mr. Park mainly focus on this year?

(A) Food presentation
(B) Waiters
(C) Menu items
(D) Customer service

76. What does the speaker want the employees to do?

(A) Contact Mr. Park directly.
(B) Ask questions after the talk.
(C) Wear their uniforms.
(D) Continue to treat customers well.

77. Where is this introduction taking place?

(A) At a board of directors meeting
(B) At a store managers meeting
(C) At a retirement dinner
(D) At a shareholders meeting

78. What is one of Mr. Nazar's accomplishments?

(A) Strengthening domestic sales
(B) Directing company policy
(C) Increasing production
(D) Reducing overhead

79. What is one of Mr. Nazar's goals in his new role?

(A) Merging operations
(B) Retraining staff
(C) Reducing expenses
(D) Expanding international sales

80. Where is it expected to rain?

    (A) Zurich
    (B) Southeastern Switzerland
    (C) The northern valleys
    (D) Geneva

81. How much snow is expected today in the mountains?

    (A) 7 centimeters
    (B) 15 centimeters
    (C) 30 centimeters
    (D) 40 centimeters

82. Where has snow already been reported?

    (A) The suburbs of Zurich
    (B) Along the Italian-Austrian border
    (C) In the southern mountains
    (D) Along the French border

83. What did Mr. Hausman do?

    (A) Published a book
    (B) Wrote the speech
    (C) Opened a bank
    (D) Introduced the speaker

84. According to the speaker, in what areas have new challenges been created?

    (A) Business and industry planning
    (B) Industry management and regulation
    (C) Financial and capital services
    (D) International markets for capital

85. What is this talk mainly about?

    (A) Regulating capital markets
    (B) The history of industry management
    (C) Financial services and business planning
    (D) Banking changes in the past 20 years

86. What kind of company does the speaker work for?

    (A) Travel agency
    (B) Construction company
    (C) Hotel chain
    (D) Customer service company

87. In what area does the business excel?

    (A) Personnel
    (B) Customer service
    (C) Interior design
    (D) Building design

88. What does the speaker ask the board of directors to make available?

    (A) A team of interior designers
    (B) New furniture for the lobbies
    (C) Money to upgrade the facilities
    (D) Customer service goals

89. What is the purpose of this announcement?

    (A) To conclude the evening's program
    (B) To introduce an guest
    (C) To advertise a product
    (D) To begin the evening's program

90. Who will be the guest next week?

    (A) A corporate vice president

    (B) Dr. McDermott

    (C) An employee motivation expert

    (D) Peter Thompson

91. What topic was probably discussed on the program?

    (A) Crisis management

    (B) Managing change

    (C) Inspiring workers

    (D) Contemporary technology

92. What is the speaker doing?

    (A) Announcing a meeting

    (B) Summarizing a previous meeting

    (C) Beginning a meeting

    (D) Interrupting a meeting

93. How many agenda items are there?

    (A) 3

    (B) 4

    (C) 5

    (D) 6

94. What is the first item on the agenda?

    (A) Welcoming new staff

    (B) Projecting budgets

    (C) Announcing job cuts

    (D) Reporting on progress

95. Who is speaking?

    (A) Captain of the flight

    (B) Lead flight attendant

    (C) Member of the ground staff

    (D) Copilot

96. Where is the flight going?

    (A) Edinburgh
    (B) Manchester
    (C) Liverpool
    (D) London

97. What delayed the flight?

    (A) A mechanical problem
    (B) A late arriving flight
    (C) Weather conditions
    (D) A security alert

98. What is the talk mainly about?

    (A) A piece of research
    (B) Annual sales figures
    (C) A proposal for a new hotel
    (D) Management techniques

99. What is the speaker's main interest?

    (A) The effects of tourism
    (B) The cost of vacation packages
    (C) How to organize hotels
    (D) The demand for tourism

100. What was measured?

    (A) Money spent
    (B) Pollution
    (C) Tourist numbers
    (D) Money earned

**Stop!** This is the end of the Listening Comprehension Section of the exam. Turn to Part V.

You will have one hour and 15 minutes to complete Parts V, VI, and VII of the exam.

## SECTION 2—READING COMPREHENSION

In the Reading Comprehension Section, you will read a variety of texts and answer different types of questions. The Reading Comprehension Section will last 75 minutes. There are three parts, and directions are given for each part. You are encouraged to answer as many questions as possible within the allotted time. Mark your answers on the separate answer sheet. Do not write them in the test book.

## PART V: INCOMPLETE SENTENCES

**Directions**: A word or phrase is missing in the following sentences. Four answer choices are given below each of the sentences. Choose the best answer to complete the sentence. Then mark the letter on your answer sheet.

101. Mr. Griffin is well known for saying _____ comes to his mind.

   (A) anything
   (B) everyone
   (C) whatever
   (D) anymore

102. All visitors must be _____ by a security officer while they are on-site.

   (A) detected
   (B) accompanied
   (C) revised
   (D) arrested

103. The factory shuts down every August for _____.

   (A) maintenance
   (B) maintain
   (C) maintained
   (D) maintainer

104. Mr. Masuyama has excelled in his new position as senior account executive; _____, he deserves a raise.

    (A) yet

    (B) or

    (C) although

    (D) thus

105. Though Mr. Ramirez is not a citizen of the United States, he has had to pay U.S. income taxes _____.

    (A) moreover

    (B) anyway

    (C) anyhow

    (D) since

106. Suzko Industries has hired additional inspectors to ensure that the highest production quality is _____.

    (A) achieve

    (B) achiever

    (C) achievement

    (D) achieved

107. For questions concerning any of the policies in this handbook, please consult _____ the head of your department.

    (A) at

    (B) with

    (C) about

    (D) for

108. During the seminar, Ms. Williams taught _____ how to calculate the annual return on an investment.

    (A) they

    (B) their

    (C) them

    (D) themselves

109. Customers have three weeks _____ report a credit dispute.

    (A) to

    (B) until

    (C) before

    (D) so

110. Dr. Allan forecasts that world demand for _____ ceramics will increase by 8 percent next year.

    (A) advance

    (B) advanced

    (C) advancing

    (D) advancement

111. Though he received the fax early Monday morning, Mr. Medina waited until Friday to _____.

    (A) rely

    (B) delay

    (C) relay

    (D) reply

112. The directors will go _____ the street to the main office to meet the department managers.

    (A) across

    (B) by

    (C) of

    (D) against

113. As economic links between the two regions _____, the flexibility of the international banking sector will be tested.

    (A) strong

    (B) strength

    (C) strengthen

    (D) stronger

114. Please send the _____ documents instead of photocopies.

    (A) original
    (B) originate
    (C) origin
    (D) originality

115. To comply with the new environmental regulations, the power plant design will need to be drastically _____.

    (A) alternated
    (B) avoided
    (C) altered
    (D) attached

116. The one _____ that sets the company apart is its self-directed team approach to management of operations.

    (A) element
    (B) elemental
    (C) elements
    (D) elementary

117. The luncheon was held to honor the senior employees who will be retiring _____ June.

    (A) at
    (B) in
    (C) among
    (D) on

118. The annual percentage rate for purchases may _____ from month to month.

    (A) vary
    (B) variety
    (C) various
    (D) varied

119. Mr. Teska _____ the weaknesses in the proposal.

   (A) entered into

   (B) joined with

   (C) signed up

   (D) pointed out

120. I support Mr. Lin's goals of more efficient management, but I object to the methods proposed to achieve _____ goals.

   (A) those

   (B) there

   (C) them

   (D) their

121. Applicants must submit two letters _____.

   (A) refer

   (B) of reference

   (C) refers to

   (D) a referred

122. Parking is limited to hotel guests, and _____ will be towed.

   (A) violated

   (B) violate

   (C) violating

   (D) violators

123. Mr. Loder was able to hand out most of the _____ items that we brought to the trade show.

   (A) promotional

   (B) promoted

   (C) promote

   (D) promotes

124. If you are late for the meeting, please enter the boardroom _____.

    (A) quieter

    (B) quietly

    (C) quietest

    (D) quiet

125. Architect Jon Rushmore _____ a huge foyer with a large marble staircase.

    (A) enlightens

    (B) entrusts

    (C) envisions

    (D) enlists

126. When facing challenges in the workplace, it is often best to prioritize tasks to put them in _____.

    (A) confirmation

    (B) perspective

    (C) satisfaction

    (D) reinforcement

127. Mr. Hamilton received a promotion _____ he developed the most successful advertising campaign of the year.

    (A) though

    (B) while

    (C) because

    (D) due

128. The designers are coming on Friday morning _____ the floors for new carpeting.

    (A) to measure

    (B) is measured

    (C) a measurement

    (D) for measurable

129. The lab has developed a novel _____ to synthesizing industrial polymers.

    (A) access

    (B) arrival

    (C) commitment

    (D) approach

130. Many workers report that they prefer being alone at the office because they can _____ more work done.

    (A) get

    (B) be

    (C) do

    (D) go

131. The store will be closed _____ Saturday and Sunday while we take inventory.

    (A) neither

    (B) both

    (C) either

    (D) and

132. Everyone agreed that Mr. Osbourne's presentation _____.

    (A) was a better

    (B) had better

    (C) has best

    (D) was the best

133. Ms. O'Hara is a good teacher because she has a lot of _____.

    (A) patience

    (B) patient

    (C) is patient

    (D) has patience

134. In her new capacity, Ms. Ricketts will _____ all financial services.

    (A) coordination
    (B) coordinating
    (C) coordinated
    (D) coordinate

135. Management blames the decrease in profits on overall lower consumer demand, _____ is linked to high inflation across all economic sectors.

    (A) there
    (B) where
    (C) who
    (D) which

136. The jurors _____ for four hours before they reached a verdict.

    (A) delivered
    (B) depended
    (C) deliberated
    (D) defined

137. In a recent poll, most people say the _____ of the personal computer has had the greatest impact on modern life.

    (A) inventive
    (B) invent
    (C) invention
    (D) inventor

138. Hiring and training salespeople who customers can trust is _____ important for our success.

    (A) valuably
    (B) critically
    (C) largely
    (D) successfully

139. Formal guidelines for bidding on contracts are _____ by the committee.

    (A) having drafted

    (B) a draft

    (C) being drafted

    (D) the draft

140. Dr. Lao's original data was found to contain significant errors, and so he has begun _____ research again from scratch.

    (A) himself

    (B) him

    (C) he

    (D) his

# PART VI: TEXT COMPLETION

**Directions**: Read the texts found in the following pages. A word or phrase is missing in the sentences below the text. Four answer choices are given below each of the sentences. Choose the best answer to complete the sentence. Then mark the letter on your answer sheet.

Questions 141–143 refer to the following email message.

From: Margaret Kim <m.kim@kr_consulting.com>
To:     Susan Parker <s_parker@parkerdesigns.com>
CC:     Kevin Rutland <k.rutland@kr_consulting.com>
Date: October 10th, 2009 11:14:21 A.M.
Subject:  Finally getting back to you . . .

Dear Susan,

So sorry that I have not been able to reply to your message earlier, but this really is the first _____ I've had in

141. (A) opening
    (B) opportunity
    (C) prospect
    (D) occurrence

a week to sit down and respond to emails. I don't know if I told you, but last week we had the auditors visit the office, and so I'm sure you can imagine how busy we were.

Anyway, I've had a look at the plans you sent and I'm really excited by them. You really seem to have understood what we are looking for. Kevin Rutland has also taken a look at them and is _____ impressed.

142. (A) just as
    (B) the same
    (C) identically
    (D) alike

There are a number of things that we'd like to discuss with you, and we think it's best if you come to our office here in Vermont. Please let us know when would be a _____ date for you.

143. (A) suited
    (B) convenient
    (C) nicely
    (D) fitted

Obviously we will cover travel and accommodation. Look forward to hearing from you soon.

Regards,
Margaret

Questions 144–146 refer to the following advertisement.

PhotoMatic

Specialists in professional quality pre-owned and refurbished photographic equipment.

WANTED

We urgently _____ your cameras, lenses, cases, and other accessories.

144. (A) ask
     (B) require
     (C) demand
     (D) invite

We have customers all over North America, Europe, and beyond searching for secondhand professional equipment _____ good condition.

145. (A) on
     (B) at
     (C) of
     (D) in

We are also interested in telescopes, binoculars, and collectable vintage cameras.

Top Prices Paid

We will buy for cash directly but are also happy to sell on your behalf on a commission _____.

146. (A) way
     (B) basis
     (C) kind
     (D) means

We can arrange to collect from you, or you can send directly to your nearest PhotoMatic outlet with shipping and handling charges covered by us.

For more details, please contact us at (212) 333-4444 or call your nearest PhotoMatic outlet, or visit us online at *www.photomatic.com*.

Questions 147–149 refer to the following warranty card.

NINDO LIMITED WARRANTY

THIS WARRANTY IS VALID ONLY FOR PRODUCTS PURCHASED IN EUROPE

For other countries, please contact the store where purchased.

This product is warranted to the original _____ to be free from defects of quality at the time of purchase and

147. (A) purchaser
(B) card
(C) seller
(D) store

for a period of 12 months after the date of purchase. If, during the warranty period, your product is found to be defective, the product will be repaired using NINDO replacement parts, _____ the product will

148. (A) so
(B) and
(C) or
(D) too

be replaced with the same or similar model within a reasonable period of time. To obtain these warranty services, you must produce this card and proof of purchase in the form of a _____ sales receipt.

149. (A) buying
(B) repaired
(C) defective
(D) valid

Questions 150–152 refer to the following review.

With this classic text, Bob Bingley has done more to alter views of *Change Management* than any other author before or since. He explains the main concepts behind the management of change with clarity, originality, and humor. _____

> 150. (A) She
> (B) He
> (C) This
> (D) That

deals with change in all its aspects and from the viewpoint of all those that _____ by change.

> 151. (A) are affected
> (B) affected
> (C) is affected
> (D) have affected

The book looks at what change means for both large-scale and small-scale organizations. Bingley successfully shows that, _____ the right techniques and a logical approach, even the most sweeping changes

> 152. (A) gives
> (B) he gave
> (C) to give
> (D) given

can be implemented without disruption. This new edition includes a preface by the author and several new chapters on the impact of technology on the management of change.

# PART VII: READING COMPREHENSION

**Directions**: In this part, you will read a selection of text, such as magazine or newspaper articles, letters, or advertisements. Each text is followed by several questions. Select the best answer for each question and mark the letter on your answer sheet.

Questions 153–154 refer to the following table.

| Abarcorporation Performance Record | | | |
|---|---|---|---|
| | Year 3 | Year 2 | Year 1 |
| Sales | $679,823 | $379,722 | $489,357 |
| Net Income | $14,805 | $19,977 | $35,465 |
| Earnings per Share | $0.75 | $1.04 | $1.89 |
| Shareholders Equity | $275,242 | $257,515 | $245,006 |
| Return on Equity [1] | 5.3% | 7.8% | 14.5% |

[1] Defined as net income divided by shareholder equity, minus extraordinary items. (Periods listed are years ending Dec. 31.)

153. How much money did each share make in Year 2?

(A) $1.04

(B) $14.50

(C) $14,805

(D) $379,722

154. What must be subtracted to determine Return on Equity?

(A) Extraordinary items

(B) Net income

(C) Shareholders equity

(D) Earnings per share

Questions 155–156 refer to the following passage.

---

**Laser Printers**

Laser printers use xerographic technology similar to that used in photocopiers. They can reproduce an almost limitless variety of type forms and sizes, as well as complex graphics. Images are electronically created on a light-sensitive drum, usually with a scanning laser. Powdered toner adheres to areas where light touches the drum and then transfers to a sheet of paper, which is briefly heated to fuse the toner to the paper permanently. They operate very quickly. A typical laser printer can print 20 color pages a minute, compared to 12 for an ink-jet printer; older dot-matrix printers can take 45 seconds to print a single page. When they were first introduced, laser printers typically cost over a thousand dollars. Now prices have dropped to only a few hundred, at most.

---

155. What is implied as an advantage of laser printers?

(A) Speed

(B) Ease of use

(C) Low ink costs

(D) Superior printing quality

156. According to the passage, how much did early laser printers cost?

(A) A few hundred dollars

(B) Approximately $500

(C) $500–$700

(D) Over $1,000

Questions 157–158 refer to the following letter.

**The
Growing
Economy
Fund**

May 12, 2009

Dear Investor:

Last week, the Board of Trustees of The Growing Economy Fund declared a 100% share dividend. This has the same effect as a 2-for-1 share split. This transaction will occur Thursday, May 24, to shareholders of record at the close of business on Wednesday, May 23.

As a result of this transaction, the number of shares you owned before the transaction will be doubled, while the net asset value will be reduced by half. The reduced net asset value makes it easier financially for people who prefer to purchase shares of the fund in 100-share increments. This does not alter the total value of your Growing Economy Fund investment. It simply means that you will own twice the number of shares at half the price per share.

If you have any questions, please avail yourself our toll-free information number. Registered brokers are available 24 hours a day.

Yours truly,

Alexandria Gadbois
Secretary for the Board of Trustees
The Growing Economy Fund

157. When will the transaction take effect?

(A) May 23
(B) May 24
(C) December 31
(D) January 1

158. What will happen to shares of the fund?

    (A) They will be reduced to half their original number.

    (B) They will double in number.

    (C) They will be offered for sale at a lower price.

    (D) They will be available to the public for the first time.

Questions 159–161 refer to the following passage.

---

**SALES FORECASTS**

Sales forecasts should be based on prices that adequately consider the market for the product, and its value to the customer versus competitive products in the marketplace.

(5) Investors sense a serious danger signal when an entrepreneur suggests there is no competition for his or her product or service. The product may be unique but there are probably other products that function similarly.

If so, the pricing has to be evaluated in light of those products.

Pricing should also reflect cost considerations. The price should produce a return sufficient to cover the level of expenses typical for a company
(10) in that industry. In high-technology businesses, for example, higher gross margins generally are needed to provide for the higher costs of research and development, as well as marketing and distribution.

---

159. According to the passage, what makes investors nervous?

    (A) Products and services that fall in value

    (B) Sales forecasts that fail to account for changes in energy prices

    (C) Entrepreneurs who set their prices too low

    (D) Claims that a product or service has no competitors

160. The term *a return* as used in line 9 of the passage is closest in meaning to

    (A) *a profit.*

    (B) *come back.*

    (C) *an expense.*

    (D) *departure.*

161. What is implied about high-technology businesses?

    (A) Their value to customers is difficult to measure.

    (B) Their product prices are more competitive.

    (C) Their sales are lower than other industries.

    (D) Their research and development costs are high.

Questions 162–164 refer to the following form.

---

**CREDIT APPLICATION FORM**

**1. Background**

Name: _Sarah P. Taylor_    Date of Birth: _Feb. 25, 1975_

Highest Educational Degree: _Master's_    # of Dependents/Ages: _2 (Ages 3 & 5)_

**2. Employment and Income**

Name of Company: _Binational Commission_    Position: _Director_    Years at Job: _4_

Address: _5 Ahmed El-Ali Street, Alexandria, EGYPT_    Years at Present Address: _2_

Telephone: _842-5001_    Monthly Wage Income: _$3,500_

Other Monthly Income: _$1,500_    Source of other Income: _Trust Annuity_

**3. Credit References**

Bank: _National Bank of Egypt_    Account Number: _34–55090_

Account Type: _Checking_    Balance: _$12,000_    Credit Card(s): _None_

Account Number(s): _N/A_    Balance: _N/A_

Other Debt: (Type) _Car loan_    Loan Institution: _National Bank of Egypt_

Balance: _$5,500_

---

162. How many years has the applicant worked for the Binational Commission?

    (A) 1

    (B) 2

    (C) 3

    (D) 4

163. How many sources of income does the applicant have?

   (A) 1

   (B) 2

   (C) 3

   (D) 4

164. How much money does the applicant owe?

   (A) $1,500

   (B) $3,500

   (C) $5,500

   (D) $12,000

Questions 165–167 refer to the following information.

---

**WARRANTY INFORMATION**

For coverage under this limited warranty, proof of the date and place of purchase must be submitted. The easiest way to do this is to complete the attached warranty card and mail it now.

If warranty service is needed, contact our customer service department at the address or phone number below. If defects appear under normal use, Umbrellas Unlimited will replace the product free of charge.

This warranty does not apply to damage that has been caused by customer abuse. Also, present color technology does not enable us to warrant against color fading over time. We suggest that the golf umbrella be stored away from direct sunlight when not in use.

This warranty is good for three years. Umbrellas Unlimited will not, under any circumstances, be liable for injury caused by misuse of any product. This warranty is not applicable outside the USA.

---

165. What must a customer do to activate the warranty?

   (A) Complete the attached warranty card.

   (B) Provide proof of purchase.

   (C) Register online.

   (D) Call the customer service department.

166. What is implied about color fading?

   (A) It can be caused by damage to the umbrella.

   (B) It has not been reported to have happened.

   (C) It is guaranteed not to happen.

   (D) It may occur over time.

167. What is *NOT* true about the company's warranty?

   (A) It does not cover damage due to customer abuse.

   (B) It is in effect for three years.

   (C) It is honored worldwide.

   (D) It promises replacement of defective products.

Questions 168–171 refer to the following passage.

---

### Subjective Prices Versus and Objective Prices

There are two ways to price items: subjectively and objectively.

A subjectively priced item is based either on what the seller perceives it is worth or what the seller thinks someone will pay for it. Generally these items have an aesthetic, rather than a utilitarian, value. Retailers of subjectively priced items include artists, some highly
(5) skilled craftspeople, and sellers of antiques and collectibles. An objectively priced item, on the other hand, is priced according to some concrete formula based on its actual cost to produce.

Almost all traditional retailers, from the corner grocer to the new car dealer, sell objectively priced items.

(10) When buying a subjectively priced item, first analyze your needs and weigh your options. This is accomplished by answering three questions: *What do I want? Is it worth my money?* and *Is it important to me?*

---

168. According to the passage, how do subjectively and objectively priced items differ?

   (A) Objectively priced items are usually more expensive.

   (B) Subjectively priced items have an aesthetic value.

   (C) Objectively priced items are less utilitarian.

   (D) Subjectively priced items are more common.

169. What is implied about antiques?

    (A) They are priced subjectively.

    (B) They were probably made by skilled craftspeople.

    (C) They are sometimes overpriced.

    (D) Their prices go up and down.

170. What can be inferred about most traditional retailers?

    (A) They set their prices based on what they perceive consumers will pay.

    (B) They set prices using a formula based on the cost to produce their goods.

    (C) They tend to make higher profits than nontraditional retailers.

    (D) They tend to analyze the needs of their customers.

171. The word *weigh* as used in line 10 of the passage is closest in meaning to the word

    (A) *decide.*

    (B) *count.*

    (C) *evaluate.*

    (D) *reduce.*

Questions 172–175 refer to the following weather report.

High pressure moving across northern Mexico will funnel cooler air down the Northwest Coast. Temperatures will be at least 3 to 6 degrees lower throughout Baja, California, and Sonora. The cooler air will not reach the Southwest, where temperatures will soar past 32, some 6 degrees above normal. Because of low humidity and a stable atmosphere, afternoon thunderstorms are unlikely. Dry conditions will also persist across Durango.

A low-pressure system will move slowly east through the northeastern region of Mexico today, spreading showers and heavy thunderstorms across Coahuila and Nuevo Leon. Winds from the north behind this system will dislodge a pool of cold air over Texas. The leading edge of this chilled air will reach Monterrey later today, but the core of the cold air will not arrive until midweek. A cold front trailing this low-pressure system will push showers and thunderstorms across the Chihuahua and Durango later today. Showers may form as far west as the eastern slopes of the Sierra Madre.

172. What conditions will northwestern Mexico experience?

    (A) Cool air

    (B) Rain

    (C) Low humidity

    (D) Dry conditions

173. Where will temperatures be higher than usual?

    (A) Baja, California

    (B) Sonora

    (C) The Southwest

    (D) The northeastern region

174. When will the majority of the cold air from Texas reach Monterrey?

    (A) That morning

    (B) Later that afternoon

    (C) The next day

    (D) Midweek

175. What will the cold front cause?

    (A) Dry air

    (B) Strong winds

    (C) Rainstorms

    (D) Snow

Questions 176–180 refer to the following report.

---

**Company Profile: Synco Corporation**

The Synco Corporation ranks among the leading international manufacturers of tires and industrial products made from rubber and plastics. Last year, it was first in tire sales in Germany, second in Europe, and fourth worldwide.

Despite last year's severe recession, lower exchange rates, and steep drops in automotive sales, Synco recorded a net income of 50 million euros on sales of 10 billion euros, an all-time high. A dividend of 3 million euros is planned.

Extensive measures to streamline production resources, cut costs, and create new products have substantially enhanced Synco earnings potential for next year and beyond. A public offering of new stock will be made July 1.

---

176. Who is the report probably written for?

   (A) Synco administrators
   (B) Prospective investors
   (C) Potential suppliers
   (D) Synco competitors

177. What is *NOT* mentioned about Synco?

   (A) Its position for plastics sales
   (B) Its rankings for tire sales
   (C) Its measures to improve performance
   (D) Its plans for paying dividends

178. What were Synco's total sales in the previous year?

   (A) 3 million euros
   (B) 50 million euros
   (C) 1 billion euros
   (D) 10 billion euros

179. What is implied about automotive sales in the previous year?

   (A) Their decline should have decreased Synco's revenues.
   (B) Their increase is responsible for Synco's record sales.
   (C) They reached an all-time high.
   (D) They were lower than expected.

180. What is expected for Synco?

   (A) Its new products will be cheaper.
   (B) Its earnings will grow.
   (C) It will expand its market share.
   (D) Its stock price will remain high.

Questions 181–185 refer to the following advertisement and letter.

**The International Employment Newsletter**

No matter where your career is headed, we can help to identify the best direction for you. *The International Employment Newsletter* is written for all professionally minded people seeking a new position or hoping to improve their current status. Each issue contains hundreds of regional, national, and international job opportunities. In addition, we offer expert career advice, such as letter and résumé writing for beginning job seekers, and negotiating and networking strategies for experienced professionals.

Regardless of where you are with your career, *The International Employment Newsletter* can help you.

Look for us at your local newsstand or subscribe today for convenient home delivery.

The International Employment Newsletter

1644 Madison Avenue

New York, NY 10017

---

December 3rd, 2008

Elizabeth Ralls

245 5th Avenue

New York, NY 10001

Dear Ms. Ralls,

Thank you for your subscription to *The International Employment Newsletter*. Your subscription is for the period January to June. However, should you be interested in extending your subscription to a full 12 months, bear in mind that we are currently making the following special offer: take out a 12-month subscription before the end of January and you will receive a 10 percent discount. If you are interested, please complete the form on the reverse of this letter and return it in the enclosed postage-paid envelope.

Remember that you can cancel your subscription at any time and we will be happy to refund your remaining balance. You'll only pay for copies of *The International Employment Newsletter* that you have actually received—no more.

Sincerely,

Heinrich Gill

Sales Manager

181. What service is offered by *The International Employment Newsletter*?

(A) Translation and interpretation

(B) Preparation for job interviews

(C) Résumé preparation

(D) Work visa applications

182. What is learned about *The International Employment Newsletter*?

(A) It is available only by subscription.

(B) It is published every two weeks.

(C) It can be read on the Internet.

(D) It can be purchased at newsstands.

183. How long is Ms. Ralls's current subscription?

(A) 3 months

(B) 6 months

(C) 1 year

(D) 2 years

184. What is available to Ms. Ralls until the end of January?

(A) A book

(B) A discount

(C) A special edition

(D) A class

185. What has been included with the letter?

(A) A coupon

(B) A survey form

(C) A sample issue

(D) An envelope

Questions 186–190 refer to the following notice and email message.

The Piano Tuners' Guild of Northern Ireland invites you to
The 10th PTGNI Convention
Friday 16th to 17th of March 2009
Bay View Hotel, Portrush, County Antrim
Registration forms and further details available from: www.ptgni.org/resgistration.html

Highlights

Opening plenary session: Friday 9:00 A.M.

Derrick Gill, UK

As chairperson of the PTGNI, Derrick opens the 10th convention and welcomes delegates to what promises to be a stimulating and enjoyable weekend.

Keynote presentation: The Apprenticeship Crisis       Friday 11:00 A.M.
James Townsend, USA.

We're proud to be able to welcome Mr. Townsend, president of the North American Association of Piano Technicians, on his second appearance at a PTGNI convention. Mr. Townsend's thought-provoking talk concentrates on the key problems facing the profession worldwide: the lack of trainee technicians entering the field, and on what can be done to halt the drain.

Hybrid Tuning Saturday 10:30 A.M.
Randy Wilson, USA

Once thought of as mutually exclusive, traditional aural tuning and high-tech digital tuning techniques can in fact be used together. Mr. Wilson will show how tradition and technology can come to the aid of the modern tuner. The session will be full of useful tips on how the two techniques can complement each other, and on how to avoid common pitfalls.

RayTone RT50—Next-generation Tuning Saturday 3:00 P.M.
Gunter Kliebermann, Germany

We are very happy to welcome Mr. Kliebermann to this year's convention. His presentation introduces the long-awaited RayTone RT50. He will discuss the key improvements of the RT50 over its predecessor, the RT40—now standard equipment for many technicians. Mr. Kliebermann's session also includes demonstrations of many of the "hidden" features of the RT series. We are grateful to RayTone for their support in making this presentation possible.

**Note:** Rooms for attendees are available at the Bay View Hotel and at the Clear Sands Hotel. Contact them directly to make reservations.

To: Mike Stern <m_stern@ptgni.org>
From: Greg Watts <g_watts@ptgni.org>
Date: Friday, January 31st, 2009
Subject: Convention Posters

Mike

Just a quick note to say that the posters for the convention have come from the printers. They look great, but the problem is that in the title it says this is our tenth convention, when in fact it's our eleventh. It's too late to do anything about it now— it will take a week to have them reprinted, and we don't have time—we're already running late on distributing these. Besides, I'm sure most people won't even notice. If they do, we'll just have to joke about it. What else can we do?

The posters have been delivered to our office, so we'll need to organize distribution. Speak to you on Monday.

Greg

186. What is *NOT* mentioned in the notice?

   (A) Which hotels attendees can stay at

   (B) What time the talks are scheduled

   (C) How much the convention costs to attend

   (D) How to get further information about the convention

187. Whose presentation is about a new piece of equipment?

   (A) Gunter Kliebermann's

   (B) Randy Wilson's

   (C) James Townsend's

   (D) Derrick Gill's

188. What is the keynote presentation about?

   (A) How to train new technicians

   (B) The difficulties of being an apprentice

   (C) The future of the piano technician profession

   (D) How the tuning profession is different in the United States

189. What can be inferred about Greg and Mike?

    (A) They are training to be piano tuners.

    (B) They will present at the convention.

    (C) They organize the convention.

    (D) They are printers.

190. What is wrong with the posters?

    (A) The dates

    (B) The size

    (C) The colors

    (D) The title

Questions 191–195 refer to the following notice and email message.

---

**CORPORATE NOTICE**

Congratulations to all employees! Our third-quarter report has just been completed, and shows a profit increase of 15% over the same quarter a year ago. With the current growing market, we anticipate an even greater increase in net profits by the end of our fiscal year this June. As you know, a profit-sharing plan is being developed, and should be ready for implementation in July. Keep up the good work!

---

To:    k.wheeler@tibs.com

From:  d.scrivner@tibs.com

Date:  April 15th, 2009 2:24:18 P.M.

Subject:  profit sharing

Hi Kate,

Just wondering if you've heard the news about the profit-sharing plan. There was a notice up on our department board announcing that profits are up 15% from the same time last year, and that the profit-sharing plan will be ready by July. Where have we heard that before! Was the notice sent to your department, too? I'll be very surprised if the plan starts in July. They've been promising it for the last two years and nothing's happened. Have you heard anything?

David

---

191. What had been completed?

    (A) A quarterly report

    (B) A profit-sharing plan

    (C) Employee evaluations

    (D) A market analysis

192. When is the profit-sharing plan expected to go into effect?

    (A) The following week

    (B) The following month

    (C) At the end of the next fiscal year

    (D) At the start of the next fiscal year

193. How did David learn about the news?

    (A) An email was sent to all employees.

    (B) A notice was posted in his department.

    (C) A colleague told him.

    (D) He read it in a newspaper.

194. What can be inferred about Kate and David?

    (A) They work in different companies.

    (B) They are not pleased about the news.

    (C) They are pleased about the news.

    (D) They work in different departments.

195. When did the company first suggest a profit-sharing plan?

    (A) Three years ago

    (B) Two years ago

    (C) A year ago

    (D) Six months ago

Questions 196–200 refer to the following letter and email message.

---

Tribune Consulting

251 Williams Street

Portsmouth, VA 23704

January 14th, 2009

Mr. John Samuels

ShredMaster Paper Shredder Corporation

1440 7th Avenue

New York, NY 10001

Dear Mr. Samuels:

We recently ordered the Personal X paper shredder from your company. After receiving it, and upon further consideration, we have determined that we require a shredder that can destroy larger volumes of paper at one time. We realize also that many of our documents will have staples or paper clips. If you carry a shredder that is better suited for high-volume commercial needs, we would appreciate your sending literature. In the meantime, I am returning the Personal X under shipping number A–135, with another copy of this letter. Upon receipt, please send a memo of credit for our records.

I apologize for any inconvenience this may have caused, but sincerely hope that we can order a larger capacity model from you soon.

Sincerely,

Anne Markowitz

Purchasing Agent

Tribune Consulting

---

| To: | Paul Steinz <p.steinz@shredmaster.com> |
|---|---|
| From: | Gina Andrews <g.andrews@shredmaster.com> |
| Date: | January 17th, 2009 2:25:02 P.M. |
| Subject: | Product return |
| Attachments: | Tribune.doc |

Paul,

A customer has just returned a Personal X shredder because it's not heavy duty enough for their needs.

They've asked if we have another model that can cope with larger volumes of paper and with staples as well. I think what they really need is the Office X, but I'm not sure if we have any in stock. Could you check? Also, can you please send her a brochure and give a quote stating our current price for the Office X?

I've scanned the original letter and attached it to this email.

Thanks

Gina

196. Why has the paper shredder been returned?

(A) It does not suit the customer's needs.

(B) It is too expensive.

(C) It is broken.

(D) It is not what the customer ordered.

197. What is probably one of Anne Markowitz's duties?

(A) Researching industry trends

(B) Handling customer complaints

(C) Buying supplies for her company

(D) Preparing her company's brochures

198. What can be inferred about the Personal X?

(A) It cannot handle documents with staples.

(B) It is no longer in stock.

(C) It can shred credit cards and CDs.

(D) It can shed up to seven pages at one time.

199. What does Gina Andrews want to know?

    (A) Which replacement model to recommend
    (B) Which models are currently in stock
    (C) Where to send the Office X
    (D) Where the invoice should be sent

200. What will Paul Steinz send to Anne Markowitz?

    (A) The Personal X
    (B) The Office X
    (C) A price quote
    (D) A letter of apology

**Stop!** This is the end of the exam. If you finish before time is called, you may go back to Parts V, VI, and VII and check your work.

# PRACTICE TEST ANSWER KEY

| Part I | Part II | Part III | Part IV | Part V | Part VI | Part VII |
|--------|---------|----------|---------|--------|---------|----------|
| 1. A | 11. C | 41. A | 71. D | 101. C | 141. B | 153. A |
| 2. C | 12. A | 42. D | 72. D | 102. B | 142. A | 154. A |
| 3. B | 13. C | 43. B | 73. C | 103. A | 143. B | 155. A |
| 4. A | 14. B | 44. B | 74. C | 104. D | 144. B | 156. D |
| 5. D | 15. A | 45. C | 75. D | 105. B | 145. D | 157. B |
| 6. A | 16. A | 46. A | 76. D | 106. D | 146. B | 158. B |
| 7. D | 17. C | 47. B | 77. B | 107. B | 147. A | 159. D |
| 8. A | 18. B | 48. D | 78. A | 108. C | 148. C | 160. A |
| 9. B | 19. C | 49. A | 79. C | 109. A | 149. D | 161. D |
| 10. A | 20. A | 50. D | 80. A | 110. B | 150. B | 162. D |
| | 21. C | 51. A | 81. C | 111. D | 151. A | 163. B |
| | 22. C | 52. B | 82. B | 112. A | 152. D | 164. C |
| | 23. A | 53. C | 83. D | 113. C | | 165. B |
| | 24. B | 54. D | 84. A | 114. A | | 166. D |
| | 25. B | 55. B | 85. C | 115. C | | 167. C |
| | 26. A | 56. A | 86. C | 116. A | | 168. B |
| | 27. C | 57. D | 87. B | 117. B | | 169. A |
| | 28. B | 58. C | 88. A | 118. A | | 170. B |
| | 29. A | 59. C | 89. A | 119. D | | 171. C |
| | 30. B | 60. A | 90. D | 120. A | | 172. A |
| | 31. A | 61. B | 91. C | 121. B | | 173. C |
| | 32. C | 62. A | 92. C | 122. D | | 174. D |
| | 33. B | 63. D | 93. D | 123. A | | 175. C |
| | 34. A | 64. A | 94. D | 124. B | | 176. B |
| | 35. B | 65. C | 95. B | 125. C | | 177. A |
| | 36. B | 66. A | 96. A | 126. B | | 178. D |
| | 37. C | 67. C | 97. C | 127. C | | 179. A |
| | 38. A | 68. C | 98. A | 128. A | | 180. B |
| | 39. C | 69. D | 99. A | 129. D | | 181. C |
| | 40. B | 70. A | 100. B | 130. A | | 182. D |
| | | | | 131. B | | 183. B |
| | | | | 132. D | | 184. B |
| | | | | 133. A | | 185. D |
| | | | | 134. D | | 186. C |
| | | | | 135. D | | 187. A |
| | | | | 136. C | | 188. C |
| | | | | 137. C | | 189. C |
| | | | | 138. B | | 190. D |
| | | | | 139. C | | 191. A |
| | | | | 140. D | | 192. D |
| | | | | | | 193. B |
| | | | | | | 194. D |
| | | | | | | 195. B |
| | | | | | | 196. A |
| | | | | | | 197. C |
| | | | | | | 198. A |
| | | | | | | 199. B |
| | | | | | | 200. C |

**KAPLAN**

# Answers and Explanations

# PART I—PHOTOGRAPHS

1. (A) A technician is using some equipment. CORRECT
   (B) The equipment is on sale. (This plays on *scale*—what we see—and *sale*.)
   (C) A technician is packing up the equipment. (This plays on *picking up* and *packing up*.)
   (D) The equipment is being unloaded from a car. (There are no cars in the picture.)

2. (A) The patio doors are open to the garden. (The doors are closed, not open.)
   (B) The flower pot is in the middle of the table. (The pot is on a stool, not a table.)
   (C) The plant is on top of the stool. CORRECT
   (D) The chair is in the corner of the room. (A stool is in the corner, not a chair.)

3. (A) He's getting up from his chair. (The man is standing, not getting up.)
   (B) He's bent over his work table. CORRECT
   (C) He's cleaning up his office. (He is working, not cleaning.)
   (D) He's turning on the desk light. (The light is pointed at the desk.)

4. (A) The truck is parked alongside the building. CORRECT
   (B) The truck is being loaded in the rain. (It is not raining, and no one is loading.)
   (C) The man is getting out of the truck. (There is no man in the photograph.)
   (D) They are moving into a new house. (There are no people in the photograph; this plays on *house/warehouse*.)

5. (A) The photographer is putting film into the camera. (He is taking a photo, not loading film.)
   (B) The scientist is watching birds through binoculars. (It is a camera, not binoculars.)
   (C) The journalist is interviewing the woman for a story. (There is no woman in the photograph.)
   (D) The man is taking a picture. CORRECT

6. (A) The dishes are arranged in the cabinet. CORRECT
   (B) The plates are on the middle shelf. (They are on the top and bottom shelves.)
   (C) There are five place settings on the table. (There is no table in the photograph.)
   (D) The dishwasher is full of clean dishes. (It is a dish cabinet, not a dishwasher.)

7. (A) The vehicles are parked side by side. (There are parked cars, but they are not side by side.)
   (B) A car is being towed away. (No cars are being towed.)
   (C) The truck is traveling the wrong way. (The vehicles are all traveling in the same direction.)
   (D) A vehicle is making a turn at the corner. CORRECT

8. (A) The people are standing behind the railing. CORRECT
   (B) The people are climbing over the railing. (They are not climbing.)
   (C) The people are seated on the railing. (They are not seated.)
   (D) The people are all holding on to the railing. (Only some of the people are holding the railing.)

9. (A) The hostess is entertaining her guests. (There are no guests in the photograph.)
   (B) The woman is slicing the meat. CORRECT
   (C) The waitress is serving her customers. (There are no customers in the photograph.)
   (D) The chef is placing the meat onto the platter. (She is cutting meat, not putting it onto a plate.)

10. (A) The woman is using a pay phone. CORRECT
    (B) She's hanging up the telephone. (She is using the phone, not hanging it up.)
    (C) The woman is talking to a crowd. (There is no crowd in the photograph.)
    (D) She's holding a microphone. (She is holding a telephone, not a microphone.)

# PART II—QUESTION-RESPONSE

11. Do you have an additional pair of bookends? (*Yes/No*)

    (A) Yes, this pear is delicious. (This plays on the homophones *pair* and *pear*.)

    (B) Yes, I have some spare time. (This is a rhyme of the words *pair* and *spare*.)

    (C) Yes, I have an extra pair. CORRECT

12. Are gratuities already added in, or are they separate? (*Choice*)

    (A) They're included in the price. CORRECT

    (B) You can pack whatever you like. (This is irrelevant.)

    (C) Yes, the price includes all meals. (This is irrelevant.)

13. Why do you want to advertise in the trade publications? (*Why*)

    (A) No, let's skip the trade show this year. (This repeats the word *trade*.)

    (B) A lot of our trade is done overseas. (This repeats the word *trade*.)

    (C) It's a good way to attract customers. CORRECT

14. What are the arrangements for publicizing the general's visit? (*What*)

    (A) We've arranged a hotel room. (This plays on the word *arrangements*.)

    (B) The television station is sending a reporter. CORRECT

    (C) All public buildings are open to visitors. (This plays on the words *visit* and *visitors*.)

15. You've had experience with this particular software, haven't you? (*Yes/No*)

    (A) No, I'm not familiar with it at all. CORRECT

    (B) Men's wear is located on the second floor. (This plays on the words *software* and *men's wear*.)

    (C) Yes, I think it's very expensive. (This plays on the words *experience* and *expensive*.)

16. Why didn't she attend the medical conference yesterday? (*Why*)

    (A) There was a conflict in her schedule. CORRECT

    (B) She will attend to it immediately. (This repeats the word *attend*.)

    (C) There wasn't any medicine in here. (This repeats the word *medical/medicine*.)

17. When will payroll be finished? (*When*)

    (A) We get paid every two weeks. (This answers a different *When* question.)
    (B) I had the last roll with my coffee. (This plays on the words *payroll* and *roll*.)
    (C) I hope to have everything done by Wednesday. CORRECT

18. Did you send an invitation to Mr. Maxwell? (*Yes/No*)

    (A) No, I registered late. (This is irrelevant.)
    (B) Yes, he was on my list. CORRECT
    (C) No, it is on backorder. (This is irrelevant.)

19. Who will be taking notes at the meeting? (*Who*)

    (A) The receptionist sent a note about the meeting. (This plays on *notes/note.*)
    (B) I'll be taking the day off. (This repeats the word *taking.*)
    (C) Mr. Lorenzo's secretary will do it. CORRECT

20. What would you like to drink with your meal? (*What*)

    (A) I'll have some iced tea. CORRECT
    (B) Could I have a piece of chocolate cake, please? (Chocolate cake is not a drink.)
    (C) I'd prefer a table next to the window, if possible. (This is irrelevant.)

21. How is your new assistant working out? (*How*)

    (A) That was a tough workout. (This plays on the words *working* and *work.*)
    (B) I need a lot of assistance. (This plays on the words *assistant* and *assistance.*)
    (C) He's learning fast and doing well. CORRECT

22. The uniforms have been ordered already, haven't they? (*Yes/No*)

    (A) Yes, the waitress took our order. (This plays on the words *ordered* and *order.*)
    (B) Yes, the soup is ready. (This plays on the words *already* and *ready.*)
    (C) Yes, they're arriving on Thursday. CORRECT

23. Who should I contact to get the sink repaired? (*Who*)

    (A) Call the building superintendent. CORRECT
    (B) There's a good car mechanic across town. (This is irrelevant.)
    (C) I like my apartment. (This is irrelevant.)

24. Where is your office in New York? (*Where*)

    (A) We moved about two months ago. (This answers a *When* question.)

    (B) Downtown, in the financial district CORRECT

    (C) We do a lot of business there. (This is irrelevant.)

25. When's a good time to telephone Mr. Boros? (*When*)

    (A) It's not what you thought. (This is irrelevant.)

    (B) It's best to call early. CORRECT

    (C) It was yesterday morning. (This response is in the incorrect tense.)

26. Are you going to print new business cards or keep your old ones? (*Choice*)

    (A) The old ones are fine for now. CORRECT

    (B) I have the printer's card in my file. (This plays on the words *business cards* and *printer's card.*)

    (C) No, you can't use the printer, because it's broken. (This plays on the words *print* and *printer.*)

27. Where did you leave the Zurich invoices? (*Where*)

    (A) I hear voices in the conference room. (This plays on the words *invoices* and *voices.*)

    (B) I am going to leave with you. (This repeats the words *leave* and *you.*)

    (C) I put them in the gray cabinet. CORRECT

28. How did you get here so quickly? (*How*)

    (A) The elevator took forever. (This is irrelevant.)

    (B) I took a taxi directly from work. CORRECT

    (C) I heard about it on the radio. (This plays on *here/heard.*)

29. You have a computer at home, don't you? (*Yes/No*)

    (A) Yes, it's a laptop. CORRECT

    (B) Yes, but I left it in my wallet. (This is illogical.)

    (C) No, I don't have a phone with me. (This is irrelevant.)

30. Would you like the lunch special, or will you stick with your regular order today? (*Choice*)

    (A) It's especially delicious. (This plays on the words *lunch* and *delicious.*)

    (B) I'll have my usual meal. CORRECT

    (C) I'll have lunch early today. (This repeats the word *lunch.*)

31. How much do we have left in our mailing budget? (*How*)

    (A) We still have 2,000 dollars. CORRECT

    (B) Because I left a copy of the budget for Mr. Wilson (This repeats the words *left* and *budget.*)

    (C) No, because the mailing costs didn't go over budget (This repeats the words *budget* and *mailing.*)

32. How much vacation do you get this year? (*How*)

    (A) In September (This answers a *When* question.)

    (B) At the shore (This answers a *Where* question.)

    (C) Two weeks CORRECT

33. I think they're going to finish before the deadline, don't you? (*Yes/No*)

    (A) Yes, the checkout line is pretty short. (This plays on the words *deadline* and *line,* and is irrelevant.)

    (B) Yes, the work seems to be going pretty fast. CORRECT

    (C) No, this street turns into a dead end. (This plays on the words *deadline* and *dead end,* and is irrelevant.)

34. When is the tour group from Brazil due to arrive? (*When*)

    (A) They should be here around noon. CORRECT

    (B) My plane lands in Brazil at 1:30. (This repeats the word *Brazil.*)

    (C) I get back from my tour on the 22nd. (This repeats the word *tour.*)

35. What's at the top of our agenda this morning? (*What*)

    (A) That's on the top shelf. (This repeats the word *top.*)

    (B) First we need to discuss pay raises. CORRECT

    (C) The agent needs the invoices by noon. (This plays on the words *agenda* and *agent,* and *morning* and *noon.*)

36. Where is the nearest bank? (*Where*)

    (A) She was genuinely thankful. (This is irrelevant.)

    (B) Just two more blocks up that way. CORRECT

    (C) No, it's closed today. (This is irrelevant.)

37. What do you think: should I bring my umbrella on the walk? (*Yes/No*)

    (A) Yes, my umbrella should be big enough. (This is illogical.)

    (B) No, the walk isn't difficult at all. (This repeats the word *walk*.)

    (C) Yes, the skies have been cloudy all morning. CORRECT

38. How long will you be in Tokyo? (*How*)

    (A) I'll be there for a week. CORRECT

    (B) They've been here for three days. (This is illogical.)

    (C) I'll be leaving this Friday. (This answers a *When* question.)

39. Who's the attorney representing them? (*Who*)

    (A) Pete Mackerel is no longer a practicing attorney. (This repeats the word *attorney*.)

    (B) He's getting ready for trial. (This answers a *What* question.)

    (C) Their own staff lawyers will handle the case. CORRECT

40. Would you like to sit in on the research meeting this afternoon? (*Yes/No*)

    (A) We could develop a new line of chairs. (There is confusion between the words *sit in* and *chairs*.)

    (B) Thank you. I'd like that. CORRECT

    (C) I don't think I've met him before. (There is confusion between the words *meeting* and *met*.)

# PART III—SHORT CONVERSATIONS

41. What are the speakers planning? (Detail)

    (A) A luncheon CORRECT

    (B) A conference (This is not mentioned.)

    (C) A seminar (This is not mentioned.)

    (D) A dinner (The time mentioned is midday.)

42. How many people are expected to attend? (Detail)

    (A) 50 (This is the original number.)

    (B) 55 (This is not mentioned.)

    (C) 60 (This is not mentioned.)

    (D) 65 CORRECT

43. What has changed? (Detail)

    (A) The time (This is mentioned, but has not changed.)

    (B) The number of people CORRECT

    (C) The venue (This is not mentioned.)

    (D) The catering company (This is mentioned, but has not changed.)

44. What are the speakers talking about? (Gist)

    (A) A conference (This is not mentioned.)

    (B) A job interview CORRECT

    (C) A project meeting (This is not mentioned.)

    (D) A presentation (This is not mentioned.)

45. Who asked questions? (Detail)

    (A) The personnel manager (The manager spoke, but did not ask questions.)

    (B) A researcher (This is not mentioned.)

    (C) The office manager CORRECT

    (D) A client (This is not mentioned.)

46. How does the man feel? (Inference)

    (A) Pleased CORRECT

    (B) Disappointed (The man does not express disappointment about his interview.)

    (C) Worried (The man does not express worry about his interview.)

    (D) Surprised (The man does not express any surprise about the events in the interview.)

47. What has Mr. Jansen called about? (Gist)

    (A) Air tickets (This is not mentioned.)

    (B) Travel insurance CORRECT

    (C) A meeting confirmation (This repeats the word *meeting.*)

    (D) A hotel reservation (This is not mentioned.)

48. Where is Ms. Brody? (Detail)

    (A) Traveling abroad (She has not traveled yet.)

    (B) At the travel agency (This is not mentioned.)

    (C) At home (This is not mentioned.)

    (D) In a meeting CORRECT

49. What does Mr. Jansen need to know regarding Ms. Brody's trip? (Detail)

    (A) Where she plans to travel CORRECT

    (B) When she will arrive (This is not mentioned.)

    (C) Which airline she is traveling with (This is not mentioned.)

    (D) What she will be presenting (This is not mentioned.)

50. Who is the man? (Inference)

    (A) A job applicant (This is not mentioned.)

    (B) An employee (This is not mentioned.)

    (C) A government official (This is not mentioned.)

    (D) A customer CORRECT

51.  Where will the speakers go? (Detail)

   (A) A factory CORRECT
   (B) A government office (This is not mentioned.)
   (C) A conference (This is not mentioned.)
   (D) A restaurant (This is not mentioned.)

52.  What does the man need to wear? (Detail)

   (A) A suit and tie (This is not mentioned.)
   (B) Safety equipment CORRECT
   (C) An ID badge (This is not mentioned.)
   (D) A microphone (This is not mentioned.)

53.  Who are the speakers talking about? (Inference)

   (A) A painter (This repeats the word *painting*.)
   (B) A writer (This is not mentioned.)
   (C) A sculptor CORRECT
   (D) An actor (This is not mentioned.)

54.  Where are the speakers? (Detail)

   (A) New York (This repeats the words *New York*.)
   (B) London (This repeats the word *London*.)
   (C) Paris (This repeats the word *Paris*.)
   (D) Glasgow CORRECT

55.  What event do the speakers refer to? (Detail)

   (A) An exhibition (This is not mentioned.)
   (B) A dinner CORRECT
   (C) A conference (This is not mentioned.)
   (D) A play (This is not mentioned.)

56. Who are the men? (Inference)

    (A) Electricians CORRECT
    (B) Plumbers (This is not mentioned.)
    (C) Movers (This is not mentioned.)
    (D) Decorators (This is not mentioned.)

57. Where is the blue box? (Detail)

    (A) In the office (This is not mentioned.)
    (B) In the kitchen (This repeats the word *kitchen*.)
    (C) In the bedroom (This repeats the word *bedroom*.)
    (D) In the truck CORRECT

58. Where are the men working? (Inference)

    (A) In an office block (This is not mentioned.)
    (B) In a factory (This is not mentioned.)
    (C) In a house CORRECT
    (D) In a school (This is not mentioned.)

59. Where are the speakers? (Inference)

    (A) At a cafe (This is not mentioned.)
    (B) In a supermarket (This is not mentioned.)
    (C) In an office CORRECT
    (D) At home (This is not mentioned.)

60. Where is the man going? (Detail)

    (A) To the bank CORRECT
    (B) To the marketing department (This repeats the words *marketing department*.)
    (C) To the post office (This is not mentioned.)
    (D) To a bookstore (This is not mentioned.)

61. What does the woman want? (Gist)

    (A) A copy of a report (This is not mentioned.)
    (B) Some food CORRECT
    (C) A book (This is not mentioned.)
    (D) Some stamps (This is not mentioned.)

62. Why is Colleen Rankin in Australia? (Detail)

    (A) She works there. CORRECT
    (B) She is on vacation there. (This is not mentioned.)
    (C) She is on a business trip there. (One of the speakers is going there for this reason.)
    (D) She has retired there. (This is not mentioned.)

63. When will the woman return from Australia? (Detail)

    (A) Thursday (This is not mentioned.)
    (B) Friday (This repeats the word *Friday*.)
    (C) Saturday (This repeats the word *Saturday*.)
    (D) Sunday CORRECT

64. Who is the man in relation to the woman? (Inference)

    (A) Her boss CORRECT
    (B) Her employee (She is the employee.)
    (C) Her customer (This is not mentioned.)
    (D) Her travel agent (This is not mentioned.)

65. What goods are the speakers talking about? (Gist)

    (A) Newspapers (This repeats the word *news*.)
    (B) Office equipment (This is not mentioned.)
    (C) Clothes CORRECT
    (D) Electrical appliances (This is not mentioned.)

66. Where has the shipment come from? (Detail)

    (A) Shanghai CORRECT
    (B) Dublin (This is not mentioned.)
    (C) Dubai (This is not mentioned.)
    (D) Hong Kong (This repeats the words *Hong Kong.*)

67. What has caused the delay? (Gist)

    (A) Payment problems (This is not mentioned.)
    (B) Bad weather (This is not mentioned.)
    (C) Customs issues CORRECT
    (D) Manufacturing problems (This is not mentioned.)

68. What are the speakers talking about? (Gist)

    (A) A desktop computer (Desktop computers don't have carrying cases.)
    (B) A printer (This is not mentioned.)
    (C) A laptop computer CORRECT
    (D) A scanner (This is not mentioned.)

69. What does the special offer include? (Detail)

    (A) A rebate (This is not mentioned.)
    (B) Extra user support (This is not mentioned.)
    (C) An extended warranty (This is not mentioned.)
    (D) Extra equipment CORRECT

70. What does the man ask for? (Detail)

    (A) A reduction in price CORRECT
    (B) A catalog (This is not mentioned.)
    (C) A product demonstration (This is not mentioned.)
    (D) A business card (This is not mentioned.)

# PART IV—SHORT TALKS

71. What event will occur on May 28? (Gist)

    (A) A speech (This is not mentioned.)

    (B) A play (This is not mentioned.)

    (C) A ballet (This is not mentioned.)

    (D) A concert CORRECT

72. How much is the cheapest ticket without the discount? (Detail)

    (A) $3 (This is not mentioned.)

    (B) $8 (This is not mentioned.)

    (C) $13 (This is not mentioned.)

    (D) $18 CORRECT

73. Where can people buy tickets? (Detail)

    (A) In local stores (This is not mentioned.)

    (B) At the student union office (This repeats the words *student union*.)

    (C) On the Internet CORRECT

    (D) From the speaker (This is not mentioned.)

74. What is Mr. Park's title? (Detail)

    (A) Head chef (This is not mentioned.)

    (B) Head waiter (This repeats the word *waiter*.)

    (C) Vice president CORRECT

    (D) Customer service representative (This repeats the word *customer*.)

75. What will Mr. Park mainly focus on this year? (Gist)

    (A) Food presentation (This is only one aspect of customer service.)

    (B) Waiters (This repeats the word *waiter*.)

    (C) Menu items (That was last year.)

    (D) Customer service CORRECT

76. What does the speaker want the employees to do? (Detail)

    (A) Contact Mr. Park directly. (This is not mentioned.)
    (B) Ask questions after the talk. (This is not mentioned.)
    (C) Wear their uniforms. (This is not mentioned.)
    (D) Continue to treat customers well. CORRECT

77. Where is this introduction taking place? (Gist)

    (A) At a board of directors meeting (This is not mentioned.)
    (B) At a store managers meeting CORRECT
    (C) At a retirement dinner. (This is not mentioned.)
    (D) At a shareholders meeting (Only managers are present.)

78. What is one of Mr. Nazar's accomplishments? (Detail)

    (A) Strengthening domestic sales CORRECT
    (B) Directing company policy (This is not mentioned.)
    (C) Increasing production (This is not mentioned.)
    (D) Reducing overhead (This is not mentioned.)

79. What is one of Mr. Nazar's goals in his new role? (Detail)

    (A) Merging operations (This is not mentioned.)
    (B) Retraining staff (This is not mentioned.)
    (C) Reducing expenses CORRECT
    (D) Expanding international sales (This is not mentioned.)

80. Where is it expected to rain? (Detail)

    (A) Zurich CORRECT
    (B) Southeastern Switzerland (This repeats the word *Switzerland*.)
    (C) The northern valleys (This is not mentioned.)
    (D) Geneva (This is not mentioned.)

81. How much snow is expected today in the mountains? (Detail)

    (A) 7 centimeters (This is not mentioned.)
    (B) 15 centimeters (This repeats the number *15*.)
    (C) 30 centimeters CORRECT
    (D) 40 centimeters (This is not mentioned.)

82. Where has snow already been reported? (Detail)

    (A) The suburbs of Zurich (This is not mentioned.)
    (B) Along the Italian-Austrian border CORRECT
    (C) In the southern mountains (This is not mentioned.)
    (D) Along the French border (This is not mentioned.)

83. What did Mr. Hausman do? (Detail)

    (A) Published a book (This is not mentioned.)
    (B) Wrote the speech (This is not mentioned.)
    (C) Opened a bank (This is not mentioned.)
    (D) Introduced the speaker CORRECT

84. According to the speaker, in what areas have new challenges been created? (Gist)

    (A) Business and industry planning CORRECT
    (B) Industry management and regulation (This is not mentioned.)
    (C) Financial and capital services (Changes here have caused challenges in other areas.)
    (D) International markets for capital (This is not mentioned.)

85. What is the talk mainly about? (Gist)

    (A) Regulating capital markets (This is not mentioned.)
    (B) The history of industry management (This is not mentioned.)
    (C) Financial services and business planning CORRECT
    (D) Banking changes in the past 20 years (There is an answer choice more specific than this.)

86. What kind of company does the speaker work for? (Detail)

    (A) Travel agency (This is related to travel, but not this aspect of it.)

    (B) Construction company (This is not mentioned.)

    (C) Hotel chain CORRECT

    (D) Customer service company (There is an answer choice more specific than this.)

87. In what area does the business excel? (Detail)

    (A) Personnel (This is not mentioned.)

    (B) Customer service CORRECT

    (C) Interior design (This is their weakness.)

    (D) Building design (This is their weakness.)

88. What does the speaker ask the board of directors to make available? (Detail)

    (A) A team of interior designers CORRECT

    (B) New furniture for the lobbies (This repeats the word *lobbies*.)

    (C) Money to upgrade the facilities (This is not mentioned.)

    (D) Customer service goals (This is not mentioned.)

89. What is the purpose of this announcement? (Gist)

    (A) To conclude the evening's program CORRECT

    (B) To introduce a guest (The program is over.)

    (C) To advertise a product (This is not mentioned.)

    (D) To begin the evening's program (This is not mentioned.)

90. Who will be the guest next week? (Detail)

    (A) A corporate vice president (This is not mentioned.)

    (B) Dr. McDermott (This is the current guest.)

    (C) An employee motivation expert (This is the current guest.)

    (D) Peter Thompson CORRECT

91. What topic was probably discussed on the program? (Detail)

    (A) Crisis management (This is not mentioned.)

    (B) Managing change (This is the topic next week.)

    (C) Inspiring workers CORRECT

    (D) Contemporary technology (This is not mentioned.)

92. What is the speaker doing? (Gist)

    (A) Announcing a meeting (They are already in a meeting.)

    (B) Summarizing a previous meeting (There is no discussion of what was covered in the previous meeting.)

    (C) Beginning a meeting CORRECT

    (D) Interrupting a meeting (The speaker is conducting the meeting.)

93. How many agenda items are there? (Detail)

    (A) 3 (This is not mentioned.)

    (B) 4 (This is not mentioned.)

    (C) 5 (The original number, one is added.)

    (D) 6 CORRECT

94. What is the first item on the agenda? (Detail)

    (A) Welcoming new staff (This is not mentioned.)

    (B) Projecting budgets (This will be discussed later.)

    (C) Announcing job cuts (This is not mentioned.)

    (D) Reporting on progress CORRECT

95. Who is speaking? (Gist)

    (A) Captain of the flight (This repeats the word *captain*.)

    (B) Lead flight attendant CORRECT

    (C) Member of the ground staff (This is not mentioned.)

    (D) Copilot (This is not mentioned.)

96. Where is the flight going? (Detail)

    (A) Edinburgh CORRECT

    (B) Manchester (This is not mentioned.)

    (C) Liverpool (This is not mentioned.)

    (D) London (The flight is departing from here.)

97. What delayed the flight? (Gist)

    (A) A mechanical problem (This is not mentioned.)

    (B) A late arriving flight (This is not mentioned.)

    (C) Weather conditions CORRECT

    (D) A security alert (This is not mentioned.)

98. What is the talk mainly about? (Gist)

    (A) A piece of research CORRECT

    (B) Annual sales figures (This is not mentioned.)

    (C) A proposal for a new hotel (This repeats the word *hotel.*)

    (D) Management techniques (This repeats the word *manager.*)

99. What is the speaker's main interest? (Gist)

    (A) The effects of tourism CORRECT

    (B) The cost of vacation packages (It is about tourism, but not this particular topic.)

    (C) How to organize hotels (This is not mentioned.)

    (D) The demand for tourism (This is mentioned, but this is not the main focus.)

100. What was measured? (Detail)

    (A) Money spent (This is not mentioned.)

    (B) Pollution CORRECT

    (C) Tourist numbers (This is not mentioned.)

    (D) Money earned (This is not mentioned.)

**KAPLAN)**

# PART V—INCOMPLETE SENTENCES

101. Mr. Griffin is well known for saying _____ comes to his mind. (*G*—pronoun)

   (A) anything

   (B) everyone

   (C) whatever CORRECT

   (D) anymore

102. All visitors must be _____ by a security officer while they are on-site. (*V*—verb)

   (A) detected

   (B) accompanied CORRECT

   (C) revised

   (D) arrested

103. The factory shuts down every August for _____. (*G*—noun)

   (A) maintenance CORRECT

   (B) maintain

   (C) maintained

   (D) maintainer

104. Mr. Masuyama has excelled in his new position as senior account executive; _____, he deserves a raise. (*V*—conjunction)

   (A) yet

   (B) or

   (C) although

   (D) thus CORRECT

105. Though Mr. Ramirez is not a citizen of the United States, he has had to pay U.S. income taxes _____. (*V*—modifier/adverb)

   (A) moreover

   (B) anyway CORRECT

   (C) anyhow

   (D) since

106. Suzko Industries has hired additional inspectors to ensure that the highest production quality is _____. (G—verb )

(A) achieve

(B) achiever

(C) achievement

(D) achieved CORRECT

107. For questions concerning any of the policies in this handbook, please consult _____ the head of your department. (V—preposition)

(A) at

(B) with CORRECT

(C) about

(D) for

108. During the seminar, Ms. Williams taught _____ how to calculate the annual return on an investment. (G—pronoun)

(A) they

(B) their

(C) them CORRECT

(D) themselves

109. Customers have three weeks _____ report a credit dispute. (V—conjunction)

(A) to CORRECT

(B) until

(C) before

(D) so

110. Dr. Allan forecasts that world demand for _____ ceramics will increase by 8 percent next year. (G—modifier/adjective)

(A) advance

(B) advanced CORRECT

(C) advancing

(D) advancement

KAPLAN

111. Though he received the fax early Monday morning, Mr. Medina waited until Friday to _____. (*V—noun*)

(A) rely

(B) delay

(C) relay

(D) reply CORRECT

112. The directors will go _____ the street to the main office to meet the department managers. (*V—preposition*)

(A) across CORRECT

(B) by

(C) of

(D) against

113. As economic links between the two regions _____, the flexibility of the international banking sector will be tested. (*G—verb*)

(A) strong

(B) strength

(C) strengthen CORRECT

(D) stronger

114. Please send the _____ documents instead of photocopies. (*G—modifier/adjective*)

(A) original CORRECT

(B) originate

(C) origin

(D) originality

115. To comply with the new environmental regulations, the power plant design will need to be drastically _____. (*V—verb*)

(A) alternated

(B) avoided

(C) altered CORRECT

(D) attached

116. The one _____ that sets the company apart is its self-directed team approach to management of operations. (*G—noun*)

    (A) element CORRECT

    (B) elemental

    (C) elements

    (D) elementary

117. The luncheon was held to honor the senior employees who will be retiring _____ June. (*V—preposition*)

    (A) at

    (B) in CORRECT

    (C) among

    (D) on

118. The annual percentage rate for purchases may _____ from month to month. (*G—verb*)

    (A) vary CORRECT

    (B) variety

    (C) various

    (D) varied

119. Mr. Teska _____ the weaknesses in the proposal. (*V—prepositional phrase*)

    (A) entered into

    (B) joined with

    (C) signed up

    (D) pointed out CORRECT

120. I support Mr. Lin's goals of more efficient management, but I object to the methods proposed to achieve _____ goals. (*G—pronoun*)

    (A) those CORRECT

    (B) there

    (C) them

    (D) their

121. Applicants must submit two letters _____ . (*G*—verb)

    (A) refer

    (B) of reference CORRECT

    (C) refers to

    (D) a referred

122. Parking is limited to hotel guests, and _____ will be towed. (*G*—noun)

    (A) violated

    (B) violate

    (C) violating

    (D) violators CORRECT

123. Mr. Loder was able to hand out most of the _____ items that we brought to the trade show. (*G*—modifier/adjective)

    (A) promotional CORRECT

    (B) promoted

    (C) promote

    (D) promotes

124. If you are late for the meeting, please enter the boardroom _____.
    (*G*—modifier/adverb)

    (A) quieter

    (B) quietly CORRECT

    (C) quietest

    (D) quiet

125. Architect Jon Rushmore _____ a huge foyer with a large marble staircase.
    (*V*—verb)

    (A) enlightens

    (B) entrusts

    (C) envisions CORRECT

    (D) enlists

126. When facing challenges in the workplace, it is often best to prioritize tasks to put them in _____. (*V*—noun)

    (A) confirmation
    (B) perspective CORRECT
    (C) satisfaction
    (D) reinforcement

127. Mr. Hamilton received a promotion _____ he developed the most successful advertising campaign of the year. (*V*—conjunction)

    (A) though
    (B) while
    (C) because CORRECT
    (D) due

128. The designers are coming on Friday morning _____ the floors for new carpeting. (*G*—verb)

    (A) to measure CORRECT
    (B) is measured
    (C) a measurement
    (D) for measurable

129. The lab has developed a novel _____ to synthesizing industrial polymers. (*V*—noun)

    (A) access
    (B) arrival
    (C) commitment
    (D) approach CORRECT

130. Many workers report that they prefer being alone at the office because they can _____ more work done. (*V*—verb)

    (A) get CORRECT
    (B) be
    (C) do
    (D) go

131. The store will be closed _____ Saturday and Sunday while we take inventory. (*V*—conjunction)

    (A) neither

    (B) both CORRECT

    (C) either

    (D) and

132. Everyone agreed that Mr. Osbourne's presentation _____. (*G*—modifier/ adjective)

    (A) was a better

    (B) had better

    (C) has best

    (D) was the best CORRECT

133. Ms. O'Hara is a good teacher because she has a lot of _____. (*G*—noun)

    (A) patience CORRECT

    (B) patient

    (C) is patient

    (D) has patience

134. In her new capacity, Ms. Ricketts will _____ all financial services. (*G*—verb)

    (A) coordination

    (B) coordinating

    (C) coordinated

    (D) coordinate CORRECT

135. Management blames the decrease in profits on overall lower consumer demand, _____ is linked to high inflation across all economic sectors. (*V*—conjunction)

    (A) there

    (B) where

    (C) who

    (D) which CORRECT

136. The jurors _____ for four hours before they reached a verdict. (*V*—verb)

    (A) delivered
    (B) depended
    (C) deliberated CORRECT
    (D) defined

137. In a recent poll, most people say the _____ of the personal computer has had the greatest impact on modern life. (*G*—noun)

    (A) inventive
    (B) invent
    (C) invention CORRECT
    (D) inventor

138. Hiring and training salespeople who customers can trust is _____ important for our success. (*V*—modifier/adverb)

    (A) valuably
    (B) critically CORRECT
    (C) largely
    (D) successfully

139. Formal guidelines for bidding on contracts are _____ by the committee. (*G*—verb)

    (A) having drafted
    (B) a draft
    (C) being drafted CORRECT
    (D) the draft

140. Dr. Lao's original data was found to contain significant errors, and so he has begun _____ research again from scratch. (*G*—pronoun)

    (A) himself
    (B) him
    (C) he
    (D) his CORRECT

# PART VI—TEXT COMPLETION

141. B    (*V*—noun)

142. A    (*V*—modifier/adverb)

143. B    (*V*—modifier/adjective)

144. B    (*V*—verb)

145. D    (*V*—preposition)

146. B    (*V*—noun)

147. A    (*V*—noun)

148. C    (*V*—conjunction)

149. D    (*V*—modifier/adjective)

150. B    (*V*—pronoun)

151. A    (*G*—verb)

152. D    (*G*—verb)

# PART VII—READING COMPREHENSION

153. How much money did each share make in Year 2? (Detail)

    (A) $1.04 CORRECT

    (B) $14.50 (This plays on *14.5%*.)

    (C) $14,805 (This is the net income in Year 2.)

    (D) $379,722 (This is the sales in Year 2.)

154. What must be subtracted to determine Return on Equity? (Detail)

    (A) Extraordinary items CORRECT

    (B) Net income (This repeats the words net income.)

    (C) Shareholders equity (This repeats the words *shareholders equity*.)

    (D) Earnings per share (This repeats the words *earnings per share.*)

155. What is implied as an advantage of laser printers? (Gist)

    (A) Speed CORRECT

    (B) Ease of use (This is not mentioned.)

    (C) Low ink costs (This is not mentioned.)

    (D) Superior printing quality (This is not mentioned.)

156. According to the passage, how much did early laser printers cost? (Detail)

    (A) A few hundred dollars (This repeats the words *a few hundred dollars.*)

    (B) Approximately $500 (This is not mentioned.)

    (C) $500–$700 (This is not mentioned.)

    (D) Over $1,000 CORRECT

157. When will the transaction take effect? (Detail)

    (A) May 23 (As of this day, they must be shareholders.)

    (B) May 24 CORRECT

    (C) December 31 (This is not mentioned.)

    (D) January 1 (This is not mentioned.)

**KAPLAN**

158. What will happen to shares of the fund? (Gist)

    (A) They will be reduced to half their original number. (This repeats the word *half.*)

    (B) They will double in number. CORRECT

    (C) They will be offered for sale at a lower price. (This is not mentioned.)

    (D) They will be available to the public for the first time. (This is not mentioned.)

159. According to the passage, what makes investors nervous? (Gist)

    (A) Products and services that fall in value (This is not mentioned.)

    (B) Sales forecasts that fail to account for changes in energy prices (This is not mentioned.)

    (C) Entrepreneurs who set their prices too low (This is not mentioned.)

    (D) Claims that a product or service has no competitors CORRECT

160. The term *a return* as used in line 9 of the passage is closest in meaning to (Vocabulary)

    (A) *a profit.* CORRECT

    (B) *come back.*

    (C) *an expense.*

    (D) *departure.*

161. What is implied about high-technology businesses? (Gist)

    (A) Their value to customers is difficult to measure. (This is not mentioned.)

    (B) Their product prices are more competitive. (This repeats the word *competitive.*)

    (C) Their sales are lower than other industries. (This is not mentioned.)

    (D) Their research and development costs are high. CORRECT

162. How many years has the applicant worked for the Binational Commission? (Detail)

    (A) 1 (This is not mentioned.)

    (B) 2 (This is not mentioned.)

    (C) 3 (This is not mentioned.)

    (D) 4 CORRECT

163. How many sources of income does the applicant have? (Detail)

    (A) 1 (This is not mentioned.)
    (B) 2 CORRECT (monthly wages and trust annuity)
    (C) 3 (This is not mentioned.)
    (D) 4 (This is not mentioned.)

164. How much money does the applicant owe? (Detail)

    (A) $1,500 (This is her other monthly income.)
    (B) $3,500 (These are her monthly wages.)
    (C) $5,500 CORRECT
    (D) $12,000 (This is the balance in her checking account.)

165. What must a customer do to activate the warranty? (Detail)

    (A) Complete the attached survey. (This is not mentioned.)
    (B) Provide proof of purchase. CORRECT
    (C) Register online. (This is not mentioned.)
    (D) Call the customer service department. (This is if service is needed, not
        to activate.)

166. What is implied about color fading? (Detail)

    (A) It can be caused by damage to the umbrella. (This repeats the words *damage*
        and *umbrella*.)
    (B) It has not been reported to have happened. (This is not mentioned.)
    (C) It is guaranteed not to happen. (This is not mentioned.)
    (D) It may occur over time. CORRECT

167. What is *NOT* true about the company's warranty? (Detail)

    (A) It does not cover damage due to customer abuse. (This is true.)
    (B) It is in effect for three years. (This is true.)
    (C) It is honored worldwide. CORRECT
    (D) It promises replacement of defective products. (This is true.)

168. According to the passage, how do subjectively and objectively priced items differ? (Gist)

    (A) Objectively priced items are usually more expensive. (This is not mentioned.)

    (B) Subjectively priced items have an aesthetic value. CORRECT

    (C) Objectively priced items are less utilitarian. (This repeats the word *utilitarian*.)

    (D) Subjectively priced items are more common. (This is not mentioned.)

169. What is implied about antiques? (Detail)

    (A) They are priced subjectively. CORRECT

    (B) They were probably made by skilled craftspeople. (This repeats the words *skilled craftspeople*.)

    (C) They are sometimes overpriced. (This is not mentioned.)

    (D) Their prices go up and down. (This is not mentioned.)

170. What can be inferred about most traditional retailers? (Gist)

    (A) They set their prices based on what they perceive consumers will pay. (This describes subjective goods; most retailers sell objective goods.)

    (B) They set prices using a formula based on the cost to produce their goods. CORRECT

    (C) They tend to make higher profits than nontraditional retailers. (This is not mentioned.)

    (D) They tend to analyze the needs of their customers. (This is not mentioned.)

171. The word *weigh* as used in line 10 of the passage is closest in meaning to the word (Vocabulary)

    (A) *decide.*

    (B) *count.*

    (C) *evaluate.* CORRECT

    (D) *reduce.*

172. What conditions will northwestern Mexico experience? (Detail)

    (A) Cool air CORRECT
    (B) Rain (This repeats the word *rain.*)
    (C) Low humidity (This repeats the words *low humidity.*)
    (D) Dry conditions (This repeats the words *dry conditions.*)

173. Where will temperatures be higher than usual? (Detail)

    (A) Baja, California (This repeats the words *Baja, California.*)
    (B) Sonora (This repeats the word *Sonora.*)
    (C) The Southwest CORRECT
    (D) The northeastern region (This repeats the words *the northeastern region.*)

174. When will the majority of the cold air from Texas reach Monterrey? (Detail)

    (A) That morning (This is not mentioned.)
    (B) Later that afternoon (This refers to the leading edge, not the core.)
    (C) The next day (This is not mentioned.)
    (D) Midweek CORRECT

175. What will the cold front cause? (Detail)

    (A) Dry air (This repeats the words *dry air.*)
    (B) Strong winds (This is not mentioned.)
    (C) Rainstorms CORRECT
    (D) Snow (This is not mentioned.)

176. Who is the report probably written for? (Gist)

    (A) Synco administrators (This is not mentioned.)
    (B) Prospective investors CORRECT
    (C) Potential suppliers (This is not mentioned.)
    (D) Synco competitors This is not mentioned.)

177. What is *NOT* mentioned about Synco? (Detail/NOT)

    (A) Its position for plastics sales CORRECT
    (B) Its rankings for tire sales (This is described.)
    (C) Its measures to improve performance (This will streamline production.)
    (D) Its plans for paying dividends (They will pay 3 million euros.)

178. What were Synco's total sales in the previous year? (Detail)

    (A) 3 million euros (This is the dividend.)
    (B) 50 million euros (This is net income.)
    (C) 1 billion euros (This is not mentioned.)
    (D) 10 billion euros CORRECT

179. What is implied about automotive sales in the previous year? (Gist)

    (A) Their decline should have decreased Synco's revenues. CORRECT
    (B) Their increase is responsible for Synco's record sales. (Automotive sales fell.)
    (C) They reached an all-time high. (This does not refer to automotive sales.)
    (D) They were lower than expected. (Information about automotive sales is not mentioned.)

180. What is expected for Synco? (Detail)

    (A) Its new products will be cheaper. (This is not mentioned.)
    (B) Its earnings will grow. CORRECT
    (C) It will expand its market share. (This is not mentioned.)
    (D) Its stock price will remain high. (This repeats the word *stock*.)

181. What service is offered by *The International Employment Newsletter*? (Detail)

    (A) Translation and interpretation (This is not mentioned.)
    (B) Preparation for job interviews (This is not mentioned.)
    (C) Résumé preparation CORRECT
    (D) Work visa applications (This is not mentioned.)

182. What is learned about *The International Employment Newsletter*? (Detail)

    (A) It is available only by subscription. (The newsletter is also at newsstands.)
    (B) It is published every two weeks. (This is not mentioned.)
    (C) It can be read on the Internet. (This is not mentioned.)
    (D) It can be purchased at newsstands. CORRECT

183. How long is Ms. Ralls's current subscription? (Detail)

    (A) 3 months (This is not mentioned.)
    (B) 6 months CORRECT
    (C) 1 year (She can extend to 12 months.)
    (D) 2 years (This is not mentioned.)

184. What is available to Ms. Ralls until the end of January? (Gist)

    (A) A book (This is not mentioned.)
    (B) A discount CORRECT
    (C) A special edition (This is not mentioned.)
    (D) A class (This is not mentioned.)

185. What has been included with the letter? (Detail)

    (A) A coupon (This is not mentioned.)
    (B) A survey form (This is not mentioned.)
    (C) A sample issue (This is not mentioned.)
    (D) An envelope CORRECT

186. What is *NOT* mentioned in the notice? (Detail/NOT)

    (A) Which hotels attendees can stay at (This is mentioned.)
    (B) What time the talks are scheduled (These are described.)
    (C) How much the convention costs to attend CORRECT
    (D) How to get further information about the convention (This is from the website.)

187. Whose presentation is about a new piece of equipment? (Detail)

    (A) Gunter Kliebermann's CORRECT

    (B) Randy Wilson's (His is on hybrid tuning.)

    (C) James Townsend's (His is on the apprenticeship crisis.)

    (D) Derrick Gill's (This is the opening speech.)

188. What is the keynote presentation about? (Detail)

    (A) How to train new technicians (This repeats the word *technicians.*)

    (B) The difficulties of being an apprentice (This repeats the word *apprentice.*)

    (C) The future of the piano technician profession CORRECT

    (D) How the tuning profession is different in the United States (This is not mentioned.)

189. What can be inferred about Greg and Mike? (Gist)

    (A) They are training to be piano tuners. (This is not mentioned.)

    (B) They will present at the convention. (This is not mentioned.)

    (C) They organize the convention. CORRECT

    (D) They are printers. (This repeats the word *printers.*)

190. What is wrong with the posters? (Detail)

    (A) The dates (This is not mentioned.)

    (B) The size (This is not mentioned.)

    (C) The colors (This is not mentioned.)

    (D) The title CORRECT

191. What had been completed? (Gist)

    (A) A quarterly report CORRECT

    (B) A profit sharing plan (This repeats the words *profit-sharing plan.*)

    (C) Employee evaluations (This is not mentioned.)

    (D) A market analysis (This is not mentioned.)

192. When is the profit-sharing plan expected to go into effect? (Detail)

    (A) The following week (This is not mentioned.)

    (B) The following month (This is not mentioned.)

    (C) At the end of the next fiscal year (It is expected at the start of the next fiscal year.)

    (D) At the start of the next fiscal year CORRECT

193. How did David learn about the news? (Gist)

    (A) An email was sent to all employees. (This is not mentioned.)

    (B) A notice was posted in his department. CORRECT

    (C) A colleague told him. (David is telling Kate about the news.)

    (D) He read it in a newspaper. (This is not mentioned.)

194. What can be inferred about Kate and David? (Detail)

    (A) They work in different companies. (They work in different departments, not companies.)

    (B) They are not pleased about the news. (This is not mentioned.)

    (C) They are pleased about the news. (This is not mentioned.)

    (D) They work in different departments. CORRECT

195. When did the company first suggest a profit-sharing plan? (Detail)

    (A) Three years ago (This is not mentioned.)

    (B) Two years ago CORRECT

    (C) A year ago (This is not mentioned.)

    (D) Six months ago (This is not mentioned.)

196. Why has the paper shredder been returned? (Gist)

    (A) It does not suit the customer's needs. CORRECT

    (B) It is too expensive. (This is not mentioned.)

    (C) It is broken. (This is not mentioned.)

    (D) It is not what the customer ordered. (This is not mentioned.)

197. What is probably one of Anne Markowitz's duties? (Detail)

    (A) Researching industry trends (This is not mentioned.)
    (B) Handling customer complaints (She is making a kind of complaint, not handling them for customers.)
    (C) Buying supplies for her company CORRECT
    (D) Preparing her company's brochures (This repeats the word *brochure*.)

198. What can be inferred about the Personal X? (Gist)

    (A) It cannot handle documents with staples. CORRECT
    (B) It is no longer in stock. (This repeats the word *stock*.)
    (C) It can shred credit cards and CDs. (This is not mentioned.)
    (D) It can shed up to seven pages at one time. (This is not mentioned.)

199. What does Gina Andrews want to know? (Gist)

    (A) Which replacement model to recommend (This is not mentioned.)
    (B) Which models are currently in stock CORRECT
    (C) Where to send the Office X (This is not mentioned.)
    (D) Where the invoice should be sent (This is not mentioned.)

200. What will Paul Steinz send to Anne Markowitz? (Gist)

    (A) The Personal X (This is being returned.)
    (B) The Office X (Only information will be sent.)
    (C) A price quote CORRECT
    (D) A letter of apology (This is not mentioned.)

# Practice Test Scoring

Your performance on the TOEIC exam is used to generate a raw score and a scaled score.

First, the test maker calculates your "raw score" by adding up the total number of correct responses in the Listening Comprehension and the Reading Comprehension sections. These two raw score totals are converted to a "scaled score" ranging from 5 to 495 for each section, with a combined total from 10 to 990.

Each administration of the TOEIC exam has a slightly different difficulty level, so the score conversion charts that ETS uses vary slightly from test to test. ***Therefore, Kaplan does not provide a conversion table for the practice tests in this book***. Any scaled score conversion table Kaplan were to provide would not be a faithful reflection of the scaled score you would get on the actual test. **Your raw score, therefore, is the most accurate representation of your performance on the exam.**

If you'd like more information on how ETS gets a scaled score, visit www.TOEIC.org. Do not use any ETS scaled-score conversion tables to get a scaled score for the Kaplan practice tests. Again, it will not give you accurate scaled score prediction.

## Calculating Your Raw Score

Your raw score is determined by the number of questions you answered correctly. Unanswered or incorrectly answered questions have no impact on your raw score.

So for example, if a student took the exam and answered 155 questions correctly, 30 incorrectly, and left the remaining 15 questions unanswered, her raw score would be 155.

# PART SIX

# Transcripts

# CHAPTER 3 TRANSCRIPTS

| | |
|---|---|
| (Narrator) | Let us begin with sample directions for the Listening Comprehension Section of the TOEIC exam. |
| (Narrator) | For each question, you will hear four statements about the picture in your test book. When you hear the statements, choose the one statement that best describes what you see in the picture. Then, find the number of the question on your answer sheet and mark your answer. The statements will not be written in your test book and will be spoken just once. |
| (Narrator) | Now listen to the four statements. |
| (Narrator) | A. |
| (Woman A) | *They're leaving the office.* |
| (Narrator) | B. |
| (Woman A) | *They're turning off the machine.* |
| (Narrator) | C. |
| (Woman A) | *They're gathered around the table.* |
| (Narrator) | D. |
| (Woman A) | *They're eating at a restaurant.* |
| (Narrator) | Choice (C), "They're gathered around the table," best describes what you see in the picture. |
| (Narrator) | Let us begin with number one. |
| (Narrator) | Number 1 |
| (Narrator) | Look at the picture marked number 1 in your book. |

(MAN A)

(A) He is sorting envelopes into the boxes.

(B) All of the boxes are filled to capacity.

(C) He is writing letters to his colleagues.

(D) The squares are stacked on top of each other.

| | |
|---|---|
| (Narrator) | Number 2 |
| (Narrator) | Look at the picture marked number 2 in your book. |

(WOMAN A)

(A) The cable is old and rusty.

(B) The wire is in front of the school.

(C) The cable is coiled on spools.

(D) The spools are being delivered by truck.

**KAPLAN**

**(Narrator)**      Number 3

**(Narrator)**      Look at the picture marked number 3 in your book.

(MAN B)

(A) Several parking spots are available.

(B) A parking attendant is counting the cars.

(C) The people are getting into their cars.

(D) The parking lot is completely filled.

**(Narrator)**      Number 4

**(Narrator)**      Look at the picture marked number 4 in your book.

(WOMAN B)

(A) The woman is watching television.

(B) The printer is out of paper.

(C) The typewriter is being used.

(D) The coffee machine is plugged in.

**(Narrator)**      Number 5

**(Narrator)**      Look at the picture marked number 5 in your book.

(MAN A)

(A) He is taking inventory at the store.

(B) He is putting pants on the hanger.

(C) He is hanging the pictures on the wall.

(D) He is hemming the pants at the shop.

**(Narrator)**      Number 6

**(Narrator)**      Look at the picture marked number 6 in your book.

(WOMAN A)

(A) He is fixing a wire in the car.

(B) He is putting a tire on the car.

(C) He is pumping air into the flat tire.

(D) He is tired of holding the car up.

(Narrator)        Number 7

(Narrator)        Look at the picture marked number 7 in your book.

(MAN B)

(A) The housekeeper is making the bed.

(B) The woman is going to bed.

(C) The sheets need changing.

(D) The maid is folding towels.

(Narrator)        Number 8

(Narrator)        Look at the picture marked number 8 in your book.

(WOMAN B)

(A) The equipment is full of dirt.

(B) The vehicle is being driven on the highway.

(C) He's working under the trees.

(D) The man is operating construction equipment.

(Narrator)        Number 9

(Narrator)        Look at the picture marked number 9 in your book.

(MAN A)

(A) The man is leaving the store with the boards.

(B) The boards are being sawed in the back room.

(C) The store sells lumber.

(D) The store is filled with many customers.

(Narrator)        Number 10

(Narrator)        Look at the picture marked number 10 in your book.

(WOMAN A)

(A) The women are being shown to their table.

(B) The waitress has spilled soup on her sleeve.

(C) The women are getting ready to leave.

(D) The waitress is serving dessert to her customers.

**(Narrator)**     Number 11

**(Narrator)**     Look at the picture marked number 11 in your book.

(MAN B)

(A) He is looking at his watch.

(B) He watches his step while he walks.

(C) He is watching something below.

(D) He is washing the glass under the railing.

**(Narrator)**     Number 12

**(Narrator)**     Look at the picture marked number 12 in your book.

(WOMAN B)

(A) The nurse is entering patient information into the computer.

(B) She attends to the sick patient all by herself.

(C) She is standing patiently while she waits for the doctor.

(D) The nurse is writing notes on the paper.

**(Narrator)**     Number 13

**(Narrator)**     Look at the picture marked number 13 in your book.

(MAN A)

(A) He is cooking meat at the restaurant.

(B) The butcher packs meat on small trays.

(C) He meets his deadline for unpacking the trays.

(D) The chef is chopping the meat into small pieces.

**(Narrator)**     Number 14

**(Narrator)**     Look at the picture marked number 14 in your book.

(WOMAN A)

(A) She is stacking boxes on top of each other.

(B) She is putting groceries on the shelf.

(C) She is getting a refund at the store.

(D) She is purchasing office supplies.

**(Narrator)**      Number 15

**(Narrator)**      Look at the picture marked number 15 in your book.

    (MAN B)

    (A) The man is buying a new tennis racquet.

    (B) The woman is writing a check for the merchandise.

    (C) The woman is helping a couple move furniture.

    (D) The woman is assisting the customers with a purchase.

**(Narrator)**      Number 16

**(Narrator)**      Look at the picture marked number 16 in your book.

    (WOMAN B)

    (A) He is driving his car to the construction site.

    (B) The truck is leaving the construction area.

    (C) He is burning garbage at the construction site.

    (D) The construction debris is being loaded into the trash container.

**(Narrator)**      Number 17

**(Narrator)**      Look at the picture marked number 17 in your book.

    (MAN A)

    (A) The shoes are stacked on the floor.

    (B) She is trying the shoes on for size.

    (C) The shoes are all on sale.

    (D) She is walking into the shoe store.

**(Narrator)**      Number 18

**(Narrator)**      Look at the picture marked number 18 in your book.

    (WOMAN A)

    (A) The material is displayed on racks.

    (B) The material is stacked on pallets.

    (C) The stack of materials is wet.

    (D) The man is stacking the material.

**(Narrator)**     Number 19

**(Narrator)**     Look at the picture marked number 19 in your book.

(MAN B)

(A) The package fell out of the truck.

(B) There is no room in the truck for the package.

(C) The package has already been opened.

(D) He's loading the package into the truck.

**(Narrator)**     Number 20

**(Narrator)**     Look at the picture marked number 20 in your book.

(WOMAN B)

(A) He wears headphones while he is on the air.

(B) The air inside the studio is chilly.

(C) He is using a remote to change the channel.

(D) He is speaking into a telephone.

**(Narrator)**     Number 21

**(Narrator)**     Look at the picture marked number 21 in your book.

(MAN A)

(A) The pharmacist is taking an order for a prescription.

(B) The farmer is buying fertilizer for her crops.

(C) The woman is reaching for a bottle from the shelf.

(D) The pharmacist is filling a customer's prescription.

**(Narrator)**     Number 22

**(Narrator)**     Look at the picture marked number 22 in your book.

(WOMAN A)

(A) The camera crew is carrying the equipment.

(B) The camera man is talking on the phone.

(C) The camera crew is taking a break.

(D) The camera man is loading film into the camera.

(Narrator)     Number 23

(Narrator)     Look at the picture marked number 23 in your book.

(MAN B)

(A) They are balancing the company's books.

(B) The woman waits while the man looks.

(C) The man and woman are reviewing a document.

(D) The woman watches the man prepare the invoice.

(Narrator)     Number 24

(Narrator)     Look at the picture marked number 24 in your book.

(WOMAN B)

(A) The boys are ignoring the speaker.

(B) The boys listen and watch while the man speaks.

(C) He's teaching the boys how to paint the fence.

(D) The man is coaching a football team.

# CHAPTER 4: TRANSCRIPTS

| | |
|---|---|
| (Narrator) | Part II |
| (Narrator) | You will hear a question or statement and three responses spoken in English. They will be spoken only once and will not be printed in your test book. Choose the best response to the question or statement and mark the letter on your answer sheet. |
| (Narrator) | Listen to a sample question: |
| (Man A) | *Where are we meeting?* |
| (Narrator) | *A.* |
| (Woman B) | *To meet the new supervisor.* |
| (Narrator) | *B.* |
| (Woman B) | *It's the second room on the left.* |
| (Narrator) | *C.* |
| (Woman B) | *No, at three o'clock.* |
| (Narrator) | Choice (B), *"It's the second room on the left,"* best answers the question. |
| (Narrator) | Number 1 |
| (Woman A) | Is there anything good on TV tonight? |

(Man B)

(A) The news comes on in about an hour.

(B) Yes, the plant is on top of the television.

(C) Please find a different station.

| | |
|---|---|
| (Narrator) | Number 2 |
| (Man A) | Why did they cancel the reception for Mr. Chang? |

(Woman B)

(A) Her secretary did.

(B) He received the invitation.

(C) He got sick.

(Narrator)      Number 3

(Woman A)      Where can I buy a magazine?

   (Man A)

   (A) A cab just went by.

   (B) The store takes credit cards, I think.

   (C) The newsstand on the corner.

(Narrator)      Number 4

(Man B)      What type of business are you in?

   (Woman A)

   (A) Because I sold the house.

   (B) I'm a banker.

   (C) I'll type it tomorrow.

(Narrator)      Number 5

(Woman B) Would you like to work overtime tonight?

   (Man A)

   (A) No thanks, I have one.

   (B) I'd rather begin at 8.

   (C) Sure, I need the hours.

(Narrator)      Number 6

(Woman A)      Where is your final destination today?

   (Man B)

   (A) I'll be flying there.

   (B) I'm leaving this afternoon.

   (C) I'm going to Rome.

**(Narrator)**      Number 7

**(Woman B)**      It'll be a long trip, won't it?

(Man B)

(A) She tripped on the stairs, yes.

(B) No, I leave next week.

(C) Yes, about four weeks.

**(Narrator)**      Number 8

**(Woman A)**      Why don't we take a short break?

(Man B)

(A) My car got new brakes last summer.

(B) Yes, Lisa broke the plate by accident.

(C) Good idea, I'm getting tired.

**(Narrator)**      Number 9

**(Man B)**      When will the earnings report be issued?

(Woman B)

(A) It will be published in the newspaper.

(B) At the end of the first quarter.

(C) Because the stock went up last week.

**(Narrator)**      Number 10

**(Man B)**      You subscribe to Business Monthly Magazine, don't you?

(Man A)

(A) No, but my office does.

(B) Yes, I heard the news on the radio.

(C) The mail is late today.

**(Narrator)**     Number 11

**(Woman B)**     How are the contract negotiations coming along?

(Woman A)

(A) Our attorneys are reviewing the proposed changes.

(B) We're almost finished with the progress report.

(C) They returned the rental car last night.

**(Narrator)**     Number 12

**(Man B)**     Who should we send to Buenos Aires?

(Woman A)

(A) I'd recommend next week.

(B) Let's send out for lunch.

(C) Jaime should go.

**(Narrator)**     Number 13

**(Man A)**     Does Ali rent that house, or does he own it?

(Woman B)

(A) He used to rent a house in Alexandria.

(B) His cousin just bought a home downtown.

(C) He has a one-year lease.

**(Narrator)**     Number 14

**(Woman B)**     Has Ms. Matala finished with the samples?

(Man A)

(A) Yes, she was right on schedule.

(B) No, she was born in Finland.

(C) She felt his action was justified.

| | |
|---|---|
| (Narrator) | Number 15 |
| (Man A) | What's the training workshop about? |

(Woman A)

(A) Sometime tomorrow afternoon.

(B) Somewhere in the new building.

(C) Something to do with team building.

| | |
|---|---|
| (Narrator) | Number 16 |
| (Man B) | Why don't you apply for that new job posting? |

(Woman B)

(A) I worked on the second shift.

(B) I don't think I'm qualified.

(C) I'm walking to the post office.

| | |
|---|---|
| (Narrator) | Number 17 |
| (Man A) | Is that pollution, or just morning haze? |

(Woman B)

(A) The latter; it should be gone by noon.

(B) The industrial zone is located in the valley.

(C) The afternoon rain keeps the air clean.

| | |
|---|---|
| (Narrator) | Number 18 |
| (Woman A) | Why don't we take a cruise for vacation? |

(Man B)

(A) Because the food is so good.

(B) So that we can get a free ticket.

(C) That might be a nice change.

**(Narrator)**       Number 19

**(Man A)**       Will Mr. Yoon write the report, or does he want me to do it?

(Woman A)

(A) He was right last time.

(B) I think he reports directly to Mr. Yoon.

(C) He'll do it himself.

**(Narrator)**       Number 20

**(Woman B)**       How many workers will we need for the Johnston building?

(Man A)

(A) Construction has been ongoing for two years.

(B) I estimate around a hundred.

(C) We'll need to work overtime to finish.

**(Narrator)**       Number 21

**(Woman A)**       Why don't you think about taking early retirement?

(Man B)

(A) I thought you retired.

(B) Actually, I've been considering it.

(C) I've worked for over thirty years.

**(Narrator)**       Number 22

**(Woman B)**       Who's your favorite author?

(Man A)

(A) I prefer short stories over novels.

(B) Her favorite books are usually fiction.

(C) It's hard for me to pick just one.

**(Narrator)**     Number 23

**(Man B)**     Don't you think interest rates will continue to go up?

(Woman B)

(A) In the short term, I suppose so.

(B) No, I am very interested.

(C) I had to drive up the hill.

**(Narrator)**     Number 24

**(Woman A)**     What should we do with these files for the Wallrock lease?

(Man A)

(A) Leave them until Tuesday.

(B) Your secretary has them.

(C) No, I sent them to Mr. Wallrock.

# CHAPTER 5: TRANSCRIPTS

| | |
|---|---|
| **(Narrator)** | Part III |
| **(Narrator)** | You will now hear a number of conversations between two people. You will be asked to answer three questions about what the speakers say. Select the best response to each question and mark the letter on your answer sheet. The conversations will be spoken only once and will not be printed in your test book. |
| **(Narrator)** | Practice 1 |
| **(Narrator)** | Questions 1 through 3 refer to the following conversation. |
| **(Man A)** | You're not working on Monday? You didn't work on Thursday, either! How many vacation days do you get? You certainly seem to get more than I do! |
| **(Woman A)** | Well, actually I get twenty-five days of vacation, just like you, but my company allows us to work weekends and trade that for week days off. I worked two Saturdays in February and three Sundays in March, so now I have five extra days to take. |
| **(Man A)** | I wish my company was flexible like that, but our office is totally closed on weekends. |
| **(Woman A)** | Oh yeah? My company just keeps on going, twenty-four hours a day, seven days a week. |
| **(Narrator)** | Number 1. What are the speakers mainly discussing? |
| **(Narrator)** | Number 2. What about the woman surprised the man? |
| **(Narrator)** | Number 3. How is the man's job different from the woman's? |

**KAPLAN**

| (Narrator) | Practice 2 |
|---|---|
| (Narrator) | Questions 4 through 6 refer to the following conversation. |
| (Woman B) | Well, Mr. Donahue, I think that's all we have to ask you. Now it's your turn to do the speaking! Do you have any questions you'd like to ask us about the job? |
| (Man B) | Well, yes there are few things. For example, you asked me earlier if I had any project management experience. Does that mean that you're looking for people with this kind of experience? |
| (Woman B) | Oh, not necessarily, although clearly it would be an advantage. But no, what we're looking for is the potential for leadership. Obviously the most important skills for the current job are the necessary computer programming expertise, but if we think someone has the necessary skills set for a leadership role in the future—things like organizational and communication skills, then we're interested. |
| (Man B) | I see. Because, you see, although I haven't actually done any project management, I did learn the principles when I was in university. |
| (Narrator) | Number 4. Who is the man? |
| (Narrator) | Number 5. What kind of experience are the speakers talking about? |
| (Narrator) | Number 6. What kind of job is being offered? |

| (Narrator) | Practice 3 |
|---|---|
| (Narrator) | Questions 7 through 9 refer to the following conversation. |
| (Man A) | I can't believe it! Someone's moved the file for that new German contract, the JDK job. I put it in the contract files cabinet only last week. Why don't people put things back where they belong? I can't understand it. |
| (Woman B) | Oh, sorry Mike. I forgot to tell you. I've changed the filing system slightly. There wasn't room anymore for all the contract files in one cabinet. You couldn't find anything, so I've split them up. |
| (Man A) | Oh, what do you mean? |
| (Woman B) | Well, I've put all the foreign contracts in a separate cabinet—that one over there by the window. You'll find the JDK file there, because it's a German contract. It's in the second drawer from the top. All the U.S. contracts are in the cabinet by your desk. And by the way, I think we need to reorganize the finance files, too! |
| (Narrator) | Number 7. Why is the man annoyed? |
| (Narrator) | Number 8. What has the woman changed? |
| (Narrator) | Number 9. Where is the JDK contract file? |

| | |
|---|---|
| (Narrator) | Practice 4 |
| (Narrator) | Questions 10 through 12 refer to the following conversation. |
| (Man B) | Now we've got your camera connected directly to the projector, so we actually don't need to copy the photos onto the computer at all. You can project directly from your camera! |
| (Woman A) | Oh, that's great. It's just that I have no idea at all how to use the projector. |
| (Man B) | Don't worry. It's really very easy. First of all, use the red button here to switch it on and off. The green button puts the projector on standby, which is very convenient for presentations and that kind of thing. These blue arrows here control the color and the brightness of the image and then there's this little wheel here. If you turn the wheel towards you, the image gets bigger, and if you turn it away from you, the image gets smaller. |
| (Woman A) | Okay, that looks easy! |
| (Narrator) | Number 10. What is the woman learning about? |
| (Narrator) | Number 11. What does the green button do? |
| (Narrator) | Number 12. How can users change the size of the image? |

| (Narrator) | Practice 5 |
|---|---|
| (Narrator) | Questions 13 through 15 refer to the following conversation. |
| (Woman B) | Oh, good evening. We're the party from Limo Car Rentals. We've reserved tables for this evening. |
| (Man B) | Oh dear, I'm sorry, but we were expecting you tomorrow. Let me just check . . . yes, Limo Cars, party of five for seven-thirty on Tuesday. The reservation was made by a Mr. Robert Jones on Friday. |
| (Woman B) | Oh yes, originally we reserved for Tuesday, but we changed the reservation for Monday instead. Didn't you get a call to change it to this evening? |
| (Man B) | No, I'm sorry, we weren't informed. At least, there's no record of that change here in the list. Perhaps Mr. Jones forgot to call us. However, don't worry too much. It's seven-thirty now and we may have a table free at eight o'clock, if you'd like to wait until then. |
| (Narrator) | Number 13. What do the speakers want to reserve? |
| (Narrator) | Number 14. When was the reservation made? |
| (Narrator) | Number 15. How long do the speakers need to wait? |

| (Narrator) | Practice 6 |
|---|---|
| (Narrator) | Questions 16 through 18 refer to the following conversation. |
| (Woman A) | Excuse me officer, I've just come from the airport and I need to get to the train station. I have absolutely no idea how to get there. Is it walking distance from here? |
| (Man A) | Well, it's not too far on foot, no, but I see you have quite a bit of luggage there. It could take ten minutes to walk from here, so I think you'd be best using public transportation to be honest. There isn't a subway station near here, but there's the number fifteen bus that stops across the street and the train station is just two or three stops down. |
| (Woman A) | Oh really? Well how frequent are the buses. I mean, will I have to wait long? |
| (Man A) | Let's see. Well, the last number fifteen came by about five minutes ago, and they're quite frequent. I mean, they come by every eight minutes or so. Yeah, there should be one coming in about three minutes. |
| (Narrator) | Number 16. Who is the woman speaking to? |
| (Narrator) | Number 17. Where does the woman want to go? |
| (Narrator) | Number 18. How many minutes will the woman need to wait for the next bus? |

| (Narrator) | Practice 7 |
|---|---|
| (Narrator) | Questions 19 through 21 refer to the following conversation. |
| (Woman B) | Rory, I've just spoken to Ann Hanson, the external consultant, and it seems that she can't make it to Thursday's planning meeting. I can't do Friday because we've got a safety inspection at the new manufacturing facility, and that can't be changed. So we'll have to postpone until next week. |
| (Man B) | Oh dear. Well, I'd better contact the people from Elgar Plastics then, and find out their availability for next week. I'll e-mail them explaining the problem. |
| (Woman B) | No, I'd prefer you to call them. They're not going to be very happy about this, and on the phone you'll be able to explain the situation better than in an e-mail message. Sometimes it's better to contact clients by phone. |
| (Man B) | Okay, but I'll also e-mail our team to announce the postponement. |
| (Narrator) | Number 19. What are the speakers mainly discussing? |
| (Narrator) | Number 20. Who will Rory call? |
| (Narrator) | Number 21. How will Rory contact their team? |

| (Narrator) | Practice 8 |
| --- | --- |
| (Narrator) | Questions 22 through 24 refer to the following conversation. |
| (Man A) | Hi Kelly. It's Tony Buckby from service supplies here. Listen, I've got a bit of a problem here and I'm not sure what to do. You see, the maintenance department is here now making some repairs, and they need a spare part for one of the lacquering machines down on the shop floor. Well, anyway we don't have that particular part in stock, and we have to order a new one. |
| (Woman A) | Oh? Well just go ahead and order one. What's the problem exactly? Don't you have the catalogue? |
| (Man A) | No, that's not the problem. It's just that last week Mr. Logan, my supervisor, told me not to order anything without asking him first . . . and he's not here today. |
| (Woman A) | Oh yes, you're right. He's away at a product training in Baltimore. |
| (Narrator) | Number 22. Where does Tony work? |
| (Narrator) | Number 23. What is Tony's problem? |
| (Narrator) | Number 24. Why are Mr. Logan and Tony not together? |

# CHAPTER 6: TRANSCRIPTS

| (Narrator) | Part IV |
|---|---|

(Narrator)   You will now hear short talks given by a single speaker. You will be asked to answer three questions about what the speaker says. Select the best response to each question and mark the letter on your answer sheet. The talks will be spoken only once and will not be printed in your test book.

(Narrator)   Practice 1

(Narrator)   Questions 1 through 3 refer to the following talk.

(Man A)   Welcome to the twelfth annual trade conference. One of the key themes of this year's conference is Ireland's position in the world marketplace. I was recently asked why I feel so strongly about Irish businesses exporting their products. My answer was straightforward and simple: If you don't sell abroad, you are selling your company short. There are lots of reasons why Irish firms should look to overseas markets to sell their goods, and it has never made more sense to be exporting than it does right now. For example, exchange rates over the last eighteen months have made our prices highly attractive to overseas buyers. Also, recent government innovations are making it easier than ever to reach foreign markets.

(Narrator)   Number 1. What is the speaker promoting?

(Narrator)   Number 2. Where does this talk take place?

(Narrator)   Number 3. According to the speaker, why are foreign buyers interested in Irish products?

| | |
|---|---|
| **(Narrator)** | Practice 2 |
| **(Narrator)** | Questions 4 through 6 refer to the following news report. |
| **(Woman A)** | Good evening and welcome to Business News Nightly. Coming up in a few minutes, the latest developments in the SmartShares fraud scandal. A judge orders the company to close, but we find out how SmartShare's creditors are reacting to the news. And later on, our East Asia correspondent has been to Thailand to learn more about the novel ways companies there are increasing the productivity of their workforces. Plus, in 20 minutes, Jane Withers reports from Berlin's twenty-first technology fair where the very latest must-have business gadgets are on display, including the world's lightest laptop computer. But first, here's Mark Francis with the latest on the stock markets. |
| **(Narrator)** | Number 4. Why is the SmartShares company in the news? |
| **(Narrator)** | Number 5. According to the report, what is improving in Thailand? |
| **(Narrator)** | Number 6. What will Mark Francis discuss? |

| (Narrator) | Practice 3 |
|---|---|
| (Narrator) | Questions 7 through 9 refer to the following advertisement |
| (Man B) | Dunthrops' big summer sale is now going on. Yes, our annual July sale bonanza starts July first, and there are literally hundreds of bargains to be had. Reductions of up to fifty percent on menswear; Men's suits have been slashed from $400 down to $300. Men's coats regularly selling for $200 are now just $150. It's crazy! But it's not just men who have reasons to be pleased. There are bargains galore for the ladies, too, with up to thirty percent off on top brand names. And this year we've extended our sale to other departments too. There are huge savings available in kitchenware and home furnishings. But don't delay! Dunthrops' big summer sale starts July first and ends July 31st! |
| (Narrator) | Number 7. What kind of store is Dunthorps? |
| (Narrator) | Number 8. What is learned about the sale at Dunthorps? |
| (Narrator) | Number 9. When does the sale end? |

| (Narrator) | Practice 4 |
|---|---|
| (Narrator) | Questions 10 through 11 refer to the following talk. |
| (Woman B) | In our next gallery you will see Island life, one of the artist's most famous works. The artist conceived of the idea while vacationing in the Caribbean, where he stayed for two months. He didn't actually begin work on the piece, however, until he had returned home to Paris. It's oil on canvas and because of its intricate design and detail, it took the artist six years to complete. You're actually very lucky to be able to see this masterwork, in fact, because the museum currently has it on loan from the Austrian National Gallery in Vienna. It will be on display here for only another two weeks and then it goes back home. |
| (Narrator) | Number 10. Where did the artist get the idea for his piece? |
| (Narrator) | Number 11. What kind of artwork is being discussed? |
| (Narrator) | Number 12. Who is the speaker addressing? |

| | |
|---|---|
| **(Narrator)** | Practice 5 |
| **(Narrator)** | Questions 13 through 15 refer to the following talk. |
| **(Man A)** | Good afternoon. I'm pleased that so many of you could attend our ceremony despite the threat of rain, and I thank you all for coming. Ira Levinson would have been proud to see our new building complete and ready for occupancy. Who could have thought that the family business he started back in 1952 would grow into the thriving company it is today, with nearly a thousand employees, or that our products would rank among the very best in the industry worldwide. This beautiful new office building will house the company headquarters, and provide workspace for a very lucky staff of 250 people., including all of you who have come this morning. And so, it's my great pleasure to name this building the Levinson Building in honor of Ira Levinson, whose innovation and hard work built the company that we know today. |
| **(Narrator)** | Number 13. Who is Ira Levinson? |
| **(Narrator)** | Number 14. How many people will work in the building? |
| **(Narrator)** | Number 15. What is the purpose of the talk? |

| | |
|---|---|
| **(Narrator)** | Practice 6 |
| **(Narrator)** | Questions 16 through 18 refer to the following news report. |
| **(Woman A)** | The number of recorded traffic violations decreased in the metropolitan area last year in keeping with a five year decline nationally. But does this mean that drivers are becoming more law-abiding? Not according to some. The transportation department suspects that the lower number is due to fewer police officers rather than fewer traffic offenders. During the last three years, traffic citations have dropped 27% in the city. The Transportation Department says budget cuts and an increasing population have led to fewer patrol hours for police throughout the metropolitan area. A police department spokesperson agreed that the figures do not necessarily indicate that drivers' behavior is changing. |
| **(Narrator)** | Number 16. For how many years have traffic violations been decreasing nationally? |
| **(Narrator)** | Number 17. Why is the number of traffic violations dropping? |
| **(Narrator)** | Number 18. What did the police spokesperson say about the figures? |

| (Narrator) | Practice 7 |
|---|---|
| (Narrator) | Questions 19 through 21 refer to the following recorded announcement. |
| (Woman B) | Thank you for calling MoneyWise Savings Bank's automated teller service. If you have a MoneyWise account, you can also access you account via our online e-banking services. For e-banking, go to w-w-w moneywise dot com. To access your savings account through our automated teller service, please press one now. To access your checking account, please press two now. To access your credit card account, please press three now. To access your retirement funds, money market accounts, or other investment accounts, please press four now. To transfer funds between accounts, please press five now. To speak with a customer service representative, please press zero now. To repeat this menu option, please press nine now. |
| (Narrator) | Number 19. Which number should a customer press for checking account access? |
| (Narrator) | Number 20. What does pressing 5 allow customers to do? |
| (Narrator) | Number 21. What do customers find out? |

(Narrator)        Practice 8

(Narrator)        Questions 22 through 24 refer to the following advertisement.

(Man B)           Jet Lines makes the difference. That's why more business people choose to fly to South East Asia destinations from New York with Jet Lines than any other airline. Perhaps it's the peace and quiet of our executive lounges, with free internet access and complementary drinks and snacks. Perhaps it's the comfort of Jet lines' business class seating, with more leg room than any of our competitors. Perhaps it's the fact that all Jet Lines business class passengers enjoy a good night's sleep on seats that recline 180 degrees to form flat beds. Perhaps it's our award-winning in-flight menus or maybe just that little extra courtesy that makes Jet Lines crews stand out from the rest. Whatever it is, Jet Lines makes a difference. Isn't it time you found out why for yourself?

(Narrator)        Number 22. Who is the intended audience for the advertisement?

(Narrator)        Number 23. What do Jet Lines executive lounges have?

(Narrator)        Number 24. What did Jet Lines win an award for?

| (Narrator) | Practice 9 |
|---|---|
| (Narrator) | Questions 25 through 27 refer to the following voicemail message. |
| (Woman A) | Hello Mr. Rushman. It's Amy Richardson here calling from Seiler Logistics. I'm sorry I wasn't able to speak to you earlier when you called. I'm afraid I was in a meeting all afternoon. I thought I might just catch you before you went home for the evening, but it seems I've just missed you. Anyway, I just wanted to let you know that we have located the missing package. I spoke to the driver who was supposed to deliver it to you today, and it seems he left the package with the security guard in the building lobby. That was at seven thirty this morning, so perhaps the guard forgot to contact you about the delivery? I'll be at my desk first thing tomorrow, so do please contact me if the item still hasn't turned up. Thank you. |
| (Narrator) | Number 25. What relationship does Mr. Rushman have with Seiler Logistics? |
| (Narrator) | Number 26. Why has Amy Richardson called? |
| (Narrator) | Number 27. When has Amy Richardson probably called Mr. Rushman? |

(Narrator)        Practice 10

**Questions 28 through 30 refer to the following announcement.**

(Man A)           Welcome aboard the Metropolitan Airport Express. This is a non-stop service for Metropolitan Airport North Terminal. We will be departing in a few moments. Our travel time will be thirty five minutes. Those of you without tickets can purchase a single fare ticket from a conductor who will be passing through the train. We accept both cash and most major credit cards. Frequent flyers may be interested to know that advance purchase discount tickets are available for the Metropolitan Airport Express, offering a ten percent discount on fares. Ask the conductor for more details. Thank you for choosing the Metropolitan Airport Express.

(Narrator)        Number 28. How long does it take to get to the airport?

(Narrator)        Number 29. What is true about the single fare tickets?

(Narrator)        Number 30. What is learned about the advance purchase discount tickets?

# PRACTICE TEST TRANSCRIPT

**(Narrator)** In the Listening Comprehension Section, you will have the chance to demonstrate how well you understand spoken English. The Listening Section will take approximately 45 minutes. There are four parts, and directions are given for each part. You must mark your answers on the separate answer sheet. Do not write them in the test book.

**(Narrator)** Directions: For each question, you will hear four statements about the picture in your test book. When you hear the statements, choose the one statement that best describes what you see in the picture. Then, find the number of the question on your answer sheet and mark your answer. The statements will not be written in your test book and will be spoken just once.

**(Narrator)** Now listen to the four statements.

**(Narrator)** *A.*

**(Woman A)** *They're leaving the office.*

**(Narrator)** *B.*

**(Woman A)** *They're turning off the machine.*

**(Narrator)** *C.*

**(Woman A)** *They're gathered around the table.*

**(Narrator)** *D.*

**(Woman A)** *They're eating at a restaurant.*

**(Narrator)** Choice (B), "They're gathered around the table," best describes what you see in the picture. Therefore, you should fill in choice (B) in your answer sheet.

**(Narrator)** Now let us begin Part I with question number 1.

**(Narrator)** Number 1

**(Narrator)** Look at the picture marked number 1 in your test book.

(Man A)

(A) A technician is using some equipment.

(B) The equipment is on sale.

(C) A technician is packing up the equipment.

(D) The equipment is in being unloaded from a car.

**(Narrator)**        Number 2

**(Narrator)**        Look at the picture marked number 2 in your test book.

(Woman A)

(A) The patio doors are open to the garden.

(B) The flower pot is in the middle of the table.

(C) The plant is on top of the stool.

(D) The chair is in the corner of the room.

**(Narrator)**        Number 3

**(Narrator)**        Look at the picture marked number 3 in your test book.

(Man B)

(A) He's getting up from his chair.

(B) He's bent over his work table.

(C) He's cleaning up his office.

(D) He's turning on the desk light.

**(Narrator)**        Number 4

**(Narrator)**        Look at the picture marked number 4 in your test book.

(Woman B)

(A) The truck is parked alongside the building.

(B) The truck is being loaded in the rain.

(C) The man is getting out of the truck.

(D) They are moving into a new house.

**(Narrator)**        Number 5

**(Narrator)**        Look at the picture marked number 5 in your test book.

(Man A)

(A) The photographer is putting film into the camera.

(B) The scientist is watching birds through binoculars.

(C) The journalist is interviewing the woman for a story.

(D) The man is taking a picture.

**(Narrator)**     Number 6

**(Narrator)**     Look at the picture marked number 6 in your test book.

(Woman A)

(A) The dishes are arranged n the cabinet.

(B) The plates are on the middle shelf.

(C) There are five place settings on the table.

(D) The dishwasher is full of clean dishes.

**(Narrator)**     Number 7

**(Narrator)**     Look at the picture marked number 7 in your test book.

(Man B)

(A) The vehicles are parked side by side.

(B) A car is being towed away.

(C) The truck is traveling the wrong way.

(D) A vehicle is making a turn at the corner.

**(Narrator)**     Number 8

**(Narrator)**     Look at the picture marked number 8 in your test book.

(Woman B)

(A) The people are standing behind the railing.

(B) The people are climbing over the railing.

(C) The people are seated on the railing.

(D) The people are all holding on to the railing.

**(Narrator)**     Number 9

**(Narrator)**     Look at the picture marked number 9 in your test book

(Man A)

(A) The hostess is entertaining her guests.

(B) The woman is slicing the meat.

(C) The waitress is serving her customers.

(D) The chef is placing the meat onto the platter.

**KAPLAN**

| | |
|---|---|
| **(Narrator)** | Number 10 |
| **(Narrator)** | Look at the picture marked number 10 in your test book. |

(Woman A)

(A) The woman is using a pay phone.

(B) She's hanging up the telephone.

(C) The woman is talking to a crowd.

(D) She's holding a microphone.

| | |
|---|---|
| **(Narrator)** | **Directions:** You will hear a question or statement and three responses spoken in English. They will be spoken only once and will not be printed in your test book. Choose the best response to the question or statement and mark the letter on your answer sheet. |
| **(Narrator)** | Listen to a sample question: |
| **(Man B)** | *Where are we meeting?* |
| **(Narrator)** | *A.* |
| **(Woman A)** | *To meet the new supervisor.* |
| **(Narrator)** | *B.* |
| **(Woman A)** | *It's the second room on the left.* |
| **(Narrator)** | *C.* |
| **(Woman A)** | *No, at three o'clock.* |
| **(Narrator)** | Choice (B), *"It's the second room on the left,"* best answers the question. Therefore, you should fill in choice (B) in your answer sheet. |
| **(Narrator)** | Now let us begin Part II with question number 11. |
| **(Narrator)** | Number 11 |
| **(Man A)** | Do you have an additional pair of bookends? |

(Woman B)

(A) Yes, this pear is delicious.

(B) Yes, I have some spare time.

(C) Yes, I have an extra pair.

**(Narrator)**     Number 12

**(Woman A)**     Why do you want to advertise in the trade publications?

(Man B)

(A) No, let's skip the trade show this year.

(B) A lot of our trade is done overseas.

(C) It's a good way to attract customers.

**(Narrator)**     Number 13

**(Woman B)**     Are gratuities already added in, or are they separate?

(Man A)

(A) They're included in the price.

(B) You can pack whatever you like.

(C) Yes, the price includes all meals.

**(Narrator)**     Number 14

**(Man B)**     What are the arrangements for publicizing the general's visit?

(Woman A)

(A) We've arranged a hotel room.

(B) The television station is sending a reporter.

(C) All public buildings are open to visitors.

**(Narrator)**     Number 15

**(Man A)**     You've had experience with this particular software, haven't you?

(Woman B)

(A) No, I'm not familiar with it at all.

(B) Men's wear is located on the second floor

(C) Yes, I think it's very expensive.

**(Narrator)**      Number 16

**(Man B)**         Why didn't she attend the medical conference yesterday?

(Woman B)

(A) There was a conflict in her schedule.

(B) She will attend to it immediately.

(C) There wasn't any medicine in here.

**(Narrator)**      Number 17

**(Woman A)**     When will payroll be finished?

(Man B)

(A) We get paid every two weeks.

(B) I had the last roll with my coffee.

(C) I hope to have everything done by Wednesday.

**(Narrator)**      Number 18

**(Woman B)**     Did you send an invitation to Mr. Maxwell?

(Man A)

(A) No, I registered late.

(B) Yes, he was on my list.

(C) No, it is on backorder.

**(Narrator)**      Number 19

**(Man B)**         Who will be taking notes at the meeting?

(Woman A)

(A) The receptionist sent a note about the meeting.

(B) I'll be taking the day off.

(C) Mr. Lorenzo's secretary will do it.

**(Narrator)**     Number 20

**(Man A)**     What would you like to drink with your meal?

(Woman A)

(A) I'll have some iced tea.

(B) Could I have a piece of chocolate cake, please?

(C) I'd prefer a table next to the window, if possible.

**(Narrator)**     Number 21

**(Woman B)**     How is your new assistant working out?

(Man B)

(A) That was a tough work out.

(B) I need a lot of assistance.

(C) He's learning fast and doing well.

**(Narrator)**     Number 22

**(Woman A)**     The uniforms have been ordered already, haven't they?

(Woman B)

(A) Yes, the waitress took our order.

(B) Yes, the soup is ready.

(C) Yes, they're arriving on Thursday.

**(Narrator)**     Number 23

**(Woman B)**     Who should I contact to get the sink repaired?

(Man A)

(A) Call the building superintendent.

(B) There's a good car mechanic across town.

(C) I like my apartment.

**(Narrator)**     Number 24

**(Man B)**     Where is your office in New York?

(Woman A)

(A) We moved about two months ago.

(B) Downtown, in the financial district.

(C) We do a lot of business there.

**(Narrator)**     Number 25

**(Man A)**     When's a good time to telephone Mr. Boros?

(Woman B)

(A) It's not what you thought.

(B) It's best to call early.

(C) It was yesterday morning.

**(Narrator)**     Number 26

**(Woman A)**     Are you going to print new business cards, or keep your old ones?

(Man A)

(A) The old ones are fine for now.

(B) I have the printer's card in my file.

(C) No, you can't use the printer, because it's broken.

**(Narrator)**     Number 27

**(Woman B)**     Where did you leave the Zurich invoices?

(Man B)

(A) I hear voices in the conference room.

(B) I am going to leave with you.

(C) I put them in the gray cabinet.

**(Narrator)**　　　Number 28

**(Man B)**　　　How did you get here so quickly?

　　(Woman A)

　　(A) The elevator took forever.

　　(B) I took a taxi directly from work.

　　(C) I heard about it on the radio.

**(Narrator)**　　　Number 29

**(Man A)**　　　You have a computer at home, don't you?

　　(Man B)

　　(A) Yes, it's a laptop.

　　(B) Yes, but I left it in my wallet.

　　(C) No, I don't have my phone with me.

**(Narrator)**　　　Number 30

**(Woman A)**　　　Would you like the lunch special, or will you stick with your regular order today?

　　(Man A)

　　(A) It's especially delicious.

　　(B) I'll have my usual meal.

　　(C) I'll have lunch early today.

**(Narrator)**　　　Number 31

**(Woman B)**　　　How much do we have left in our mailing budget?

　　(Man A)

　　(A) We still have about 2,000 dollars.

　　(B) Because I left a copy of the budget for Mr. Wilson.

　　(C) No, because the mailing costs didn't go over budget.

**KAPLAN**

**(Narrator)** Number 32

**(Man B)** How much vacation do you get this year?

(Woman B)

(A) In September.
(B) At the shore.
(C) Two weeks.

**(Narrator)** Number 33

**(Man A)** I think they're going to finish before the deadline, don't you?

(Woman A)

(A) Yes, the checkout line is pretty short.
(B) Yes, the work seems to be going pretty fast.
(C) No, this street turns into a dead end.

**(Narrator)** Number 34

**(Woman B)** When is the tour group from Brazil due to arrive?

(Man B)

(A) They should be here at noon.
(B) My plane lands in Brazil at 1:30.
(C) I get back from my tour on the 22nd.

**(Narrator)** Number 35

**(Woman A)** What's at the top of our agenda this morning?

(Man B)

(A) That's on the top shelf.
(B) First we need to discuss pay raises.
(C) The agent needs the invoices by noon.

**(Narrator)** Number 36

**(Woman B)** Where's the nearest bank?

(Man A)

(A) She was genuinely thankful.

(B) Just two more blocks up that way.

(C) No, it's closed today.

**(Narrator)** Number 37

**(Man B)** What do you think: should I bring my umbrella on the walk?

(Woman A)

(A) Yes, my umbrella should be big enough.

(B) No, the walk isn't difficult at all.

(C) Yes, the skies have been cloudy all morning.

**(Narrator)** Number 38

**(Man A)** How long will you be in Tokyo?

(Woman A)

(A) I'll be there for a week.

(B) They've been here for three days.

(C) I'll be leaving this Friday.

**(Narrator)** Number 39

**(Man B)** Who's the attorney representing them?

(Woman B)

(A) Pete Mackerel is no longer a practicing attorney.

(B) He's getting ready for trial.

(C) Their own staff lawyers will handle the case.

| | |
|---|---|
| (Narrator) | Number 40 |
| (Man A) | Would you like to sit in on the research meeting this afternoon? |

(Woman A)

(A) We could develop a new line of chairs.
(B) Thank you. I'd like that.
(C) I don't think I've met him before.

| | |
|---|---|
| (Narrator) | You will now hear a number of conversations between two people. You will be asked to answer three questions about what the speakers say. Select the best response to each question and mark the letter on your answer sheet. The conversations will be spoken only once and will not be printed in your test book. |
| (Narrator) | Now let us begin Part III with question number 41. |
| (Narrator) | Questions 41 through 43 refer to the following conversation. |
| (Man A) | We need to know the final count before we can call the caterer. Originally we were supposed to have fifty, but I know the number has gone up since last week. Do you have any idea how many we're going to have? |
| (Woman A) | It's sixty five. Ms. Colby also invited the instructors to lunch, so that's another eight people. Plus we've decided to invite people from the administration team, so that's another seven. |
| (Man A) | Thanks. And are we staying with the same time? |
| (Woman A) | Yes, that hasn't changed; we're still scheduled to start serving at one-thirty. |
| (Narrator) | Number 41. What are the speakers planning? |
| (Narrator) | Number 42. How many people are expected to attend? |
| (Narrator) | Number 43. What has changed? |
| (Narrator) | Questions 44 through 46 refer to the following conversation. |
| (Woman B) | Jane told me that your interview went quite well. Who interviewed you? |
| (Man B) | The office manager, but the personnel director dropped by to explain some procedures. He didn't ask me any questions though. It was the office manager who did all the interviewing, but she was very nice. I think it all went very well, actually so I'm happy about that. |
| (Woman B) | That's encouraging. I bet the office manager doesn't interview every applicant. Did you get a chance to talk about the research you've been doing recently? |

| | |
|---|---|
| (Man B) | Yes, I did. She asked me a lot of questions about it and she seemed pretty impressed. |
| (Narrator) | Number 44. What are the speakers talking about? |
| (Narrator) | Number 45. Who asked questions? |
| (Narrator) | Number 46. How does the man feel? |
| (Narrator) | Questions 47 through 49 refer to the following conversation. |
| (Man A) | Hello. My name's Eric Jansen from API insurance. I'd like to speak to Kate Brody, please. |
| (Woman A) | I'm sorry, but Ms. Brody's in a meeting right now. Would you like to leave a message? |
| (Man A) | Yes, could you please tell her that she's covered for her trip to China next week, but that she needs to send me a message with the details of her trip—I mean the cities that she'll be visiting. It's urgent, so she needs to get those details to me before the end of today. If she wants to call me, I'll be in the office all day. She has my number. |
| (Woman A) | Okay, Mr. Jansen. I'll let her know. Thanks for calling. |
| (Narrator) | Number 47. What has Mr. Jansen called about? |
| (Narrator) | Number 48. Where is Ms. Brody? |
| (Narrator) | Number 49. What does Mr. Jansen need to know regarding Ms. Brody's trip? |
| (Narrator) | Questions 50 through 52 refer to the following conversation. |
| (Woman B) | I always think it's a good idea for customers to see how we run our production process, so if you have time, Mr. Bidwell, I thought I'd show you around the plant. |
| (Man B) | That's a great idea. I don't have much time, though. How long will it take? If it's not more than half an hour, that should be fine. |
| (Woman B) | Not long—about twenty minutes or so. I'm afraid I'll have to ask you to put on this hard hat, though. It's government regulations . . . we can't risk having you getting injured. |
| (Man B) | No, I understand, no problem. |
| (Narrator) | Number 50. Who is the man? |

KAPLAN

| | |
|---|---|
| (Narrator) | Number 51. Where will the speakers go? |
| (Narrator) | Number 52. What does the man need to wear? |
| (Narrator) | Questions 53 through 55 refer to the following conversation. |
| (Man A) | I hear that her work is exhibited all over the world. She must be very well known. |
| (Woman B) | Oh yes, she's quite a celebrity in the art world. Her works are in most of the big galleries in New York, London, and Paris. Although, I have to admit that until a week ago I'd never heard of her. |
| (Man A) | Me neither, but then I don't know much about sculpture. I prefer paintings. Anyway, it's quite an honor to have someone so famous come and speak here in Glasgow. |
| (Woman B) | Yes, she's supposed to be a very entertaining speaker. I think it will really make a big difference to the dinner. |
| (Narrator) | Number 53. Who are the speakers talking about? |
| (Narrator) | Number 54. Where are the speakers? |
| (Narrator) | Number 55. What event do the speakers refer to? |
| (Narrator) | Questions 56 through 58 refer to the following conversation. |
| (Man A) | I'm going to need ten more feet of wire to install these overhead lights. This piece doesn't reach the ceiling. We've got some more in a blue box in the truck. Could you go and bring it, Greg? |
| (Man B) | Yeah, sure. Do you want me to bring the whole box or just cut ten feet? |
| (Man A) | Well, bring the whole box. We'll need some more wire for the switches in the bedrooms and the kitchen. |
| (Man B) | Okay. I'll be right back. |
| (Narrator) | Number 56. Who are the men? |
| (Narrator) | Number 57. Where is the blue box? |
| (Narrator) | Number 58. Where are the men working? |
| (Narrator) | Questions 59 through 61 refer to the following conversation. |

| | |
|---|---|
| **(Man B)** | I'm just popping out to the bank to deposit a check in my account. Do you want me to pick anything up for you while I'm out? |
| **(Woman A)** | Well, actually, if you pass by the mini-market could you get me a sandwich for lunch? Cheese if you can find one, chicken if not. Hang on a moment and I'll get some money. |
| **(Man B)** | No, no. My treat! I'll pick up sandwiches for us both on my way back. Oh, and by the way, I'm expecting a call from the marketing department. If they call, could you tell them I'll be back at my desk in half an hour or so? |
| **(Woman A)** | Okay. I'll do that. |
| **(Narrator)** | Number 59. Where are the speakers? |
| **(Narrator)** | Number 60. Where is the man going? |
| **(Narrator)** | Number 61. What does the woman want? |
| **(Narrator)** | Questions 62 through 64 refer to the following conversation. |
| **(Man A)** | I just received an e-mail from Colleen Rankin. She said she'd love to see you when you're in Australia next week. Do you think you'll have time? |
| **(Woman B)** | I'm not sure, to be honest. I'd love to see her, but it's going to be a very busy three days. I've got meetings with five different clients, plus I'll be at the Trade and Commerce Center. Still, it would be a shame to go all the way there and not see Colleen. I'll e-mail her and tell her my program. Maybe we can meet up on Friday evening before my flight back on Saturday. |
| **(Man A)** | Yes, I think you should . . . Listen, why don't you stay an extra night and fly back on Sunday? As your boss, I can approve the cost of another night's accommodation this afternoon. After all those years working out there, I'm sure that Colleen has some useful contacts and it would be good for us if you could meet with her. |
| **(Woman B)** | Really! That's a great idea. Thanks, Jim. |
| **(Narrator)** | Number 62. Why is Colleen Rankin in Australia? |
| **(Narrator)** | Number 63. When will the woman return from Australia? |
| **(Narrator)** | Number 64. Who is the man in relation to the woman? |
| **(Narrator)** | Questions 65 through 67 refer to the following conversation. |
| **(Woman A)** | Have you heard any news on that shipment of sportswear from Shanghai? I'm getting a bit worried. The ad campaign is due to start in two weeks and we need to deliver to stores well before then. |

| (Man B) | Don't worry, Jane. The ship hasn't sunk in Hong Kong harbor or anything like that. The container's actually here in Dublin, but there's been a problem in customs—they needed extra time to review the paperwork, or something, I didn't understand the issue, exactly. |
|---|---|
| (Woman A) | So when can we expect delivery to the stores? |
| (Man B) | The official I spoke to said we should get customs clearance by Wednesday, and then all the stores will receive delivery by Friday at the latest. |
| (Narrator) | Number 65. What goods are the speakers talking about? |
| (Narrator) | Number 66. Where has the shipment come from? |
| (Narrator) | Number 67. What has caused the delay? |
| (Narrator) | Questions 68 through 70 refer to the following conversation. |
| (Man A) | I've heard you have a special deal on the Verity 540. Can you tell me more about it? |
| (Woman B) | Yes, that's right, sir. If you buy the 540 we'll throw in a free carrying case and a choice between a memory upgrade or a graphics software package. |
| (Man A) | Oh, I see. And how much is the software or the memory upgrade worth in dollars? I mean, can't I just get a reduction in the price instead of the software or the memory upgrade? To be honest I don't really need either of those . . . |
| (Woman B) | Well, the offer is worth about 120 dollars, but I'm afraid a straight discount isn't available with this particular model. And to be honest, this is already a great price on a quality laptop. You won't find one with the same features for much cheaper. |
| (Narrator) | Number 68. What are the speakers talking about? |
| (Narrator) | Number 69. What does the special offer include? |
| (Narrator) | Number 70. What does the man ask for? |
| (Narrator) | **Directions:** You will now hear short talks given by a single speaker. You will be asked to answer three questions about what the speaker says. Select the best response to each question and mark the letter on your answer sheet. The talks will be spoken only once and will not be printed in your test book. |
| (Narrator) | Questions 71 through 73 refer to the following talk. |
| (Woman B) | We hope you will come and help us welcome the Colombian National Symphony for the first time to Seattle on Saturday May 28th at 7 o'clock at the Municipal Concert Hall. Tickets are 18, 24, and 30 dollars. A ten percent discount is available |

to holders of student union membership cards and to school or university staff. Tickets are available at the Municipal Concert Hall. You can also buy seats for all our events online, at w-w-w dot Seattle arts dot com where you can search for details of upcoming concerts and reserve seats.

| | |
|---|---|
| (Narrator) | Number 71. What event will occur on May 28th? |
| (Narrator) | Number 72. How much is the cheapest ticket without the discount? |
| (Narrator) | Number 73. Where can people buy tickets? |
| (Narrator) | Questions 74 through 76 refer to the following announcement. |
| (Man A) | Tomorrow, John Park, the vice president, will be coming to make an inspection that he would like to include as a part of his annual report. As some of you may remember from last year, his reports are very thorough. Last year he focused on our menu items, and this year he will be concentrating on customer service. This means he will be carefully observing the host, waiters, bus boys, and anyone else who has direct contact with the customers. He will also be looking at how we present the food. I hope you will work hard, smile, and demonstrate how well we treat our customers. |
| (Narrator) | Number 74. What is Mr. Park's title? |
| (Narrator) | Number 75. What will Mr. Park mainly focus on this year? |
| (Narrator) | Number 76. What does the speaker want the employees to do? |
| (Narrator) | Questions 77 through 79 refer to the following introduction. |
| (Woman A) | I'd like to introduce you to our new vice president of operations, Mr. Frank Nazar. Mr. Nazar has been with the company for 15 years. He started as an account representative and then quickly moved up to sales executive. For the last five years he has been Regional Manager and under his direction domestic sales have increased by 30 percent. As vice president of operations, Mr. Nazar will be looking at ways to lower expenses and increase production. I'm sure all of the store managers will join me in welcoming Mr. Nazar. |
| (Narrator) | Number 77. Where is this introduction taking place? |
| (Narrator) | Number 78. What is one of Mr. Nazar's accomplishments? |
| (Narrator) | Number 79. What is one of Mr. Nazar s goals in his new role? |
| (Narrator) | Questions 80 through 82 refer to the following weather report. |
| (Man B) | The weather in Zurich today: rain at times, highs in the lower teens. In the central valley, a mostly cloudy day with some areas of mixed rain and snow over the mountains, highs around nine degrees. In the southern mountains, lots of |

snow, possibly 30 centimeters today with the snow level around elevations of 1,000 meters. And in southeastern Switzerland, snow there too, about 15 to 25 centimeters are possible today. Seven to 13 centimeters of snow are already reported along the Italian-Austrian border.

| | |
|---|---|
| **(Narrator)** | Number 80. Where is it expected to rain? |
| **(Narrator)** | Number 81. How much snow is expected today in the mountains? |
| **(Narrator)** | Number 82. Where has snow already been reported? |
| **(Narrator)** | Questions 83 through 85 refer to the following talk. |
| **(Woman A)** | Thank you for that introduction, Mr. Hausman. Today I would like to speak about financial services and how they affect the planning process for business and industry. As we are aware, tremendous changes have been made in the financial services sector over the past decade, and they are set to continue. These changes, especially those in the areas of regulation and industry management, have created new challenges for business planning. |
| **(Narrator)** | Number 83. What did Mr. Hausman do? |
| **(Narrator)** | Number 84. According to the speaker, in what areas have new challenges been created? |
| **(Narrator)** | Number 85. What is this talk mainly about? |
| **(Narrator)** | Questions 86 through 88 refer to the following talk. |
| **(Man A)** | As you know I just returned from Europe where I spent two months visiting our hotel units. I spent approximately three days at each unit, evaluating the services, staff, and accommodations. My goal was to evaluate the architectural structure of both the interiors and exteriors. Very briefly, we surpass the competition in customer service, but many of our units need structural updating. I feel we should have a team of interior designers redecorate the lobbies and rooms. I'd like to suggest to the board that they make these improvements a priority and that sufficient sums be allocated for each unit. |
| **(Narrator)** | Number 86. What kind of company does the speaker work for? |
| **(Narrator)** | Number 87. In what area does the business excel? |
| **(Narrator)** | Number 88. What does the speaker ask the board of directors to make available? |
| **(Narrator)** | Questions 89 through 91 refer to the following announcement. |
| **(Woman B)** | Well folks, that concludes our show for this evening. You have been listening to "Contemporary Management," broadcast every Monday night on these affiliated radio stations. We have been talking with Dr. Julia McDermott, the renowned |

management consultant and expert in the field of employee motivation. Dr. McDermott's new book is *Motivating Your Staff*. Please listen again next week when we will visit with Mr. Peter Thompson, the noted author of the best-selling book, *Managing Change*. Until next week, thank you for listening.

**(Narrator)**  Number 89. What is the purpose of this announcement?

**(Narrator)**  Number 90. Who will be the guest next week?

**(Narrator)**  Number 91. What topic was probably discussed on the program?

**(Narrator)**  Questions 92 through 94 refer to the following announcement.

**(Man B)**  Thanks for coming, everyone. As usual, I'm going to begin by briefly summarizing what we'll try and cover over the next hour. You can see that there are five agenda items on the meeting invitation I sent out, but there's also another important item to add to the list, which Katherine wants to talk to you about towards the end of today's meeting. She'd like to talk about project budgets for the next financial year. The first item, however, is an update. It's been two weeks since I last spoke to you, and I'm sure you've all made a lot of progress since then, so I thought we could just go around the table here and each of us could update the rest of us on developments regarding your respective projects.

**(Narrator)**  Number 92. What is the speaker doing?

**(Narrator)**  Number 93. How many agenda items are there?

**(Narrator)**  Number 94. What is the first item on the agenda?

**(Narrator)**  Questions 95 through 97 refer to the following announcement.

**(Man A)**  Good morning ladies and gentlemen. On behalf of Captain Smith and the rest of the crew, I'd like to welcome you aboard LinkLines flight L-K nine seventy from London Gatwick to Edinburgh. My name is James Watts and I'm your lead flight attendant on today's flight. We'd like to apologize for the slight delay this morning, which has been due to fog grounding flights most of the morning up in Edinburgh. We thank you for your patience and understanding. I'm pleased to be able to report that the fog has lifted now and we'll be pushing away from the gate in the next few minutes.

**(Narrator)**  Number 95. Who is speaking?

**(Narrator)**  Number 96. Where is the flight going?

**(Narrator)**  Number 97. What delayed the flight?

### Questions 98 through 100 refer to the following talk.

(Woman A)     This next slide shows how the different elements of our research fit together. First of all we have the stakeholder interviews. The principle stakeholders were the tour operators, the hotel managers and their clients—that is, the tourists themselves. However, we also interviewed local residents because the industry has a huge impact on their lives, too. And this actually leads into the second of our research elements, which involved empirical measurement of the impact visitors have on the local environment. We did this in a number of ways. One was to gather data on changes in demand for local resources such as water and electricity. Other quantifiable data came from measurements of erosion on pathways and increases in pollution of various kinds. Next slide, please.

(Narrator)     Number 98. What is the talk mainly about?

(Narrator)     Number 99. What is the speaker's main interest?

(Narrator)     Number 100. What was measured?

(Narrator)     This is the end of the Listening Comprehension Section of the exam. Turn to Part V in your test book.

(Narrator)     End of recording.